CIM

PRACTICE & REVISION KIT

Diploma

International Marketing Strategy

BPP Publishing
September 2000

First edition 1999
Second edition September 2000

ISBN 0 7517 4914 1 (previous edition 0 7517 4929 X)

British Library Cataloguing-in-Publication Data
A catalogue record for this book
is available from the British Library

Published by

BPP Publishing Limited
Aldine House, Aldine Place
London W12 8AW

www.bpp.com

in association with

Nottingham Business School
Nottingham Trent University

Printed in England by DACOSTA PRINT
35-37 Queensland Road
London, N7 7AH
(0207 700 1000)

All our rights reserved. No part of this publication may be reproduced, stored in a retrieval system or transmitted, in any form or by any means, electronic, mechanical, photocopying, recording or otherwise, without the prior written permission of BPP Publishing Limited.

We are grateful to the Chartered Institute of Marketing for permission to reproduce in this Kit the syllabus, the specimen paper and past examination paper questions.

Author
John Stewart

Series editor
Paul Brittain, Senior Lecturer in Marketing and Retailing at Nottingham Business School, Nottingham Trent University

©
BPP Publishing Limited
2000

CONTENTS

	Page
Question and answer checklist/index	(iv)
About this kit	(vii)
Revision	(viii)
Question practice	(ix)
Exam technique	(x)
Approaching mini-cases	(xii)
The exam paper	(xv)
Syllabus	(xix)
QUESTION BANK	3
ANSWER BANK	37
TEST YOUR KNOWLEDGE	
Questions	167
Answers	169
TEST PAPER	
June 2000 questions	173
June 2000 suggested answers	181
TOPIC INDEX	197
ORDER FORM	
REVIEW FORM & FREE PRIZE DRAW	

Question and answer checklist/index

The headings indicate the main topics of questions, but questions often cover several different topics.

Tutorial questions, listed in italics, are followed by **guidance notes** on how to approach the question, thus easing the transition from study to examination practice.

A date alone (6/99, say) after the question title refers to a past examination question.

Questions marked by * are **key questions** which we think you must attempt in order to pass the exam. Tick them off on this list as you complete them.

		Marks	Time allocation mins	Page number Question	Answer
PART A: INTERNATIONAL STRATEGIC ANALYSIS					
The world trading environment and comparative analysis					
*1	*Tutorial question: Strategic importance of international marketing*	-	-	4	37
2	Political risk (12/96)	20	32	4	39
*3	Effect of EU (6/96)	20	32	4	40
*4	Macro factors (12/98 & specimen paper)	20	32	4	41
*5	Identifying opportunities (6/95)	20	32	4	42
6	Global/local (6/97)	20	32	4	43
*7	*Tutorial question: Key factors in comparative analysis*	-	-	4	45
*8	Levels of development (12/99)	20	32	5	47
9	New market economy (6/99)	20	32	5	48
*10	*Tutorial question: Product portfolio analysis*	-	-	5	50
SLEPT factors					
*11	*Tutorial question: Differences between domestic and international marketing*	-	-	7	51
12	International finance	20	32	7	53
'C' factors					
13	*Tutorial question: Culture*	-	-	7	54
*14	Cultural differences (12/99)	20	32	7	56
Buyer behaviour					
*15	*Tutorial question: Buyer behaviour*	-	-	7	57
16	Government buyer behaviour (12/95)	20	32	7	60
Marketing research and agency selection					
17	*Tutorial question: Marketing information systems for international markets*	-	-	7	61
*18	Segmenting international markets (12/98 & specimen paper)	20	32	8	63
19	Market research in developing countries (6/98)	20	32	8	64
*20	Internet and segmentation (specimen paper)	20	32	8	65
*21	Priorities for market entry (12/97)	20	32	8	66
22	Emerging markets research (6/97)	20	32	8	68

(iv)

Question and answer checklist/index

	Marks	Time allocation mins	Page number Question	Answer

PART B: INTERNATIONAL STRATEGIC PLANNING

Market entry

★ 23	Tutorial question: Foreign market entry criteria	-	-	10	69
24	Overseas expansion (12/97)	20	32	10	71
★ 25	Market entry (6/98)	20	32	10	73
★ 26	Modes of entry (12/95)	20	32	10	74
★ 27	Risk and revenue (6/99)	20	32	10	76
28	Co-operation between firms (12/96)	20	32	10	77

Standardisation v adaptation

★ 29	Tutorial question: Standardised approach to international marketing	-	-	10	78
★ 30	Standardisation (6/98)	20	32	11	79
31	Marketing and financial implications of a move from differentiated to standardised marketing	20	32	11	80
32	Globalisation (6/98)	20	32	11	82
★ 33	Evolving operations (6/99)	20	32	11	83
★ 34	Going global (12/99)	20	32	11	84
35	Transnational versus multinational marketing	20	32	11	86

International marketing planning

★ 36	Tutorial question: Strategy development	-	-	13	87
★ 37	Planning international marketing (12/97)	20	32	13	89
38	Electronic commerce (6/99)	20	32	13	90
39	Three year plan (6/95)	20	32	13	91

Managing resources

40	Global workforce (12/99)	-	-	13	92
★ 41	Expatriate staff (12/98 & specimen paper)	20	32	13	94
★ 42	Knowledge based organisations (12/99)	20	32	13	95
★ 43	Databases (12/99)	20	32	13	96
★ 44	Tutorial question: Effects of organisation structure on product standardisation	-	-	14	97
★ 45	Retailing differences (6/98)	20	32	14	98

PART C: INTERNATIONAL STRATEGY IMPLEMENTATION AND CONTROL

International product management

★ 46	Tutorial question: Criteria for selection of international products	-	-	16	100
47	New products and international inputs (6/96)	20	32	16	101
48	New product development (6/97)	20	32	16	102
49	Economic development and product design	20	32	16	103

Question and answer checklist/index

		Marks	Time allocation mins	Page number Question	Answer
50	Packaging decisions	20	32	16	104
*51	Marketing services (6/97)	20	32	16	105

Marketing communications

		Marks	Time allocation mins	Page number Question	Answer
*52	Strategic marketing communications (12/97)	20	32	18	106
53	Global positioning (12/98 & specimen paper)	20	32	18	108
54	Pan-regional advertising (12/96)	20	32	18	110
*55	Intelligence bases (specimen paper)	20	32	18	111
56	Planning an international advertising campaign (6/98)	20	32	18	113
57	Global communications (6/99)	20	32	18	114
*58	Adapting global brands (6/97)	20	32	18	115

Distribution and logistics

		Marks	Time allocation mins	Page number Question	Answer
*59	*Tutorial question: Selecting distributors and agents*	-	-	20	116
*60	Logistics and distribution (12/96)	20	32	20	118
61	Developments in distribution and logistics (12/98 & specimen paper)	20	32	20	119
*62	Retailers and international activities (6/95)	20	32	20	120
63	Distribution in the global village (12/97)	20	32	20	121

Pricing

		Marks	Time allocation mins	Page number Question	Answer
*64	*Tutorial question: Export prices*	-	-	22	124
65	Pricing considerations (6/99)	20	32	22	125
66	Trading bloc and pricing (12/95)	20	32	22	126
*67	International pricing strategy (12/96)	20	32	22	127
*68	Incoterms and their use (12/95)	20	32	22	128
*69	International financial risk (12/97)	20	32	22	129

Evaluation and control

		Marks	Time allocation mins	Page number Question	Answer
70	*Tutorial question: Evaluation and control in a multinational*	-	-	24	131
*71	Strategy breakdown (12/99)	20	32	24	132
72	Evaluating marketing strategies in countries at different levels of economic development	20	32	24	133
73	Knowledge based system (specimen paper)	20	32	24	134
*74	Control system (12/98 & specimen paper)	20	32	24	135

MINI-CASES

		Marks	Time allocation mins	Page number Question	Answer
*75	King Carpets (6/97)	40	64	25	136
*76	McDonald's and globalisation (12/97)	40	64	26	141
*77	Harley Davidson (6/98)	40	64	27	147
*78	Sri Lankan Tea (12/98 & specimen paper)	40	64	29	151
*79	Zimflowers (6/99)	40	64	30	155
*80	Levi Strauss (12/99)	40	64	31	159

About this kit

ABOUT THIS KIT

You're taking your professional CIM exams in December 2000 or June 2001. You're under time pressure to get your exam revision done and you want to pass first time. Could you make better use of your time? Are you sure that your revision is really relevant to the exam you will be facing?

If you use this BPP Practice & Revision Kit you can be sure that the time you spend revising and practising questions is time well spent.

The BPP Practice & Revision Kit: International Marketing Strategy

The BPP Practice & Revision Kit, produced in association with Nottingham Trent University Business School, has been specifically written for the syllabus by an expert in marketing education, John Stewart.

- We give you a **comprehensive question and answer checklist** so you can see at a glance which are the key questions that we think you should attempt in order to pass the exam, what the mark and time allocations are and when they were set (where this is relevant)
- We offer **vital guidance** on revision, question practice and exam technique
- We show you the **syllabus** examinable in December 2000 and June 2001. We **analyse the papers** set so far, with summaries of the examiner's comments
- We give you a **comprehensive question bank** containing:
    - *Do You Know* checklists to jog your memory
    - *Tutorial questions* to warm you up
    - *Exam-standard questions*, including questions set up until December 1999 and the new syllabus specimen paper
    - *Full suggested answers* - with summaries of the examiner's comments
- A **Test Your Knowledge quiz** covering selected areas from the entire syllabus
- A **Test Paper** consisting of the June 2000 exam, again with full suggested answers, for you to attempt just before the real thing
- A **Topic Index** for ready reference

The Study Text: further help from BPP

The other vital part of BPP's study package is the Study Text. The Study Text features:

- Structured, methodical syllabus coverage
- Lots of case examples from real businesses throughout, to show you how the theory applies in real life
- Action programmes and quizzes so that you can test that you've mastered the theory
- A question and answer bank
- Key concepts and full index

There's an order form at the back of this Kit.

Help us to help you

Your feedback will help us improve our study package. Please complete and return the Review Form at the end of this Kit; you will be entered automatically in a Free Prize Draw.

BPP Publishing
September 2000

To learn more about what BPP has to offer, visit our website: www.bpp.com

Revision

REVISION

This is a very important time as you approach the exam. You must remember three things.

> **Use time sensibly**
> **Set realistic goals**
> **Believe in yourself**

Use time sensibly

1. **How much study time do you have?** Remember that you must EAT, SLEEP, and of course, RELAX.

2. **How will you split that available time between each subject?** What are your weaker subjects? They need more time.

3. **What is your learning style?** AM/PM? Little and often/long sessions? Evenings/ weekends?

4. **Are you taking regular breaks?** Most people absorb more if they do not attempt to study for long uninterrupted periods of time. A five minute break every hour (to make coffee, watch the news headlines) can make all the difference.

5. **Do you have quality study time?** Unplug the phone. Let everybody know that you're studying and shouldn't be disturbed.

Set realistic goals

1. Have you set a **clearly defined objective** for each study period?
2. Is the objective **achievable**?
3. Will you **stick to your plan**? Will you make up for any **lost time**?
4. Are you **rewarding yourself** for your hard work?
5. Are you leading a **healthy lifestyle**?

Believe in yourself

Are you cultivating the right attitude of mind? There is absolutely no reason why you should not pass this exam if you adopt the correct approach.

- **Be confident** - you've passed exams before, you can pass them again
- **Be calm** - plenty of adrenaline but no panicking
- **Be focused** - commit yourself to passing the exam

(viii)

QUESTION PRACTICE

Do not simply open this Kit and, beginning with question 1, start attempting all of the questions. You first need to ask yourself three questions.

> **Am I ready to answer questions?**
> **Do I know which questions to do first?**
> **How should I use this Kit?**

Am I ready to answer questions?

1 Check that you are familiar with the material on the **Do you know?** page for a particular syllabus area.

2 If you are happy, you can go ahead and start answering questions. If not, go back to your BPP Study Text and revise first.

Do I know which questions to do first?

1 **Start with tutorial questions.** They warm you up for key and difficult areas of the syllabus. Try to produce at least a plan for these questions, using the guidance notes following the question to ensure your answer is structured so as to gain a good pass mark.

2 Don't worry about the time it takes to answer these questions. Concentrate on producing good answers. There are 15 tutorial questions in this Kit.

How should I use this Kit?

1 Once you are confident with the Do you know? checklists and the tutorial questions, you should try as many as possible of the exam-standard questions; at the very least you should attempt the **key questions,** which are highlighted in the **question and answer checklist/index** at the front of the Kit.

2 Try to **produce full answers under timed conditions**; you are practising exam technique as much as knowledge recall here. Don't look at the answer, your BPP Study Text or your notes for any help at all.

3 **Mark your answers to the non-tutorial questions as if you were the examiner.** Only give yourself marks for what you have written, not for what you meant to put down, or would have put down if you had had more time. If you did badly, try another question.

4 Read the **Tutorial notes** in the answers very carefully and take note of the advice given and any **comments by the examiner.**

5 When you have practised the whole syllabus, go back to the areas you had problems with and **practise further questions.**

6 When you feel you have completed your revision of the entire syllabus to your satisfaction, answer the **test your knowledge** quiz. This covers selected areas from the entire syllabus and answering it unseen is a good test of how well you can recall your knowledge of diverse subjects quickly.

7 Finally, when you think you really understand the entire subject, **attempt the test paper** at the end of the Kit. Sit the paper under strict exam conditions, so that you gain experience of selecting and sequencing your questions, and managing your time, as well as of writing answers.

Exam technique

EXAM TECHNIQUE

Passing professional examinations is half about having the knowledge, and half about doing yourself full justice in the examination. You must have the right approach to two things.

> **The day of the exam**
> **Your time in the exam hall**

The day of the exam

1. Set at least one alarm (or get an alarm call) for a morning exam.
2. Have something to eat but beware of eating too much; you may feel sleepy if your system is digesting a large meal.
3. Allow plenty of time to get to the exam hall; have your route worked out in advance and listen to news bulletins to check for potential travel problems.
4. Don't forget pens, pencils, rulers, erasers.
5. Put new batteries into your calculator and take a spare set (or a spare calculator).
6. Avoid discussion about the exam with other candidates outside the exam hall.

Your time in the exam hall

1. **Read the instructions (the 'rubric') on the front of the exam paper carefully**

   Check that the exam format hasn't changed. It is surprising how often examiners' reports remark on the number of students who attempt too few - or too many - questions, or who attempt the wrong number of questions from different parts of the paper. Make sure that you are planning to answer the right number of questions.

2. **Select questions carefully**

   Read through the paper once, then quickly jot down key points against each question in a second read through. Select those questions where you could latch on to 'what the question is about' - but remember to check carefully that you have got the right end of the stick before putting pen to paper.

3. **Plan your attack carefully**

   Consider the order in which you are going to tackle questions. It is a good idea to start with your best question to boost your morale and get some easy marks 'in the bag'.

4. **Check the time allocation for each question**

   Each mark carries with it a time allocation of 1.6 minutes (including time for selecting and reading questions). A 20 mark question therefore should be completed in 32 minutes. When time is up, you must go on to the next question or part. Going even one minute over the time allowed brings you a lot closer to failure.

5. **Read the question carefully and plan your answer**

   Read through the question again very carefully when you come to answer it. Plan your answer to ensure that you keep to the point. Two minutes of planning plus eight minutes of writing is virtually certain to earn you more marks than ten minutes of writing.

(x)

6 Produce relevant answers

Particularly with written answers, make sure you answer the question set, and not the question you would have preferred to have been set.

7 Gain the easy marks

Include the obvious if it answers the question and don't try to produce the perfect answer.

Don't get bogged down in small parts of questions. If you find a part of a question difficult, get on with the rest of the question. If you are having problems with something, the chances are that everyone else is too.

8 Produce an answer in the correct format

The examiner will state in the requirements the format in which the question should be answered, for example in a report or memorandum.

9 Follow the examiner's instructions

You will annoy the examiner if you ignore him or her. The examiner will state whether he or she wishes you to 'discuss', 'comment', 'evaluate' or 'recommend'.

10 Present a tidy paper

Students are penalised for poor presentation and so you should make sure that you write legibly, label diagrams clearly and lay out your work neatly. Markers of scripts each have hundreds of papers to mark; a badly written scrawl is unlikely to receive the same attention as a neat and well laid out paper.

11 Stay until the end of the exam

Use any spare time checking and rechecking your script.

12 Don't worry if you feel you have performed badly in the exam

It is more than likely that the other candidates will have found the exam difficult too. Don't forget that there is a competitive element in these exams. As soon as you get up to leave the exam hall, forget that exam and think about the next - or, if it is the last one, celebrate!

13 Don't discuss an exam with other candidates

This is particularly the case if you still have other exams to sit. Even if you have finished, you should put it out of your mind until the day of the results. Forget about exams and relax!

Approaching mini-cases

APPROACHING MINI-CASES

What is a mini-case?

The mini-case in the examination is a description of an organisation at a moment in time. You first see it in the examination room and so you have 64 minutes to read, understand, analyse and answer the mini-case.

The mini-case (Part A of the paper) carries 40% of the available marks in the examination.

As mini-cases are fundamental to your exam success, you should be absolutely clear about what mini-cases are, the CIM's purpose in using them, and what the examiner seeks; then, in context, you must consider how best they should be tackled.

The purpose of the mini-case

The examiner requires students to demonstrate not only their knowledge of the fundamentals of marketing, but also their ability to use that knowledge in a commercially credible way in the context of a 'real' business scenario.

The examiner's requirements

The examiner is the 'consumer' of your examination script. You should remember first and foremost that a paper is needed which makes his or her life easy. That means that the script should be well laid out, with plenty of white space and neat readable writing. All the basic rules of examination technique discussed earlier must be applied, but because communication skills are fundamental to the marketer, the ability to communicate clearly is particularly important.

An approach to mini-cases

Mini-cases are easy once you have mastered the basic techniques. The key to success lies in adopting a logical sequence of steps which, with practice, you will master. You must enter the exam room with the process as second nature, so you can concentrate your attention on the marketing issues which face you.

Students who are at first apprehensive when faced with a mini-case often come to find them much more stimulating and rewarding than traditional examination questions. There is the added security of knowing that there is no single correct answer to a case study.

Suggested mini-case method

You have about 64 minutes in total.

Stage		Minutes
1	Read the mini-case and questions set on it very quickly.	2
2	Read the questions and case again, but carefully. Make brief notes of significant material. Determine key issues in relation to the questions etc.	5
3	Put the case on one side and turn to your notes. What do they contain? A clear picture of the situation? Go back if necessary and concentrate on getting a grip on the scenario outlined.	4
4	Prepare an answer structure plan for question (a) following exactly the structure suggested in the question, highlighting your decisions supported by case data and theory if appropriate. Follow the process outlined for question (b), etc.	3
5	Prepare a timeplan for each part of the question, according to the marks allocated.	1
6	Write your answer.	44
7	Read through and correct errors, improve presentation.	5
		64

(xii)

Approaching mini-cases

A good answer will be a document on which a competent manager can take action.

Notes

(a) It is not seriously suggested that you can allocate your time quite so rigorously! The purpose of showing detailed timings is to demonstrate the need to move with purpose and control through each stage of the process.

(b) Take time to get the facts into your short term memory. Making decisions is easier once the facts are in your head.

(c) Establish a clear plan and you will find that writing the answers is straightforward.

(d) Some candidates will be writing answers within five minutes. The better candidates will ignore them and concentrate on planning. This is not easy to do, but management of your examination technique is the key to your personal success.

(e) Presentation is crucial. Your answer should be written as a final draft that would go to typing. If the typist could understand every word and replicate the layout, then the examiner will be delighted and it will be marked highly.

Handling an unseen mini-case in the examination

The following extract is taken from a Chartered Institute of Marketing's Tutor's/Student Guide to the treatment of mini-cases.

Tutor's/Student Guide to the treatment of mini-cases

'It needs to be stated unequivocally that the type of extremely short case (popularly called the mini-case) set in the examinations for Certificate and Diploma subjects cannot be treated in exactly the same way as a long case study issued in advance. If it could there would be little point of going to all the trouble of writing an in-depth case study.

'Far too many students adopt a maxi-case approach using a detailed marketing audit outline which is largely inappropriate to a case consisting only of two or three paragraphs. Others use the SWOT analysis and simply re-write the case under the four headings of strengths, weaknesses, opportunities and threats.

'Some students even go so far as to totally ignore the specific questions set and present a standard maxi-case analysis outline including environmental reviews through to contingency plans.

'The "mini-case" is not really a case at all, it is merely an outline of a given situation, a scenario. Its purpose is to test whether examinees can apply their knowledge of marketing theory and techniques to the company or organisation and the operating environment described in the scenario. For example answers advocating retail audits as part of the marketing information system for a small industrial goods manufacturer demonstrate a lack of practical awareness. Such answers confirm that the examinee has learned a given MIS outline by rote and simply regurgitated this in complete disregard of the scenario. Such an approach would be disastrous in the real world and examinees adopting this approach cannot be passed, ie gain the confidence of the Institute as professional marketing practitioners. The correct approach to the scenario is a mental review of the area covered by the question and the *selection* by the examinee of those particular parts of knowledge or techniques which apply to the case. This implies a rejection of those parts of the student's knowledge which clearly do not apply to the scenario.

'All scenarios are based upon real world companies and situations and are written with a fuller knowledge of how that organisation actually operates in its planning environments. Often the organisation described in the scenario will not be a giant fast moving consumer goods manufacturing and marketing company since this would facilitate mindless

Approaching mini-cases

regurgitation of textbook outlines and be counter to the intention of this section of the examination.

'More often the scenarios will involve innovative small or medium sized firms which comprise the vast majority of UK companies which lack the resources often assumed by the textbook approach. These firms do have to market within these constraints however and are just as much concerned with marketing communications, marketing planning and control and indeed (proportionately) in international marketing, particularly the Common Market, as are larger enterprises.

'However, as marketing applications develop and expand and as changes take root, the Institute (through its examiners) will wish to test students' knowledge and awareness of these changes and their implication with regard to marketing practice. For example in the public sector increasing attention is being paid to the marketing of leisure services and the concept of "asset marketing" where the "product" is to a greater extent fixed and therefore the option of product as a variable in the marketing mix is somewhat more constrained.

'Tutors and students are referred to Examiners' Reports which repeatedly complain of inappropriateness of answer detail which demonstrates a real lack of *practical* marketing grasp and confirms that a leaned by rote textbook regurgitation is being used. Examples would include:

- the recommendation of national TV advertising for a small industrial company with a local market;
- the overnight installation of a marketing department comprising Marketing Director, Marketing Manager, Advertising Manager, Distribution Manager, Sales Manager, etc into what has been described as a very small company;
- the inclusion of packaging, branded packs, on-pack offers, etc, in the marketing mix recommendations for a service.

'It has to be borne in mind that the award of the Diploma is in a very real sense the granting of a licence to practice marketing and certainly an endorsement of the candidate's practical as well as theoretical grasps of marketing. In these circumstances such treatments of the mini-case as described above cannot be passed and give rise to some concern that perhaps the teaching/learning approach to mini-cases has not been sufficiently differentiated from that recommended for maxi-cases.

'Tutors/distance-learning students are recommended to work on previously set mini-cases and questions and review results against published specimen answers. They are also advised to use course-members' companies/organisations as examples in the constraints/limitations of marketing techniques and how they might need to be modified.

'Students are also advised to answer the specified questions set and if for example a question was on objectives, then undue reference to market analysis and strategies would be treated as extraneous.'

The exam paper

THE EXAM PAPER

Format of the exam

	Number of marks
Part A: one compulsory case study, with two questions	40
Part B: three questions from six (equal marks)	60
	100

Time allowed: 3 hours

Section A is a mini-case scenario against which students should recommend action, or alternatively an extract from an article on International issues to be commented on and action recommended. Generally the answer will need to be written in a report format.

Section B will contain questions testing across the whole syllabus range, and knowledge will need to be applied to the context of the question set.

Analysis of past papers

The analysis below shows the topics which have featured in papers set under the old and new syllabus since 1997.

June 2000

Part A

1 Management consultancy specialising in advising on the use of intellectual assets

   (a) Write a report indicating the types of market information it will need to help it decide where to locate its headquarters and what online services it should offer

   (b) Write an international marketing plan

Part B

2 Mergers and global competitive advantage
3 Market intelligence for a tourism company
4 Branding and Manchester United Football Club
5 Marketing between developed and developing countries
6 *Either* Planning and control developments
   or Planning in a turbulent environment
7 *Either* Marketing software
   or Marketing databases

> This paper forms the Test Paper at the end of this Kit, so only an outline of its contents is given here.

Question number in this Kit

December 1999 (first new syllabus sitting)

Part A

1 International marketer and manufacturer of jeans facing competition and reversal of fortune.

   (a) Environmental variables - use of marketing information system
   (b) Strategic 10 year international marketing plan   80

The exam paper

Part B

		Question number in this Kit
2	Marketing to developed and less developed countries	8
3	Internal factors when deciding to go global	34
4	*Either:* Knowledge based organisations	42
	or: Use of databases in gaining competitive advantage	43
5	Cultural differences and the international marketing mix	14
6	Motivation of a global workforce	40
7	Global standardisation strategy	71

> *Examiner's comments.*
>
> The overall standard was quite similar to the June 1999 results. The major problems were as follows.
>
> - Lack of an international or strategic dimension
> - Checklist or bullet point answers
> - Insufficient use of supporting concepts or theories
> - Failure to answer the whole question
> - Answering more than was required
> - Illegibility, poor expression and poor grammar
> - Using material from the minicase to answer questions in Part B
> - Using the same examples in every answer
>
> Students should read publications such as the Economist and Financial Times in order to keep up with contemporary issues.

June 1999

Part A

Zimbabwe flower growing industry seeking new markets

1   (a)   Factors to consider when entering the European or ASEAN market

      (b)   Design a generic marketing strategy   79

Part B

2	Risk and revenue as a form of global partnering	27
3	Satellite broadcasting and global advertising	57
4	Market and distribution channel development in young economies	9
5	Electronic commerce: impact, dangers and opportunities	38
6	The pricing decision in the international market	65
7	Organisational change from domestic to global operator	33

> *Examiner's comments*
>
> It is essential to note the following reasons why the overall standard of pass rate did not improve over previous sessions.
>
> - Lack of an international dimension
> - Insufficient underpinning with relevant theory and examples
> - Too much use of checklists
> - Poor writing style
> - Superficial and general answers
> - Failure to answer the whole question
> - Poor time management
> - Lack of a strategic dimension, with far too much operational detail
>
> Lack of reading beyond set texts is all too evident. Candidates should read the quality press and other journals to provide a wide range of examples.

The exam paper

December 1998/New syllabus specimen paper

Question number in this Kit

Part A

1   Sri Lankan tea production and international marketing

    (a)   Preparation of a UK market entry plan

    (b)   Operational, human resource, production and financial considerations   78

Part B

2	*Either:* Segmentation of international markets	18
	or: Use of internet in segment identification	20
3	Developments in distribution and logistics	61
4	Use of expatriates rather than locals in overseas branches	41
5	*Either:* Global positioning, planning and control	53
	or: Intelligence bases	55
6	Macro influences on world trade and the effect on marketing strategies	4
7	*Either:* Effective control systems for international planning	74
	or: Knowledge based control systems	73

Examiner's comments

The overall standard achieved was similar to June 1998. Where poor results were achieved, this was generally due to the following factors.

- failure to answer the required number of questions
- failure to answer the question set
- superficiality
- lack of strategic insight or international dimension
- poor writing style and grammar
- little application of relevant concepts, theories or examples
- use of bullet point checklists

Of all these points, the lack of an international dimension to many answers was particularly worrying and indicates a need to read more widely. See the commentary on individual questions.

June 1998

Part A

1   International marketing strategy of Harley Davidson

    (a)   Strategic issues to be faced when planning overseas expansion

    (b)   Options for a market entry strategy in a chosen area   77

Part B

2	Limits to product standardisation	30
3	Globalisation process and market entry methods	25
4	International marketing research and its problems	19
5	Planning, executing and controlling an international advertising campaign	56
6	Retailers in developing v. developed countries; impact on marketing plan	45
7	Definition and development of 'globalisation'	32

The exam paper

> *Examiner's comments*
>
> The overall standard was comparable to that of 1996-97. The main problems included a tendency not to focus on the question set, or to write "all I know about X" answers which were not selective or properly applied to the question. Examples from the marketing world were thin on the ground, and were often repeated throughout the answers. Many markers commented upon the frequent lack of an international dimension. Lack of knowledge of basic concepts and definitions was also in evidence.
>
> Questions which required analysis and application as opposed to regurgitation of book knowledge were poorly answered. Candidates must take the time to read around the topic areas to gain up to date knowledge. More practice at past questions would also help greatly.
>
> Having said that, there were a number of good answers which addressed the questions with relevant information, concepts and examples and brought in evidence of reading beyond the standard texts.

December 1997   *Question number in this Kit*

Part A

Global fast foot chain faces competitors

1   (a) Market analysis
    (b) Planning, implementation and control of a response to competitors   76

Part B

2   Market entry criteria   24
3   Communications   52
4   Distribution   63
5   Financial risk   69
6   Self reference criteria   37
7   Underdeveloped country markets   21

> *Examiner's comments*
>
> There was evidence of overall improvement in the standard of answers. The areas where improvement is still needed continue to include failure to address the specific requirements of the question, too often ignoring the international implications. Presentation is often weak. Particularly in the mini-case, there needs to be greater emphasis on structure and focus. Candidates who think about and plan their answers tend to score well.
>
> Candidates seem to fail to appreciate that this is a strategic subject, and strategic issues must be given prominence.

June 1997

Part A

Californian-based carpet firm is seeking to enter Europe via a franchise agreement.

1   (a) Research programme to underpin launch
    (b) Planning and control issues   75

Part B

2   Marketing services internationally   51
3   Managing the transition from domestic to global operations   -
4   Adapting global brands to local/regional cultures   58
5   New product development   48
6   Emerging markets research   22
7   Organisational issues of globalisation and localisation   6

SYLLABUS

Aims and objectives

- To provide students with an understanding of the application of fundamental marketing principles and concepts within a variety of organisations
- To enable students to develop a thorough understanding of international marketing theory and key concepts
- To develop a knowledge and understanding of vocabulary associated with international/global marketing strategy in different types of economies, organisations and market situations
- To appreciate the complexities of international and global marketing in a mix of economies
- To create an awareness of processes, context and influences associated with international and global marketing strategies in a range of economies
- To develop students' appreciation of strategies and plans for a mix of international and global economies
- To develop an understanding of the implications for implementation, monitoring and control of the international marketing planning process.

Learning outcomes

On successful completion of this unit students will be able to:

- Demonstrate an understanding of the changing nature of the international trading environment, the major trends, strategic and contextual, affecting the global decision, and the different business and social/cultural conventions which affect buying behaviour and marketing approaches in international markets
- Determine marketing strategies appropriate to industrialised, developing and lesser developed economies, and identify and explain the relevant sources of information and analysis necessary to support the appropriate strategy
- Formulate strategies for export, international, multi-national, transnational and global marketing operations and evaluate the relevant organisational changes as an organisation moves through the export to global spectrum
- Select and justify an appropriate marketing strategy, marketing mix and evaluate the financial, human resource, operational and logistical implications of different international strategies
- Determine the appropriate control measures in international operations

Indicative content and weighting

1 International Strategic analysis *(study weighting 30%)*

1.1 Identifying and analysing opportunities in the international trading environment. Changing patterns of trade globally and types of markets (product/service/commodity/not for profit).

1.2 The strategic and contextual elements of global operations – organisational and external. Global and multinational marketing as a strategic decision. Strategic networking and the international supply chain.

1.3 The changes in the world trading environment: countries, world, regions (eg European Union, ASEAN etc) and trading blocs.

1.4 The SLEPT factors: social/cultural, legal, economic, political, technological and ethical, green and other environmental considerations. The role and effect of pressure groups.

Syllabus

1.5 The 'C' factors: countries, currency, competitors and their effect on international marketing planning.

1.6 Evaluating customers' buying behaviour (consumer, business, institutional) in different countries at different stages of economic and political development. Using marketing research to identify opportunities, similarities and differences.

1.7 Market research agency selection for international marketing support, the use of databases, intelligent and expert systems. Government initiatives and the importance of cross-cultural analysis.

1.8 The use of competitive/absolute/comparative analysis in international market appraisal.

1.9 The consequences of a more ethically responsible approach including green and environmental issues and their effect on global corporate operations.

2 International strategic planning *(study weighting 30%)*

2.1 Differences in international marketing planning between developed countries and Lesser Developed Countries (LDCs) and developing and emergent economies.

2.2 The organisational and management issues pertinent to the export to globalisation spectrum decision, organisation structures, cultures, capabilities and the leveraging of core competencies and capabilities.

2.3 The globalisation process: partnering, alliances, mergers and their effect on the structure of industry and the competitive environment.

2.4 The organisation as a learning organisation and non-linear approaches to planning, including expert and database systems, emergent strategies and 'muddling through'.

2.5 The crosscultural dimensions of global activity and cultural sensitivity.

2.6 The effect of market/economic transience on global operations and within the host country environment – social, supply chain, labour and economic factors.

2.7 Managing and controlling in-house and external resources. The expatriate, national and global staff.

2.8 Standardisation and differentiation: the issues of globalisation in international marketing.

2.9 The determination of market entry choices, selection and decision and the implications for strategy and sources of global finance to support entry strategies.

3 International strategy implementation and control *(study weighting 40%)*

3.1 Identifying and selecting a product management strategy.

3.2 Determining pricing strategies for international markets: skimming and penetration pricing; currency considerations in exporting and international marketing. Price escalation in the value chain, the futures market, hedging/forward buying, tendering and bartering. The meaning and specifics of Incoterms and specific pricing methods.

3.3 Determining international marketing communications issues relating to international positioning strategies. The importance of cultural differences and similarities.

Syllabus

3.4 The selection of a distribution and logistics strategy. Foreign channel management. Channel members' expectations and performance; customer service levels. The evolving forms of distribution, eg e-business.

3.5 Global technological developments and their strategic competitive effect eg e-commerce, internet in general and global media.

3.6 The process and evidence of global operations – strategies, humans and their physical transactional activities.

3.7 Assessing the people elements of global operations – cross/inter cultural dimensions and transaction activity and human involvement.

3.8 The role of a relationship marketing approach as complementary to a traditional marketing mix approach.

3.9 Implementing international/global marketing strategy across different countries and the strategic implications. The tactical and operational issues relevant to different countries and situations.

3.10 Establishing criteria for control and evaluation of marketing and other business functions including self assessment, benchmarking, best practice and the balanced scorecard. The strategic implications of differing rates of implementation across the developed and developing world.

Question bank

DO YOU KNOW?

INTERNATIONAL STRATEGIC ANALYSIS

THE WORLD TRADING ENVIRONMENT AND COMPARATIVE ANALYSIS

Check that you know the following points before you attempt any questions. If in doubt you should go back to the BPP Study Text and revise first.

- There are many decisions to make regarding '**going international**'. Some of the **key decisions** are:
    - Whether to market abroad at all
    - Where to market
    - The mode of entry
    - The design of the marketing programme
    - The development of the marketing organisation

- International trade can present countries with **balance of payments** problems due to a mismatch between the flow of exports and the flow of imports.

- International trade in goods and services results in demand for and supply of **currencies** for foreign exchange.

- **Exchange rates** are determined by the supply and demand conditions for the currency of countries.

- Other factors affecting exchange rates are speculation, balance of payments, government exchange rate policy.

- The two routes taken to develop international trade have been **import substitution** and **export-led growth**.

- The **global market** for some products is more extensive than others.

- The role of the **major international institutions** (WTO, IMF, World Bank, UNCTAD, regional trading groups) and agreements (GATT, free trade areas, customs unions, economic unions) should be understood.

- Increasing **specialisation** of production **lowers costs** of producing goods, through economies of scale and improving the knowledge and expertise related to production.

- The principle of **comparative advantage** demonstrates that international trade is beneficial to all countries that engage in it, providing there are 'free' trading relationships; that is, trade without protective barriers.

- **Comparative advantage** is based on two beliefs
    - Countries specialise in what they produce best
    - International trade should take place without restrictions

- **Comparative analysis** of countries is essential to locate the markets with the best potential.

- Bases for comparative analysis must include restrictions on trade (tariff and non tariff barriers), the stability of the currency, market size, and the ability of customers to pay.

- A variety of **sources of information** are available in the UK to assist in the preparation of a comparative analysis, including OTS, public databases etc.

- Scoring models are useful tools for evaluating the suitability of markets.

- **Product portfolio analysis** can be used to assist in the development of international marketing strategies.

- Country attractiveness/competitive position matrices can be used to evaluate the **suitability of markets.**

Question bank

1 TUTORIAL QUESTION: STRATEGIC IMPORTANCE OF INTERNATIONAL MARKETING

(a) Identify and critically review the reasons for the growing strategic importance of international marketing in the world economy.

(b) Explain how barriers to trade influence the development of international trade.

Guidance note

Distinguish between world trade and internal organisational dynamics.

2 POLITICAL RISK (12/96) *32 mins*

A survey of Chief Executive Officers in the USA indicated that a major concern for multinationals is political risk. What are the main methods of assessing the level of this risk and how might a multinational corporation adapt the management of its business in a country identified as having a high political risk? **(20 marks)**

3 EFFECT OF EU (6/96) *32 mins*

In what ways does the European Union affect a firm's global marketing strategy in Europe? Why have some firms reacted by acquiring and merging with other European firms?

(20 marks)

4 MACRO FACTORS (12/98, Specimen paper) *32 mins*

What are the macro factors underpinning the shaping and development of world trade? Making reference to examples, illustrate how these are being reflected in the way companies are planning and implementing their international marketing strategies. **(20 marks)**

5 IDENTIFYING OPPORTUNITIES (6/95) *32 mins*

Examine the ways in which an international company should identify and analyse opportunities across a wide spread of country markets. **(20 marks)**

6 GLOBAL/LOCAL (6/97) *32 mins*

Kenichi Ohmae writes of the need to 'think global, act local'. What are the organisational issues for a company in achieving this and how might they reconcile the conflicting pressures? **(20 marks)**

7 TUTORIAL QUESTION: KEY FACTORS IN COMPARATIVE ANALYSIS

What are the key factors which should be examined to provide a comparative analysis of potential consumer markets, in a number of countries, for a company looking to expand its international marketing effort?

Guidance note

The question refers specifically to *consumer* markets.

8 LEVELS OF DEVELOPMENT (12/99) *32 mins*

What differences, if any, are there in marketing products and/or services from:

(a) A developed to another developed country?

(b) A developed to a less developed country?

How might these differences be overcome? Illustrate your answer by choosing a product or service of your choice. **(20 marks)**

9 NEW MARKET ECONOMY (6/99) *32 mins*

In terms of potential market and channel development, what are the implications for organisations which are intending to market their products or services in countries which are experiencing World Bank inspired change from a 'command' to a 'market' economy?

(20 marks)

10 TUTORIAL QUESTION: PRODUCT PORTFOLIO ANALYSIS

Examine the problems of using product portfolio analysis in international marketing.

DO YOU KNOW?

INTERNATIONAL STRATEGIC ANALYSIS

SLEPT AND 'C' FACTORS, BUYER BEHAVIOUR MARKETING RESEARCH AND AGENCY SELECTION

Check that you know the following points before you attempt any questions. If in doubt you should go back to the BPP Study Text and revise first.

- The relationship between the **SLEPT** factors of social, legal, economic, political, and technological forces and changes has a significant impact on international trade.

- The relationship between the **'C' factors** also has a significant impact. The primary 'C' factors are customs, countries, currencies and competition.

- **Culture** is the complex set of interactions of shared beliefs, artefacts and behaviour patterns to which people are exposed in their day to day lives.

- Cultures are characterised by language, religious customs, value systems, education, legal systems, aesthetic values and taboos.

- The importance of **analysing and understanding culture** cannot be overstated in the context of international marketing and trade.

- Culture has a significant impact on **buyer behaviour**, both consumer and business-to-business buyers.

- Different cultures have different approaches to **doing business**. Anglo-Saxon buyers tend to be rapid decision makers, while Japanese buyers are slow decision makers.

- **International marketing research** is more complex than domestic marketing research due to the cultural differences.

- Cultural differences can distort the results of marketing research unless full account is taken of the differences in the research design.

- Using a **research agency** in the target market may be more advisable than using one based in the home country.

Question bank

11   TUTORIAL QUESTION: DIFFERENCES BETWEEN DOMESTIC AND INTERNATIONAL MARKETING

It has sometimes been suggested that marketing internationally is essentially the same as marketing in a domestic market. Discuss the validity of this view.

Guidance note

The question does not require a simple true/false assessment.

12   INTERNATIONAL FINANCE   *32 mins*

Analyse the ways in which an understanding of the international financial environment assists the development of successful international marketing planning.   **(20 marks)**

13   TUTORIAL QUESTION: CULTURE

What training and familiarisation procedures would you propose for sales people, experienced and successful in the UK, to enable them to be effective in sales negotiations in a foreign country with a different culture and language?

Guidance note

This needs to be adapted specifically to the selling task.

14   CULTURAL DIFFERENCES (12/99)   *32 mins*

Implementing an International Marketing Mix is merely a matter of finely adjusting the various mix elements to cultural differences. Giving examples, show how far you agree with this statement.   **(20 marks)**

15   TUTORIAL QUESTION: BUYER BEHAVIOUR

It has been suggested that cultural, social, personal and psychological factors affect buyer behaviour. Use examples to illustrate how these factors are of significance to the international marketer.

Guidance note

This question allows you to display your broad awareness of international marketing issues.

16   GOVERNMENT BUYER BEHAVIOUR (12/95)   *32 mins*

Explain how buyer behaviour at government level is influenced by cultural and other factors. Your answer should be in the form of briefing notes to your marketing director.

(20 marks)

17   TUTORIAL QUESTION: MARKETING INFORMATION SYSTEMS FOR INTERNATIONAL MARKETS

Analyse the reasons for using a marketing information system for international markets. What are the main information sources you would expect to use?

Guidance note

You need a framework for the type of information you need.

Question bank

18   SEGMENTING INTERNATIONAL MARKETS (12/98, Specimen paper)   *32 mins*

The task of the international researcher is potentially enormous. But perhaps most important is the search for similar segments of customers across geographically dispersed regions/countries. Outline what you consider are the key tasks that need to be undertaken in segmenting international markets and how market research might contribute to this.

(20 marks)

19   MARKET RESEARCH IN DEVELOPING COUNTRIES (6/98)   *32 mins*

What are the problems encountered by companies carrying out international market research in developing countries? How might these companies deal with the issue of information gaps?   **(20 marks)**

20   INTERNET AND SEGMENTATION (Specimen paper)   *32 mins*

Discuss the way in which the Internet can be used to identify globally similar segments. How can this both simplify and make more effective the market research process in segment identification?   **(20 marks)**

21   PRIORITIES FOR MARKET ENTRY (12/97)   *32 mins*

Identify the principal methods that companies might use in assessing and reviewing underdeveloped country markets, and suggest how the information generated might be used to prioritise countries for decisions on market entry.   **(20 marks)**

22   EMERGING MARKETS RESEARCH (6/97)   *32 mins*

Many companies are looking to emerging markets in their internationalisation programmes. What are the problems involved in researching these markets? How, if at all, might they be overcome?   **(20 marks)**

DO YOU KNOW?

INTERNATIONAL STRATEGIC PLANNING
MARKET ENTRY, STANDARDISATION VS ADAPTATION

Check that you know the following points before you attempt any questions. If in doubt you should go back to the BPP Study Text and revise first.

- The three ways of entering foreign markets are: **indirect** exports, **direct** exports, **overseas manufacture**.

- The **strategic options** for overseas manufacture are
    - Licensing/Franchising
    - Central Manufacture
    - Joint Venture
    - Wholly owned facilities

- The **choice of mode of entry** will be affected by:-
    - The firm and its products
    - The target market and its characteristics
    - The degree of involvement the firm wants in the target market

- **Standardisation and globalisation** issues apply to communications as well as products.

- **Globalised or adapted** products are more environmentally sensitive (in relation to the SLEPT factors) than **standardised** products.

- Organisations with a globalised or **geocentric** (regiocentric) structure usually have staff with higher motivation than organisations that control totally from headquarters.

- Organisations with an **ethnocentric** approach offer a standardised marketing mix to international markets and are environmentally insensitive (in relation to the SLEPT factors).

- A geocentric approach applies **standardisation where possible** and globalisation or **adaptation where necessary**.

- A **polycentric** approach is an extreme application of globalisation.

Question bank

23 TUTORIAL QUESTION: FOREIGN MARKET ENTRY CRITERIA

What are the key criteria, both financial and non-financial, you would use to appraise the viability of entering a new foreign market?

Guidance notes

You should outline a variety of factors, each of which should be considered, although it is unlikely that any one factor will decide the issue.

24 OVERSEAS EXPANSION (12/97) *32 mins*

Selecting the market entry strategy is the key decision many companies have to take in expanding into overseas markets. Explain why this decision is so critical and identify the criteria that should be used in choosing between the alternatives. **(20 marks)**

25 MARKET ENTRY (6/98) *32 mins*

Outline the market entry methods and the levels of involvement associated with the development of a company's globalisation process from initial exporting through to becoming a global corporation. Specify what you consider to be the important criteria in deciding the appropriate entry method. **(20 marks)**

26 MODES OF ENTRY (12/95) *32 mins*

Identify the main market entry methods used in international marketing. For *two* market entry methods of your choice explain the financial implications of their implementation.

(20 marks)

27 RISK AND REVENUE (6/99) *32 mins*

Projects which involve large amounts of development money, for example a new aero engine, are sometimes undertaken on a 'risk and revenue' basis. Explain the rationale behind this form of global partnering and outline the major advantages and disadvantages of this arrangement. **(20 marks)**

28 CO-OPERATION BETWEEN FIRMS (12/96) *32 mins*

Licensing, joint ventures and strategic alliances are becoming increasingly more important in terms of market entry strategies for multinational companies. Briefly describe each entry strategy and explain why it is becoming more popular with multinationals. What are the control and strategic management issues of each method?

(20 marks)

29 TUTORIAL QUESTION: STANDARDISED APPROACH TO INTERNATIONAL MARKETING

What would be the advantages of a standardised approach to international marketing?

Guidance note

This refers to the entire marketing process not just the product element of the marketing mix.

30 STANDARDISATION (6/98) *32 mins*

In an ideal world, companies would like to manufacture a standardised product. What are the factors that support the case for a standardised product and what are the circumstances that are likely to prevent its implementation? Support your argument with examples.

(20 marks)

31 MARKETING AND FINANCIAL IMPLICATIONS OF A MOVE FROM DIFFERENTIATED TO STANDARDISED MARKETING *32 mins*

You have been asked by your company to assess the key financial and marketing implications of its intended change of strategy from product and marketing adaptation in different markets to a strategy of standardised marketing. Write your answer in the form of an outline of the key points you would wish to make. **(20 marks)**

32 GLOBALISATION (6/98) *32 mins*

Many key authors like Levitt, Keegan, Ohmae and others state the necessity to develop a global strategy. State what you consider to be the definition of 'globalisation' and outline the forces driving its development. **(20 marks)**

33 EVOLVING OPERATIONS (6/99) *32 mins*

As an organisations evolves from a domestic to a global operator what are the principal changes in organisational form, resources and operations from a marketing point of view? Discuss the major implications of these changes on host countries. **(20 marks)**

34 GOING GLOBAL (12/99) *32 mins*

Using an organisation of your choice, what internal factors should be considered when a company operating solely in a domestic market decides to go global?

(20 marks)

35 TRANSNATIONAL VERSUS MULTINATIONAL MARKETING *32 mins*

How would a trans-national company differ in its marketing approach to a multinational enterprise (MNE)? **(20 marks)**

Question bank

DO YOU KNOW?

INTERNATIONAL STRATEGIC PLANNING
INTERNATIONAL MARKETING PLANNING, MANAGING RESOURCES

Check that you know the following points before you attempt any questions. If in doubt you should go back to the BPP Study Text and revise first.

- **International marketing planning** can often be the 'poor relation' of home marketing planning.

- The **assumptions** needed to develop international marketing plans are usually difficult to make due to fragmented markets, cultural differences, legal factors, payment terms etc.

- The **orientation** of the organisation is an important aspect of planning the marketing programme and managing the resources.

- The **ethnocentric** approach ignores differences between countries and assumes that the home marketing programme will work internationally. It is an approach which does not fully exploit the opportunities which may exist.

- The **polycentric** approach recognises the differences between countries and so the marketing programmes are **adapted** for each local environment. Whilst being a totally customer orientated approach, it does carry the risk of **too much differentiation** resulting in loss of economies of scale.

- The **geocentric** (or regiocentric) approach synthesises ethnocentrism and polycentrism. This approach realises that there are similarities and differences which can be incorporated into regional (regiocentric) or world (geocentric) objectives and strategies. The geocentric approach considers the issues of **standardisation and adaptation on merit** in order fully to exploit markets and minimise overall costs.

- **Control** of marketing plans must be general enough to allow comparison between markets, but must be tailored to each market.

- **Resources** can be managed centrally (ie international marketing management integrated with home marketing) or the international marketing function and resources can be managed separately.

- **Information is the key resource** for each phase of the marketing planning process to enable:
    - analysis and screening to match company and country needs
    - the marketing mix to be adapted for the target markets
    - the development of effective plans
    - implementation and control

Question bank

36 TUTORIAL QUESTION: STRATEGY DEVELOPMENT

Discuss the pattern of stages that companies tend to evolve through in the development of their international marketing strategies.

37 PLANNING INTERNATIONAL MARKETING (12/97) *32 mins*

In planning domestic marketing the marketer can readily adapt the Self Reference Criteria (SRC) confident in meeting customer desires. What are the different issues involved in planning international marketing? **(20 marks)**

38 ELECTRONIC COMMERCE (6/99) *32 mins*

Evaluate the impact and opportunity of 'electronic commerce' developments (eg Internet etc) on the marketing strategy of a global consulting organisation. What are the potential dangers of electronic commerce? **(20 marks)**

39 THREE YEAR PLAN (6/95) *32 mins*

You have been appointed as an international marketing manager. Write a briefing paper for your director on which you regard as the essential elements of a three year international marketing plan. **(20 marks)**

40 GLOBAL WORKFORCE (12/99) *32 mins*

It is often asserted that people make strategies work, not processes or systems. Identify and describe the ways in which a global marketer might try to ensure that its global workforce is kept highly motivated. **(20 marks)**

41 EXPATRIATE STAFF (12/98, Specimen paper) *32 mins*

Your company is considering establishing a new territory outside of its home-base. As International Brand Manager you have been asked to look at the strengths and weaknesses of the use of head office, home-based expatriate sales people, as opposed to using local nationals. What training and familiarisation procedures would you propose for home-based expatriates for them to be effective in sales negotiations in a foreign country with a different language and culture? **(20 marks)**

42 KNOWLEDGE BASED ORGANISATIONS (12/99) *32 mins*

It has been often said that the turn of the century is seeing the dawn of the 'knowledge based' organisation. In what ways can such an organisation, in a global context, compete to gain competitive advantage? Use examples as a basis for your answer. **(20 marks)**

43 DATABASES (12/99) *32 mins*

As the new century approaches, organisations are increasingly using databases to compete and gain competitive advantage in a global context. Show using existing relevant examples the ways organisations are using databases to such an effect. **(20 marks)**

Question bank

44 TUTORIAL QUESTION: EFFECTS OF ORGANISATION STRUCTURE ON PRODUCT STANDARDISATION

Studies have shown that products are more likely to be standardised in international marketing than most other elements of the marketing mix. How might organisational structure influence product standardisation in the new product development process?

Guidance note

There are three elements to this question and a good answer will have to balance all three: NPD, standardisation and organisation structure.

45 RETAILING DIFFERENCES (6/98) *32 mins*

Describe the factors which typically differentiate between retailers in developing and developed countries. Show how the marketing plan would require modification with reference to a product of your choice. **(20 marks)**

DO YOU KNOW?

INTERNATIONAL STRATEGY IMPLEMENTATION AND CONTROL
INTERNATIONAL PRODUCT MANAGEMENT

Check that you know the following points before you attempt any questions. If in doubt you should go back to the BPP Study Text and revise first.

- A product's stage in its **product life cycle** will vary from country to country.

- **Marketing strategies** must reflect the position of the product in its life cycle in a particular market.

- The product (ie the physical object) can have different **meanings and uses** in different countries.

- You should know the criteria that need to be considered to make the choice between

    (a) **standardising the product**, to maximise the benefits from economies of scale of production

    (b) **adapting the product** to maximise the flexibility in responding to customers' needs in the target market.

- Adaptation may be unavoidable due to meeting the **legal requirements** of a market.

- **Packaging, labelling**, and **branding** must be sensitive to local conditions.

46 TUTORIAL QUESTION: CRITERIA FOR SELECTION OF INTERNATIONAL PRODUCTS

A firm in the UK has a well-established diversified product range. What criteria would it be likely to use in order to select particular products for an overseas operation?

47 NEW PRODUCTS AND INTERNATIONAL INPUTS (6/96) *32 mins*

What are some potential sources of ideas for new product development? How can a firm obtain international inputs? Contrast the new product possibilities of a company that only exports with those of a company that has several wholly owned foreign plants.

(20 marks)

48 NEW PRODUCT DEVELOPMENT (6/97) *32 mins*

Facing an increasingly competitive international environment, how might companies speed up their new product development process? **(20 marks)**

49 ECONOMIC DEVELOPMENT AND PRODUCT DESIGN *32 mins*

Show how the levels of economic development in various countries could affect the design of a particular product to be marketed in such countries. **(20 marks)**

Guidance note

Where a question uses an expression like 'particular product', it usually means that the examiner is expecting *you* to choose a particular product to use as an example in the answer.

50 PACKAGING DECISIONS *32 mins*

In what ways do the demands of international marketing influence packaging decisions? Use examples to illustrate your answer. **(20 marks)**

51 MARKETING SERVICES (6/97) *32 mins*

What are some of the distinguishing characteristics of services? Explain why these characteristics make it difficult to market services in foreign markets. **(20 marks)**

DO YOU KNOW?

INTERNATIONAL STRATEGY IMPLEMENTATION AND CONTROL

MARKETING COMMUNICATIONS

Check that you know the following points before you attempt any questions. If in doubt you should go back to the BPP Study Text and revise first.

- The decision criteria that need to be considered in order to adopt a **standardised communication strategy** across all markets are devised from the overall policy of standardisation or adaptation.

- The decision criteria that need to be considered in order to adopt an **adapted communication strategy** for each market should also be familiar.

- Verbal and non-verbal communication, aesthetics, dress and appearance, family roles and relationships, beliefs, learning and work habits are the **dimensions of culture** with particular reference to communications.

- **Media availability and access** vary significantly between each market. Media conventions applicable in the home market usually do not apply in the target market.

- Each market will have its own **restrictions** applying to advertising, packaging, sales promotion, direct marketing and publicity.

- Factors will influence the choice between using **local agencies** or **home based agencies** with subsidiaries or alliances in the target market or region.

- The importance of using a **selection process** for an international advertising agency covers aspects such as:
    - Expertise in handling international campaigns
    - Compatibility of management styles
    - Types and range of services provided
    - Response to the brief

- The current preference for large companies is to choose **agencies with international coverage** rather than local agencies on a country to country basis.

Question bank

52 STRATEGIC MARKETING COMMUNICATIONS (12/97) *32 mins*

Marketing communications is frequently the most difficult part of the international marketing mix to plan and control. Making reference to examples, show why this is so and how a marketing communications programme might best be managed strategically.

(20 marks)

53 GLOBAL POSITIONING (12/98, Specimen paper) *32 mins*

In today's global village, companies such as Levi, Nike, McDonalds and Virgin are seeking to create a global position. In a presentation report format identify the potential developments in global positioning and the implications for international planning and control. You should include examples to demonstrate your understanding of these key areas. **(20 marks)**

54 PAN-REGIONAL ADVERTISING (12/96) *32 mins*

Select an economic region eg EU or ASEAN (or another). Identify the advantages and disadvantages of pan-regional advertising. Taking the element of control, show how you might manage a pan-regional campaign for a product/service of your choice. **(20 marks)**

55 INTELLIGENCE BASES (Specimen paper) *32 mins*

Show how companies like Levi, Nike, McDonalds and Virgin are using 'intelligence bases' to create a global position. Discuss the development of this positioning approach and its implications on international planning and control. **(20 marks)**

56 PLANNING AN INTERNATIONAL ADVERTISING CAMPAIGN (6/98) *32 mins*

What are the key issues in planning, executing and controlling an international advertising campaign? Indicate your knowledge of the topic with reference to either the European Union or ASEAN. **(20 marks)**

57 GLOBAL COMMUNICATIONS (6/99) *32 mins*

The growth of satellite broadcasting has brought a whole new dimension to regional and global advertising. With reference to specific examples evaluate the strategic and tactical advantages of such a development on an organisation's global communications strategy.

(20 marks)

58 ADAPTING GLOBAL BRANDS (6/97) *32 mins*

Making references to examples, show how and why companies adapt their global brands to meet the local/regional culture environment. **(20 marks)**

DO YOU KNOW?

INTERNATIONAL STRATEGY IMPLEMENTATION AND CONTROL

DISTRIBUTION AND LOGISTICS

Check that you know the following points before you attempt any questions. If in doubt you should go back to the BPP Study Text and revise first.

- The system of **distribution** operating in the selected foreign market will affect the choice of the **mode of market entry**.

- The identification and location of the '**key player**' in the **distribution channel** will indicate the position in the channel where it will be most appropriate to enter the foreign market.

- Logistics approaches which consider the whole of the supply chain enable companies to implement **just-in-time techniques**.

- **Competitive advantage** is gained from getting new products to the market quickly. For these benefits to be achieved, a logistics approach needs to be taken to ensure that the whole of the supply chain is adequately responsive.

- The major **terms of trade** (eg ex works, FOB, CIF and DDP) can be used to enhance the **customer orientation** of the organisation.

- Accurately completed sets of **export documentation** improve the level of customer service and speed the movement of goods across national borders.

- The **purchasing culture** within a country is often a reflection of the distribution system. A slow purchasing culture usually reflects a complex, multistage distribution channel which is not responsive to change. A rapid purchasing culture usually reflects a dynamic and responsive distribution channel.

- The **costs and benefits** to both supplier and customer of the **transport methods** used will affect the prices charged for the products. A more expensive, but faster, method of transport such as airfreight may allow lower prices to be charged due to the speed of delivery and payment.

Question bank

59 TUTORIAL QUESTION: SELECTING DISTRIBUTORS AND AGENTS

(a) Why is great care necessary in choosing a firm's representatives in a foreign market? What procedures might be followed in selecting foreign distributors?

(b) What steps would you take to ensure that agents are operating both effectively and efficiently as the distribution part of the export marketing mix of a company relying totally on agents as its export distribution channel?

60 LOGISTICS AND DISTRIBUTION (12/96) *32 mins*

Moving goods from country to country is expensive. Up to 35% of the total cost of a product can be accounted for by logistics and distribution. What are the main influences impacting on logistics and distribution strategy for international companies?

(20 marks)

61 DEVELOPMENTS IN DISTRIBUTION AND LOGISTICS (12/98, Specimen paper)

32 mins

Distribution and logistics are increasingly becoming the new battleground in international marketing as companies seek to gain the competitive edge. As International Marketing Manager for a multi-national organisation, write a short report identifying the major developments that are taking place in this important field of international marketing. Making reference to examples, explain what your international organisation should do to stay ahead of the competition. **(20 marks)**

62 RETAILERS AND INTERNATIONAL ACTIVITIES (6/95) *32 mins*

Evaluate the marketing factors that influence the attempts by retailers to become more international. **(20 marks)**

63 DISTRIBUTION IN THE GLOBAL VILLAGE (12/97) *32 mins*

The arrival of the global village has had a major impact on companies' distribution methods. Identify four major factors involved and explain how each has influenced distribution. **(20 marks)**

DO YOU KNOW?

INTERNATIONAL STRATEGY IMPLEMENTATION AND CONTROL

PRICING

Check that you know the following points before you attempt any questions. If in doubt you should go back to the BPP Study Text and revise first.

- Prices can be based on costs, demand, or what competitors are charging.
- **Pricing strategies** (skimming and penetrating) can vary from country to country. An ethnocentric organisation may set a standard price to be effective in all countries (eg a Boeing 747 of a given specification is the same price in dollars world-wide). A geocentric organisation may allow its subsidiaries to set the local price, where necessary.
- **International pricing decisions** are more complex than home market pricing decisions, in part due to the difficulties of obtaining appropriate information.
- The **currency** chosen for international marketing pricing will have an impact on the **profitability** of the organisation due to **exchange rate movements**.
- Organisations operating internationally need to protect themselves from the vagaries of **exchange rate movements**.
- **Countertrade or barter** is frequently used when access to hard currency is restricted. It is not a preferred means of trade due to administrative and logistical difficulties.
- Use of **Incoterms**

Question bank

64 TUTORIAL QUESTION: EXPORT PRICES

Describe the advantages and disadvantages of adopting a standard pricing policy in all export markets.

65 PRICING CONSIDERATIONS (6/99) *32 mins*

The recent collapse of economies in some South-East Asian countries has highlighted the difficulties of the 'pricing' decision in global marketing. What are the major considerations in pricing goods and services for the international market, and what contingencies should be planned to offset currency collapses? **(20 marks)**

66 TRADING BLOC AND PRICING (12/95) *32 mins*

Examine the pricing consequences for companies within and outside the bloc, in the following situation. A trading bloc has just established a common tariff of 4 per cent. Before this, each country in the trading bloc established its own tariff levels, these ranged from 1 per cent to ten per cent. **(20 marks)**

67 INTERNATIONAL PRICING STRATEGY (12/96) *32 mins*

Explain the factors companies need to take into account in establishing an international pricing strategy. **(20 marks)**

68 INCOTERMS AND THEIR USE (12/95) *32 mins*

Prepare a report to show how various Incoterms could be used to monitor and improve customer service levels in international marketing. **(20 marks)**

69 INTERNATIONAL FINANCIAL RISK (12/97) *32 mins*

'Going international' involves increased financial risk. Identify the major types of international financial risk facing international business and how companies might plan to manage this risk. **(20 marks)**

DO YOU KNOW?

INTERNATIONAL STRATEGY IMPLEMENTATION AND CONTROL

EVALUATION AND CONTROL

Check that you know the following points before you attempt any questions. If in doubt you should go back to the BPP Study Text and revise first.

- **Control** is the process of ensuring that the results from implementing the international marketing plan conform to the goods established in the plan.

- A **general control** system will comprise:
    - Formulation and setting of standards
    - The measurement of performance against these standards
    - Procedures for corrective action

- **Corrective** action might include:
    - Changes to aspects of the marketing plan
    - The development of personnel associated with understanding the plan
    - Adjusting the standards to reflect changed environmental circumstances

- Methods of **measuring performance** are either direct through meetings, or indirect through reports.

70 TUTORIAL QUESTION: EVALUATION AND CONTROL IN A MULTINATIONAL

Examine the view that marketing evaluation and control is essentially the same for multinational business as it is for domestic business.

71 STRATEGY BREAKDOWN (12/99)   *32 mins*

A global standardisation strategy depends on every link, function and person acting or performing to exactly the same performance standards. In what ways can a global strategy break down, and how might a global marketer attempt to prevent this? Illustrate your answers with examples. **(20 marks)**

72 EVALUATING MARKETING STRATEGIES IN COUNTRIES AT DIFFERENT LEVELS OF ECONOMIC DEVELOPMENT   *32 mins*

What are the key differences and difficulties you would expect to find in evaluating the performance of the marketing strategies of a company operating in two countries with different levels of economic development. **(20 marks)**

73 KNOWLEDGE BASED SYSTEM (Specimen paper)   *32 mins*

Discuss the way in which a 'knowledge based system' of control can provide the foundations for future international planning. What are the potential difficulties of planning in this way? **(20 marks)**

74 CONTROL SYSTEM (12/98, Specimen paper)   *32 mins*

Control is described as one of the major building blocks of planning, providing the foundation on which the future can be constructed. From an international perspective identify the factors which should be taken into account in developing an effective control system. What might affect the degree and effectiveness of such a control system? **(20 marks)**

Question bank

> **DO YOU KNOW? - MINICASES**
>
> If you are in any doubt as to how you should tackle a mini-case go back to page (xii).
>
> The mini-case is compulsory and comprises 40% of the marks. You must be confident in handling such questions.
>
> Consequently, all the mini-cases below should be attempted.

75 KING CARPETS (6/97)   *64 mins*

King Carpets - franchising in Europe

The background

Max King started his carpet business in Los Angeles, California in 1988 with a brainwave idea, 'Why do customers need to travel to out of town stores in order to buy their carpets - why doesn't the store come to them' he thought. So hiring a van equipped with samples he travelled the city door to door selling carpets direct and contracting out the fitting to local carpet fitters. The venture 'took off' and soon he had more business than he could cope with. Not having the capital to expand himself, he hit on another brainwave - why not franchise the business? In return, King Carpets as the company was called would supply the training, the sales techniques and the samples. In less than six years over 500 franchises had been appointed in the USA and King Carpets is now established as one of the Top 100 privately owned business. Its slogan, 'The Carpet Store to your Door', had clearly taken the USA by storm.

Details of the offer

The key factors of the success of King Carpets are convenience, value and customer service. With a range of over 1,500 carpets and other floor coverings such as wood, vinyl and ceramic tiles, the customer choice is extremely comprehensive. But more than that, the range can be inspected under actual home conditions to enable customers to get a feel for what the product might look like against the background of their furniture, curtains and wallpaper. Even more persuasive is the unique 'King computers imaging system' whereby customers can see the room to be carpeted on a computer screen replicating exactly how it would appear after being fitted with the choice of each carpet under consideration.

With no retailer or middlemen, low staff overheads and no heavy stock to carry King Carpets can pass on much of the saving to the customers guaranteeing lower prices than carpet shops, whilst at the same time making higher profits.

Expansion into Europe

Having conquered America, Max King began to eye the overseas market. From his base in Los Angeles he decided that Europe would be his next stage of development. He called in his most successful Californian franchisees for a discussion and on discovering that Luis Pedraza of Mexican parentage could speak Spanish, appointed him as European Vice President - although Luis had never been to Europe. The meeting in Los Angeles concluded that Europe would be a good place to go. After all 'it is all one single market now, isn't it?'.

In any case said Max, 'I've licked the problem in the USA and I'll do the same in Europe'. He didn't believe there were any differences between Americans and Europeans apart from the language and that would be overcome by appointing local franchisees. So it was agreed to launch into the 15 countries of the European Union in mid 1997.

Question bank

Franchisees would be sought and appointed on the following basis.

An up front fee of £15,000 would be paid to King Carpets.

Franchisees would need to lease a mid sized van, eg Ford Transit, Toyota Hiace, Renault Trafic or local equivalent.

Each franchisee would be given an exclusive operating territory of 15,000 households.

King Carpets would hold training sessions in how to handle the computer software that generated the in-house simulation imagery in European capital cities.

Required

(a) As an international consultant advise King Carpets on a research programme to underpin the successful launch in Europe. (16 marks)

(b) What strategic planning and control issues does the company need to address in undertaking the Pan-European launch? (24 marks)

(40 marks)

76 MCDONALD'S AND GLOBALISATION (12/97) *64 mins*

McDonald's - A Challenge to Globalisation

The golden arches of McDonald's rank first among the world's best known corporate symbols, assuring customers that their Big Mac will look and taste the same whether ordered in Manchester or Malaysia. That rigorous consistency has been a key factor in helping McDonald's build the biggest and most successful fast food brand in the world.

However, others envious of McDonald's success have started to carve their own niche in the burger market, some making inroads into what was McDonald's domain. This is the normal course of business as successful innovation in any market will attract competition. The example that follows is one of several instances where McDonald's success has created an opportunity for the competition.

Jollibee Foods, a family owned chain in the Philippines, has borrowed every trick from McDonald's marketing know-how, but instead of selling a generic burger acceptable to any market in the world, Jollibee caters to a local preference for sweet-and-spicy flavours. 'We've designed our products to suit the Filipino palate,' says Mr Bibonia, Jollibee's vice president of marketing.

The secret of success - Rice and Spice

The combination of first class service and matching and sometimes beating McDonald's in delivery of the product in-store, plus the creation of tailored menus, has resulted in Jollibee out-performing McDonald's in the Philippines. Indeed, according to the market researchers A C Neilsen, in 10 years Jollibee has grabbed 46% of the market versus McDonald's 16% based on the share of total number of visits. Whereas McDonald's have stabilised the number of stores as a result of a corporate decision taken when the Philippines was undergoing political change in the late 1980s, and early 1990s, Jollibee have surged ahead and now has 177 outlets - roughly double McDonald's total of 90, with another 36 added in 1996/97. Jollibee's strategy in distribution has been to locate alongside McDonald's and with their superior store numbers, to 'surround McDonald's'. Additionally, the fact that Jollibee's prices are 5% lower on average than McDonald's doesn't hurt either.

The Jollibee burger isn't that different from McDonald's. The basic product is broadly similar but the sauce (or spice if you like) is different. 'It's familiar to customers - it's the spice a Filipino mother would cook at home,' says Tessa Puno, a consumer analyst. Besides the spicy sauces, Jollibee offers, rice and spaghetti as an alternative to French fries, though these are also available.

Local promotion

Just like McDonald's, Jollibee works hard to attract kids with in-store play activities and a line of heavily advertised characters, including a hamburger-headed boxer called Champ and a spaghetti haired girl named Hetty. Licensed toys, towels and other novelties promoting the characters are on sale in stores. Again, the characters have a local expression and have a Filipino feel to them as does the television advertising. Here again Jollibee feels it has the edge in communicating local values to local customers creating the position of being like McDonald's in broad terms, but being Filipino in the style and manner of delivery.

Breaking out

With sales of £170m (US $250m) in 1996, Jollibee is the second largest consumer goods company in the Philippines - but minuscule compared with McDonald's £20bn ($30bn US) world-wide sales. But it can see opportunities overseas in niche markets. Already it has pilot ventures in S E Asia as well as in the Gulf states and plans to open a total of 40 restaurants there by the end of 1997. It has already opened in California and thinks Chicago, New York and Miami with their Asian and Hispanic populations could offer good prospects. The threat to McDonald's might just get serious.

McDonald's response

Jollibee's success has not gone unnoticed although McDonald's subsidiary in Manila has not commented officially, and corporate headquarters had little to say. 'We focus on our customers there just as anywhere else' has been the response. McDonald's may have been handicapped by the fact that government legislation has prohibited foreign companies from owning retail chains, restricting the company therefore to a franchise operation. But this constraint is in the process of being lifted allowing McDonald's to operate its own stores. Furthermore money is no object. The company could pour in advertising and attempt to overwhelm Jollibee's, reminding other upstart burger-chains around the world of the might of the Golden Arches. Whatever its response McDonald's is unlikely to resist retaliation for long and when it comes it will be serious.

Required

You have been asked to head a task force at McDonald's headquarters in Illinois with the brief to plan, implement and control the company's response to Jollibee's. No budget has been set and the time frame is three years from January 1998. Specifically the brief covers two critical areas.

(a) An analysis of the market. You should therefore prepare a report identifying the areas that you would need to investigate in order to gain the detailed understanding of the market that would allow a planned and strategic response to Jollibee's to be developed.

(16 marks)

(b) The planning and implementation of your response over a three year period. You are therefore required to develop an outline of a plan which includes issues broader than just the 7 Ps of marketing and must incorporate issues of control. (24 marks)

(40 marks)

77 HARLEY DAVIDSON (6/98) *64 mins*

Harley Davidson began manufacturing motorcycles in the USA at the turn of the century. Virtually from the beginning they had a unique design with a powerful, robust engine.

Thus from the outset, Harley had created a style that would become a familiar part of their heritage today.

Steadily, through the first 50 years or so of the company's history, they destroyed domestic competition until, in the early 1960s, they dominated the US market. Then, in the early 1960s, the Honda Motor Company of Japan entered the US market. Initially no one, including Harley Davidson, paid any attention to the tiny motorcycles that Honda imported. They were not taken seriously and appeared to pose no threat to Harley's seemingly impregnable position. But the Honda initiative sparked a motorcycle craze and Honda, having established the beachhead with small motorcycles, then started importing larger motorcycles. In less than 10 years financial problems forced Harley Davidson into a take-over by AMF, an American conglomerate with no motorcycle heritage. However, by the end of the 1970s, after 10 years of ownership, AMF's interest in Harley Davidson waned. For Harley Davidson the picture looked bleak. Japanese competition (for Yamaha, Kawasaki and Suzuki had now entered the US market) accounted for 70% of what was previously Harley Davidson's key market segment - the super heavyweight motorcycle (defined as cycles with over 700cc capacity). Then in the early 1980s, Harley Davidson's management managed to buy the company back from AMF and so began the first stage of the recovery.

Throughout the 1980s the company focused on improving quality, cutting costs, and monitored closely the relationship between the product and the customer. By 1993, the position had changed with Harley Davidson once again dominating the super heavy motorcycle market sector and proving that the Japanese onslaught could be halted.

1993 Market share (USA)

Harley Davidson	63%
Honda	26%
Others	11%

Harley Davidson's strategy

Harley Davidson has focused on its key market sector - the heavyweight motorcycle market. Unlike the Japanese, who concentrated on a global standardisation strategy to get economies of scale, Harley concentrated on highly differentiated sub-niches. Based on individual customer needs, Harley produced a range of tailor-made models based on a few basic types, appealing to the older, educated, executive type customer in the upper income bracket, prepared to pay a high price for uniqueness.

Harley's market research suggested that its customers did not see 'other motorcycles' as its competition - but products like conservatories, swimming pools and luxury cruises. When buying a Harley Davidson, price was not a factor. Its competitive advantage was 'nostalgia' based on the dream and legendary mystique of owning an American classic. Customers did not buy a motorcycle, but the dream of 'escaping from business' and 'the freedom of the open road'.

International expansion

Harley Davidson has been a long time exporter of its products. Curiously one of the earliest overseas countries to import Harleys was Japan, capitalising on American occupation following World War II. However, faced with a deteriorating domestic market position, Harley Davidson virtually abandoned the overseas market. With its recovery in the USA and the retrieval of its position of dominance, coupled with a saturation of demand, the company has in recent years once again focused its attention on overseas markets. With a very limited overseas marketing budget, Harley has seen exports rise steadily and today sales in overseas markets account for around 30% of turnover, caused by the steady growth of the 'executive' sector in the world market with rising capital income and increased leisure and recreational activities.

The company has recently established a 3 year goal of overseas sales accounting for 50% of its turnover, with a strong ambition to be represented in the European Union, and South East Asia, including Japan.

Harley Davidson is a uniquely American company. The heritage, the product, the production facility, the marketing and the dealership network are all handled from corporate headquarters in Milwaukee, USA. It has very little overseas experience. All it knows - via unsolicited enquiries and its emerging very small scale international distribution network, is that there is a demand. What is not known is the nature of the customer, the degree of competition, state of the development of the market and the role and contribution of marketing. One of the key considerations is whether the company needs to manufacture overseas in order to lower its cost base.

Required

(a) What are the major strategic issues Harley Davidson has to face in planning its 3 year overseas expansion programme? (10 marks)

(b) *Select either Europe or South East Asia (including Japan) as your chosen area for overseas development. Do not attempt to write about both.*

Having identified your chosen area, outline the options Harley Davidson might consider in developing a comprehensive market entry strategy. Make a recommendation, which must be justified. Then, explain (again in outline), how in marketing and management terms, Harley Davidson might implement its strategy.

(30 marks)

(40 marks)

78 SRI LANKAN TEA (12/98, Specimen paper) — 64 mins

Sri Lanka is an island state situated to the south east of India. It is a beautiful country whose major exports consist of tea and clothing. Herein lies the problem. In both cases production is based mainly at the commodity end of the process. Tea for example, is exported in bulk quantities to the United Kingdom where it is processed by the major manufacturers into packages sold in supermarkets either under national brand names such as Typhoo and PG Tips or as private label brands for the major supermarkets. Whilst the same is not true for clothing the principle of UK companies adding value and increasing the profitability remains unchanged. It is a fact that where commodity activities occur, anywhere in the world, prices are falling for the producers of the basic product. In the global economy there is a world price for basic goods.

Given the beauty and the attractiveness of Sri Lanka it has naturally attracted considerable tourism. However, the success of this industry has been blighted by internal strife within Sri Lanka as the northern part of the country seeks independence. Moreover, tourism has inadvertently created a second problem. Tourist demand has increased the price of goods and services which has compounded the situation faced by tea and clothing producers by also accelerating wage claims.

The problem faced by tea producers can be, therefore, summarised as:

(a) falling profitability as wages rise in Sri Lanka; a commodity cycle, with a world price for tea forcing down the price paid to producers;

(b) limited knowledge by consumers of the superb quality of Sri Lankan tea.

Question bank

The Opportunity

Sri Lankan tea ranks among the best in the world. Its production takes place inland in the general vicinity of the city of Kandy. Here, on relatively cool hillsides, tea is grown and picked by hand on 'estates' which have been established for generations. The question is, can Sri Lankan tea be marketed globally as a Sri Lankan branded tea and sold in small packets to the end consumer through the normal grocery channels or supermarkets? This would improve profitability dramatically for the producers in Sri Lanka.

The UK has been selected to pioneer this new initiative as it is a major tea consuming nation. Preliminary investigations into the UK market have taken place to establish if there were any similar examples that the Sri Lankan producers might learn from. So far one has been identified - the wine market. Many countries produce wine which is exported. Much is standard unbranded wine which is sold to supermarkets at commodity prices. Yet there is ample evidence that skilful marketeers have created brands, enhancing profitability. For example, ten years ago, Australian wine was virtually unknown in the UK but today the Jacobs Creek brand is the number one seller in the market. A similar opportunity might be available for Sri Lankan branded tea.

No detailed work has yet been carried out in the UK in relation to consumer preferences in terms of the taste and variety of tea, the choice of brand names, the nature and form of the packaging (eg tea bags and loose leaf tea), nor the design or even the true impact and value of the country of origin effect. Clearly there is much to be done. What has occurred is the creation of a consortium of a number of the larger tea producers from Sri Lanka to market their teas which has secured approval and some financial backing for the project from the Sri Lankan government. The commitment and finance is, therefore, available for an initial three year period.

Required

(a) You are a marketing consultant to the consortium. You have been asked to prepare a UK market entry plan which includes all aspects of the marketing task. (20 marks)

(b) The implementation of the market entry plan will require you to consider operational, human resource management, production and financial issues. Explain how each of these might be affected by your international marketing decisions and what control mechanisms you consider to be appropriate. (20 marks)

(40 marks)

79 ZIMFLOWERS (6/99) *64 mins*

Encouraged by increasing European demand, and the success of its neighbours (particularly Kenya), Zimbabwe began an increasingly lucrative flower production and exporting industry in the 1980s. Climatic conditions were ideal, and the construction of glass or polythene houses, whilst expensive, was relatively easy. In the early 1990s the success continued, especially in the export of roses. 'Special occasion' purchasing (eg Valentine's Day), made roses a lucrative proposition. More and more farmers and growers entered the industry, until a number of these regularly supplied the Dutch flower auction market and exported directly to Frankfurt in Germany, and the United Kingdom. Gradually the infrastructure (eg cool stores at the airport), was improved. Exports of cut flowers stood at 3,985 tonnes in 1992/3 and the industry predicted a rise to 8,200 tonnes by the millennium.

The major world exporters of cut flowers in 1993 were the Netherlands (via agents and the auction market), followed by Columbia, Israel and Italy. In Africa, Kenya was a major player, much bigger than Zimbabwe, but in roses Zimbabwe began to give Kenya cause to notice.

The principal success factors in the growing and exporting of flowers are infrastructure (eg cool stores, cool transport facilities), government support (eg providing a 'climate' for the industry to flourish), importers (eg providing market information on prices, demand etc) and uplift facilities (air transport to major markets). Whilst Zimbabwe had experienced these success factors to some degree it was not as advanced as Kenya (exports in 1992/3 some 16,000 tonnes). In addition Kenya had other advantages; some growers belonged to multinationals (eg Brooke Bond), and had far better and more frequent uplift facilities into the major markets. Zimbabwe had only one national carrier, which sometimes was unreliable. The country was also served by a few other international carriers (eg Lufthansa), most of which flew North/South. Table 1 gives the comparative air freight rates from selected flower exporting countries, into Europe in 1992.

Table 1

Country	Air Freight Rates US $ per kg
Columbia	1.85 + 7%
Israel	1.48
Kenya	1.59 to 2.00
Malaysia	3.46
Africa	1.85
Zimbabwe	2.00

During the early 1990s there was a feeling amongst the traders that Zimbabwe should be looking for markets elsewhere. This was partly due to more production coming in from competing countries. There was also a feeling in the industry that the growers were not getting as good a price as they could in selling into the Dutch auction, and that with the Dutch re-exporting to other parts of the world Zimbabwe was losing out on some market opportunities. Typically both Dutch agents and the auction would add 25% to the Cost Insurance Freight (CIF) price. Wholesalers to whom the Dutch exported would then add 20-25% to the agent's auction price. Finally, the florists and supermarkets to whom the wholesalers sold on would set a retail price up to double their delivered price. In this way the final retail price could be 2 to 3 times the original CIF price from the same growing country.

In 1993 the Horticultural Promotion Council in Zimbabwe, a body promoting the interests of many growers, decided it was time to explore new markets as alternatives alongside its traditional ones.

Required

(a) Choosing either other European or ASEAN countries as possible new market destinations, outline the factors which the Horticultural Promotion Council should consider before entering the market. (20 marks)

(b) For the region chosen above, design a generic marketing strategy for the Zimbabwe flower exporting industry. (20 marks)

(40 marks)

80 LEVI STRAUSS (12/99) — *64 mins*

By the mid 1990s, with a turnover of $6 billion, there was no doubt that the USA West Coast based organisation, Levi Strauss, was a world leader in manufacturing and marketing jeans.

The product originally started life as a unique, riveted waste overall. In fact, the idea of rivets on the pockets was patented, and it was the only blue denim with this feature up until the early 1900s. In the 1930s the product became standard wear of the American cowboy, but it was not until the late 1950s that jeans exploded as a cult phenomenon - worn by such matinee idols as Marlon Brando and James Dean. However, in the early 1980s a new clothes line became fashionable - that of the polyester suit - which contributed to a sales decline in denim.

All this changed with the arrival of Robert Haas, the Chairman and CEO. He took over when the company was at a low point in 1984. He gathered a lot of talented people around him and decided to re-focus the company on its core product - the Levi 501 brand. He took a big gamble on a single product strategy that worked - due in some considerable way to the clever positioning strategy of its advertising. The advertising portrayed the gritty and urban image of 501s, with the backing of some very appropriate blues music. In fact, the astute use of music has played a big part in the 501 strategy. The advertising showed real people doing real things and sales began to increase.

With the success, Robert Haas decided on a leveraged buy out of the company and to target international markets. The brief in London fell to the advertising agency BBH. The product was to move from a 'mainstream' to a premium product, with a focus on the Levi 501 brand as the original American blue jean. A string of successful advertisements (mainly based on sex appear), including the famous Nick Kamen 'man in the laundrette' advert, accompanied by great music, made the brand a runaway success. Levi's sales rocketed 800%, but strangely, so did other brand manufacturers who did not spend a penny on advertising.

As a result of the successful advertising campaign Levi's attained a premium position and was successfully able to charge a retail premium. The 501 brand sold for US$85 equivalent in London, $50 in New York and $30 in a discount store in San Francisco. Levi's were making a healthy profit on basically a product which was in many ways no different, nor expensive to make, than its competitors' products. Like Pepè or Wrangler, the product was based on good quality control and good yarn. In fact, in a 1993 consumer test report, the Levi 501 was outperformed in many test categories by its competitors.

The challenge in the early 1990s was to maintain the number one global position in the world. How could a leading market producer stay in the dominant position? Rivals, like the Diesel brand, had shown what could be done by being a niche player - being very successful in a narrow market niche. Levi's branched out into the 'Dockers' brand, a diversification built on the trend to smart office wear clothes - a good move to avoid the 'saturation' point which might be rapidly approaching for the mainstream brand. Levi's pioneered the concept of 'casual Friday,' a new idea which allowed workers to attend their place of work casually dressed for one day each week. If it failed, Dockers would not harm the 501 main line, as it was promoted differently. Levi's also created their own stores to sell exclusive Levi lines.

Robert Haas believed in a company culture not based on private jets and limousines, but on a code of ethics which made employees see themselves as stakeholders in the business - even if not actually a stockholder. However, this philosophy was put to the test with the closure in 1990 of one of the San Antonio sewing factories, and very importantly, the realities of a global business were brought home - such as a need to stay cost competitive.

In early 1996, with 1 billion cash surplus, Haas bought back even more stock and shares changed hands 53 times over their 1986 values. The company had reached a high point.

What a difference two years can make! In late 1998 it was reported that four European factories and two US plants were to close. A total of 1,500 staff in Belgium and France and 991 staff in the US were made redundant. Revenue had fallen to $3 billion and it just wasn't 'cool' to slip into Levi's. Competition had taken its toll, with fashion item multinationals such as Calvin Klein and Lee Jeans brands doing well, and upmarket jeans like Armani and Yves St Laurent becoming the 'coolest' jeans.

The company strategy in developing the Dockers brand and new rigid hard wearing denim, plus their emphasis on product focused advertising, seemed to be out of touch with current consumer tastes. For an historically successful international company faced with such a reversal of fortune the major concern now is how to re-establish themselves to their former leading position.

Required

(a) What environmental variables contributed to the 1998 position of Levi's? How could a sensitive and informative Marketing Information System have helped to identify these environmental factors and inform a change in strategy? (20 marks)

(b) Given the situation at the end of 1998, devise a Strategic International Marketing plan for Levi's covering the period 1999 to 2002. State clearly any assumptions you wish to make in devising your marketing plan. (20 marks)

(40 marks)

Answer bank

Answer bank

1 TUTORIAL QUESTION: STRATEGIC IMPORTANCE OF INTERNATIONAL MARKETING

(a) World trade developed through exploiting **comparative advantage** (to simplify, a country should specialise in what it does best). During the 20th century world trade has grown significantly as **multi-national companies** have been created which exploit on a greater scale the resources of particular countries or regions. This has had the effect of creating a **'global village'** for some products and commodities, due to multi-national companies considering the world as a single market.

As the level of **competition** increases on a global scale, both between countries and companies operating within countries, there is a need for organisations to identify more closely with their customers. Hence the growing importance of **international marketing**.

National incomes are highly dependent on **international trade**. Thus governments actively seek partner countries with which to develop **trading links** and to exploit natural comparative advantage. Organisations such as GATT (now the WTO) have been created to allow the development of world trade. Regional trading blocs, such as the EU, NAFTA and ASEAN have been created to increase trade between neighbouring countries within the trading blocs, and also to exploit opportunities between trading blocs.

Companies, and in particular multinational companies, are continually seeking **growth opportunities** in order to increase **profits** and their **shareholders' wealth**. Hence, in order to achieve and maintain competitive advantage, companies and countries are applying the concepts of international marketing to obtain differentiation and increase income.

Strategic importance of IM

The major reasons for the strategic importance of international marketing are as follows.

(i) **Economies of scale**

Price is still a major component of competitive advantage and, the greater the volume that can be produced, then the lower the price that can be charged. This can lead to a greater market share on a global scale. This requires **marketing research** to be conducted on a global basis, to identify and locate the customers and their needs.

The successful exploitation of the phenomenon of economies of scale will depend upon whether a **product standardisation strategy** can be adopted, as this will allow the maximum economies of scale to be achieved. Should a product adaptation strategy be required, then international marketing research will enable the maximum benefits to be obtained.

(ii) **Product life cycles**

Technological changes are leading to shorter product life cycles and increasing **research and development** (R & D) expenditures. To lengthen product life cycles, and to amortise the R & D costs over the largest possible volume of production, opportunities have to be found on a global scale. Multinational companies are in a strong position to lengthen product life cycles through the movement of **production techniques and facilities** to those areas which need the products and which will produce the highest financial returns.

Answer bank

(iii) **Improving global communications**

With improved **communications,** particularly using the **Internet,** satellite broadcasting and more freedom to **travel, demand** is being created on a global scale for products that once may have been considered suitable only for the markets of the 'developed' world. **International marketing techniques** need to be applied to identify the **requirements** of these new customers and to determine the manner by which the requirements can be met and exploited.

(b) Tariffs involve the imposition of specific or ad valorem **taxes and duties** on imported goods. As Keynes noted, the resulting increase in price leads to a **reduction in demand** and on a worldwide basis the lessening of economic activity. Thus one effect of a tariff is to reduce demand for that item in the country of import, which is exactly what the government desired.

(i) **Tariff barriers**

Exporters who wish to improve trade with a country imposing high tariff barriers may do several things.

(1) They can export the item in a **form** where the value is reduced.

(2) They may seek a **third party country** which has favoured trading status with the target market, and export via the favoured nation to the target market to obtain reduced tariffs.

(3) A final and more drastic solution is to **manufacture** within the target country and so avoid the tariffs altogether.

(ii) **Non tariff barriers**

Non-tariff barriers pose similar problems, and create similar distortions to trading patterns. Examples of such barriers include:

(1) **'Buy local' campaigns**

Such campaigns can lead to exporters setting up local manufacturing facilities, especially when the campaign is allied to government grants for inward investment. It is often practised by developing countries wishing to protect and develop indigenous industries.

(2) **Specific local technical requirements**

The astute exporter produces to the highest technical standards to satisfy the requirements of his markets.

(3) **Specific local legal requirements**

Legal restrictions may also subject the enterprise to licensing and quotas on certain goods, or to currency controls, all of which put pressure on the exporter to establish a source of supply within the country.

(4) **Bureaucratic obstruction**

Bureaucratic obstruction is more difficult to overcome. Such pressure is applied to reduce imports and to encourage direct investment, or to protect local industry.

These are some of the more frequently encountered barriers to trade. The work of GATT and the WTO over the last 45 years has done much to reduce the levels of tariff barriers to encourage growth in world trade.

2 POLITICAL RISK

> **Examiner's comments.** Most avoided this question. Too many discussed the topic in broad terms, without suggesting how a multinational firm might deal with such risks.

Political risk encompasses not only **political factors** within a country and relations between that country and perhaps the HQ country of the multinational, but it will also be measured in terms of both **economic** and **social** factors within the country which may affect business patterns and behaviour.

In short political risk indicators fall under these headings.

(a) **Political**: relationships with neighbours; degree of authorisation required for action; legitimacy of government; military control and foreign conflict.

(b) **Social**: religious fundamentalism; ethnic tension; complexity of culture and urbanism (including shanty towns).

(c) **Economic**: GDP per head; inflation; capital flight; foreign indebtedness; dependence on particular commodity exports and food output.

There may be complete political breakdown or the threat of it, or the level of political risk may be measured in terms of the time to the next general election and a possible change of government to the disfavour of multinational operations.

Methods of **assessing risk levels** will depend partly upon the level of involvement in a country - where there is a subsidiary, regular reports will be required if it is believed the level of risk is high or escalating. Independent assessments may be bought on a consultancy basis.

Collection of information from **international agencies** or the head offices of international banks will also contribute to the level of knowledge concerning an individual country. Senior corporate managers will also talk with their counterparts in other multinational organisations both informally and through specialist seminars.

High risk countries

In countries which are perceived to have a **high risk profile** it is important to have a range of **contingency options** available, both for medium and long-term operations and in the face of short-term problems.

Where there is already a **high level of risk** and the company has no presence, there will be a need to keep a low profile with little or no physical presence in that country in terms of capital, manpower, or even a significant customer base. The multinational would be well advised to deal primarily **via third parties** and generally deal at a **high level of authority**.

Very **careful monitoring of existing commitments** and plans will be necessary on a continuing basis, and short-term deals should be made with payments specified in a **stable currency**.

There should always be **contingency plans** in any well run organisation for foreseeable changes, and **scenario planning** for less foreseeable possibilities. In a situation where it is well known that there is a high political risk, the status of such contingency planning should be stepped up. The **responsibility** for this kind of planning should be lodged very high in the organisational hierarchy.

Where entry is envisaged in a high risk country, the **market entry strategy** should be prepared as flexibly as possible, with least resources put at risk at any stage and, wherever possible, **transactions and payments should be insured**. Clearly the risk levels need to be

Answer bank

assessed against the possible reward levels, since potential profits may be high in this kind of situation.

It should also be borne in mind that many international marketing decisions have a very **long time horizon** and, therefore may be seriously affected by even relatively minor changes in political stability over a long period. Some of the abrupt changes to the pattern of government seen in Hong Kong show that even where a particular event may be foreseen a long time in advance, the actual changes are not always clearly understood.

Some **products** are more liable to political debate than others and therefore some multinationals (oil-based, construction companies or transport-based organisations for instance) are more prone to **political instability** than others and should be more wary as a result.

Issue based risk

Some note should also be taken of the political risk associated with **specific issues,** which may or may not be country specific. Recent examples that spring to mind are the positive benefits which have accrued to companies headquartered in countries which adopted a hostile stance towards apartheid in the years before the recent emergence of South Africa in its new guise as a democratically accountable country.

In the other direction one might also look at the troubles of Shell in Nigeria and also their handling of the environmental issues surrounding the potential dumping of an oil platform in the deep ocean. On both counts, Shell was subject to boycotts in some of their key markets.

3   EFFECT OF EU

> **Examiner's comments**. This question was attempted by many - but 'few did justice to themselves'. It was not a textbook question about the EU as such, but what was needed was an awareness of international business conditions. 'All students should read *The Economist* and the *Financial Times* (perhaps not every day, but frequently).'

The creation of the **European Union** resulted in a market of between 300 and 400 million people who are amongst the most wealthy in the world. The tariff barriers that existed between each of the individual member states were removed on the 1st January 1993, and many of the technical barriers (non-tariff barriers) are in the process of being removed. Competition laws, designed to restrain abuse of dominant market power by large companies, provide another example of on-going activity. To the outside world the European Union presents a **single tariff** and a more consistent environment within the union.

The EU will have generated significant **internal economies of scale**. This may make the EU a more attractive market place for indigenous firms than other, more distant, markets and trading blocs such as NAFTA and ASEAN. Thus, the creation of the EU may have had an impact on the level of **competition** in other market areas. For companies in countries outside the EU, its creation presents potentially the biggest market in the world for their products and services, with very significant economies of scale to be achieved and the benefits of an emerging **consistent business environment**.

For non-EU companies, notably Japanese automotive manufacturers and consumer durable manufacturers, the creation of the EU has encouraged them to **invest in manufacturing facilities** within the EU. This inward investment will have had a significant impact on the individual Japanese company's **global marketing strategy**. Most Japanese companies with manufacturing facilities in the EU now view themselves as global companies. Many consumers in the EU now view the products of Japanese companies as high quality locally (EU) made. Thus, there has been a significant shift in buyers' **perception** of goods formerly imported from Japan, with the undoubted consequence that the Japanese companies will have altered their **marketing mix** to take account of, and to exploit, this favourable shift in buyer perception and behaviour.

The above comments apply, in particular, to the UK market which, of all the countries in the EU, has attracted the largest amount of Japanese inward investment. Although the products from UK based Japanese manufacturing plants can be **freely marketed** EU wide, the success of the marketing campaigns of the Japanese companies in other parts of the EU, notably France, Italy, and Germany is not quite so spectacular.

For other non EU global companies the EU presents an opportunity for them to produce products to fill **excess production capacity.** For others the opportunity to invest more in R & D to create products for this large market will be irresistible.

For all firms the creation of the EU changes the way they view the world. Some will see **opportunities** from the larger market, while others will see more **competitive conditions** and respond accordingly. Some organisations will view **legislation** aimed at harmonising the EU as an opportunity and others will see it as a threat.

The **merger and acquisition** of European companies within the European Union will be a response to the changed competitive environment. The acquisition of European companies by non-EU companies allows the non EU company unlimited and tariff free access to the European market. However, the EU does not represent a market with a common **language** and a common **culture**. Thus, the organisation of the marketing function within the merged or acquired firms will need to take account of the **significant regional differences** that remain.

Whilst **consumer behaviour** within the EU is changing due to the emergence of European wide **brands** (often a subset of global brands) with a common underlying **promotional theme** that can be exploited, evidence suggests that most consumers prefer to believe that they are buying a product that satisfies their particular needs. In many instances this desire for **individuality** by consumer groups can be satisfied best by the **merging** of companies (say a firm in Spain with a firm in France) so that the indigenous loyalties of consumers in each country will not be lost.

Economies in management may be achieved at the corporate level rather than the operations level. In the case of acquisition, providing the acquiring firm does not try to swamp the marketing activities the acquired firm (which will be geared to the local culture) then significant gains can be made in the economies of satisfying consumer needs whilst recognising regional differences.

4 MACRO FACTORS

> **Examiner's comments**: Many candidates misinterpreted this question as referring to PEST or SLEPT factors, rather than the major trends supporting and shaping the development of world trade. There were consequently few references to factors like global trading bloc developments or the WTO.

All the **macro factors** of sociological/cultural, economic, legal, political, and technological have a significant impact on world trade, and can be seen to be affecting the way in which companies develop and implement their international marketing strategies.

The **global consumer** is emerging as a focal point for many companies, and identifying these consumers whose needs can be met with a **single global product** is a major driving

Answer bank

force for many companies, such as Kodak and Microsoft. Other companies approach their global consumers with a **global brand**, and **adapt** the product to suit local tastes and preferences, eg Coca Cola and McDonalds. The **world youth market** is an example of a set of global consumers developing out of a **convergence** of the social, cultural, and economic factors aided by the technological developments in global communications.

As the world gets richer due to international companies moving their **value adding activities** to the most suitable locations, world wide **travel** has come within the reach of larger segments of the world population. As travel increases so the **needs and wants** of consumers for their familiar products and brands expand globally. The designer brands and products of North America and the European Union are available in the countries of South East Asia. Similarly, the cuisine and artefacts (so far without strong brand identities) of the countries of South East Asia are widely available in North America and the European Union.

The reduction of **tariffs** through the continual action of the members of the World Trade Organisation (formerly GATT) during the last 50 years has significantly increased the volume of world trade. More recently the formation of **trading blocks** such as the EU, NAFTA and ASEAN is having a significant impact on the structure of world trade, as trade within the blocks becomes easier and trade between the blocks becomes the subject of longer and longer negotiations.

To overcome any difficulties of trading between blocks, companies are setting up facilities to gain **access** to markets which may otherwise be closed. These developments will significantly reduce the flow of goods around the world between the blocks, but greatly increase the flow of **money and information**. The emerging **information technologies** will have an increasing impact on the way trade between countries is conducted. Key to this is the development and influence of the **Internet**, particularly in business-to-business dealings over the supply chain.

Political developments such as the collapse of the centrally planned economies of Central and Eastern Europe have created many opportunities for international companies. Car makers have acquired car plants in this area (eg VW bought Skoda), brewers have bought breweries, and more recently retailers have started to acquire businesses in these countries, such as Tesco in Prague.

Information technology is allowing the countries of the world to become more interconnected and **interdependent**. World trade was affected in 1999 by the fall in the value of the currencies of many of the countries of South East Asia, which created a general lack of **consumer confidence** world wide.

IT with its ability to provide the world with **real time information** is causing companies to completely rethink their business strategies with respect to what they order, when they order, how much they order, when they pay and in what currency. IT is also providing consumers with information on what is fashionable, and altering their **buying habits** and patterns.

5 IDENTIFYING OPPORTUNITIES

> **Examiner's comments.** Students should have demonstrated the use of models and perhaps discussed points relating to evaluation of opportunities, prioritisation and even segmentation prior to consideration of in-depth immersion into market research.

Comparative analysis is a description of the ways in which companies can identify and analyse opportunities across a wide spread of country markets. International companies use comparative analysis to decide upon their **marketing strategy** and where **resources** should be concentrated. Smaller companies would use comparative analysis to decide which countries offer the best opportunities for export.

A large international company first has to identify and locate the **information** needed on which to base the analysis. Primary research is far too expensive for this very general first stage of comparative analysis. Therefore **secondary data** needs to be collected from sources such as government statistics, trade journals, company records, and general commercial data. This information gathering process should ensure that the most recent data is obtained and complemented by comprehensive historic data. These will be used to determine trends and to provide forecasts of future potential.

The most important piece of information the company will want to know is the **size of the market** for their product in each of the countries under consideration, and the **rate of growth** in each of the markets chosen. Growth rates in terms of population trends, trends in wage rates and levels of disposable income all help to give an indication of the suitability of the market. **Reliable statistics** may not be available or there may be a problem in defining the market area, particularly in large countries such as the USA, Australia or Russia.

Import/export statistics will also be very useful, particularly if a target country is a net importer of the products being considered. Then it will be known that other companies have managed to export there and opportunities will exist, albeit possibly highly competitive. These statistics also indicate that domestic customers are prepared to purchase foreign goods and the barriers to entry are probably not too high.

Economic factors

The stage of **economic development** of the country will be important in comparing opportunities. Are they highly industrialised, newly industrialised, or developing? This has an influence on other important factors such as infrastructure and education levels.

The **Gross National Product** will allow countries to be ranked according to their total income. This statistic can also be expressed on a **per capita basis**. Care needs to be taken with such figures, as some countries such as India have very affluent market segments which are worth exploiting, but which would never be detected from an analysis of GNP per capita. **Aggregate figures** used for comparative purposes tend not to identify potential profitable niches.

Geography and climate may influence opportunities: the market may be vast, or spread out over a large area which would incur increased **distribution costs** for the new entrants. Extremes of climate would affect both the country's attractiveness as a market and the suitability of the product for that market.

The competitive level within different countries could be measured and assessed using **Porter's Five Forces model**, the **SLEPT + C factors** and the country attractiveness/ business performance portfolio analyses.

When the information is gathered a comparative analysis can be undertaken, ranking or selecting countries on a consistent basis. The outcome of a comparative analysis is to **identify** those countries for which it is appropriate to undertake **more detailed research**.

6 GLOBAL/LOCAL

> **Examiner's comments**. A 'catch all' question, handled moderately well, but answers would have benefited from better general business knowledge as available in the *Economist* or the *Financial Times*.

Answer bank

All organisations (which sociologists and behavioural scientists define as collections or groups of people) are created within the **ethnocentric framework** of their country of origin, and as such, reflect, for example, the 'Britishness' of doing things. Sometimes organisations created in one country can transfer the characteristics of that organisation to other countries without any adaptation.

The Romans were successful in transferring many of their organisations (both government and commercial organisations) and ways of doing things to most of Europe, the Middle East and North Africa, and succeeded in putting a Roman 'spin' to local life, some of which has been retained with some refinements to the present time. More recently, European countries transferred their ways of doing things to their overseas colonies. The UK was the last great colonising power to transfer its way of doing things around the world.

In total contrast during the 20th century, **commercial organisations** in the USA started to transfer their organisations and ways of doing things around the world in a non- colonising way. The motor companies were in the vanguard of this commercial organisational transfer and they quickly learned that success in Europe would be achieved through making and selling cars suitable for the European environment. Thus, some fifty years before Kenichi Ohmae's exultation to 'think global, act local', one industry sector had put the principle into practice.

The motor companies realised that cars designed and built to suit the fledgling transport infrastructure in the USA would not be suitable for the well established transport infrastructure in Europe. Thus, Ford had to **adapt its product strategy** and create vehicle design and development teams in the UK and Germany to satisfy the needs of the emerging European motorist. Hence, what could be seen as a duplicate design and development organisation had to be created in Europe to ensure success in Europe. Any potential for **global 'economies of scale'** in the design, development, and production of Ford cars *had to* wait for around sixty years, with the introduction of the Mondeo as Ford's first 'world car'.

The alternative approach used by General Motors, during the infancy period of the motor industry, of acquiring local companies did not result in any obvious economies of scale. Vauxhall in the UK designed, developed and built cars primarily for the UK market and exported to all other markets of the world, whilst Adam Opel in Germany did exactly the same but primarily for the German market and exported to all other markets of the world.

Thus one of the key issues facing organisations is one of duplication of activities to satisfy **local needs** when operating on a **global scale**.

However, not all products are as complicated as cars. Other factors (which have enabled the introduction of Ford's world car mentioned above), have had an impact on all organisations. These factors include the oil crises of the 1970's and 1980's, the need to protect the **physical environment** and consume fewer natural resources, the need to reduce pollution, improvements in **communication and transport** systems, increasing levels of **affluence** and increasing **convergence of needs** as a result of improved communications. All of these factors have created conflicts within organisations between the **standardised approach** (one product all markets - think global) and the **adaptive approach** (different product for each market - act local).

As **globalisation** of products increases (some would argue that it is the brand that is globalised), resulting primarily from the convergence of needs, organisations will have to think through how they are going to satisfy those needs and address issues relating to the **degree of control** that will be extended to the local operations.

Globalisation can be seen as providing a standard product across all markets, eg an Olympus camera, but with the marketing **adapted** (particularly the **communications**) to

Answer bank

suit the needs of individual countries and their customers. Thus design, development and production may be concentrated and standardised in one location, with each country/market having **local responsibility** for marketing activities relating to local pricing, promotion and distribution within the guidelines of a **corporate global marketing strategy**.

Organisations operating on a global scale continually need to review the **trade-offs** between combinations of standard or adapted **product strategies** promoted with standard or adapted **communication strategies.**

Reconciliation of the conflicting pressures between thinking global, and wanting to offer the world a standard product using a standard communications strategy to extract the maximum economies of scale, and acting local, and satisfying as closely as possible all customer needs, will depend primarily on the motivation of the senior management and other stakeholders in the organisation towards maximising their wealth.

7 TUTORIAL QUESTION: KEY FACTORS IN COMPARATIVE ANALYSIS

The ideal factors for examination in a comparative analysis of potential consumer markets are the following.

- The consumer profile
- The market profile
- The media profile

In the UK, organisations such as Mintel and Euromonitor publish regular **reports** on a wide range of **consumer products** which include profiles of consumers by a variety of variables, eg geographic (TV region), age, gender, type of use (light, medium, heavy for consumable products), socio-economic groups etc. These reports also contain **market profiles** which highlight **trends** in consumption patterns, price movements, competition and changes in the pattern of distribution. **Media profiles** are examined to give levels of advertising expenditure by channel (TV, newspapers, display etc). Although the information provided is **secondary information** and invariably historic, the **frequency** with which these market research companies report on products gives an adequate benchmark for designing primary research programmes.

On a European scale, the **Economic Intelligence Unit (EIU)** produces regular comparative reports on a selected range of products in countries in Europe covering consumer profiles, market profiles and media profiles.

In the absence of these ideal factors being analysed and published by market research companies, the profiles will have to be **constructed** from **key factors** in original data. Consumer markets are highly dependent **on people**, hence the primary key factors relate to people: population size, age distribution of population, gender distribution, geographic distribution etc.

(a) **Population size**

This will give an indication of the potential **market size** in terms of number of consumers, which will need combining with a measure of **income data** to establish the **viability** of the market. For example, a country with a large population (China) may look attractive from the point of view of numbers of consumers, but as the income level is so low attention must be focused on smaller segments which display greater potential.

(b) **Age distribution**

The age distribution of population gives indications of the **types of product** potentially in demand. A population with a bias towards the young should be attracted to new, innovative products, be less resistant to change and be more aware of and susceptible to the latest communication technologies. Also, a population biased to the young is potentially a growth market for household durables. The number of marriages recorded can act as a surrogate measure of the numbers of households formed in a given time period.

A population biased towards middle and old age will present different challenges (many European markets are experiencing this **population age shift**). With households established and demand for durables from established households being on a replacement basis, other markets will emerge such as travel or financial services.

(c) **Geographic distribution**

The geographic distribution of a population will give indications of the potential **infrastructure** of the market. A population which is largely urban or suburban is likely to have a fairly high level of **retail concentration**. A population which is largely rural will have a totally different **physical distribution** system and will present different challenges.

(d) **Income distribution**

An appreciation of income distribution or preferably **disposable income distribution** is a vital factor in comparative analysis. At the macro level, measures of GNP or GDP per capita mask many potential niche markets, particularly when the population is large. For example, the GNP per capita of India is very low, but due to its large population (nearly 1 billion) the wealthiest 10% represent a market equal in size to the largest market in the EU. Hence there is a need for careful **segmentation** of income data to enable effective comparative analyses to be made.

(e) **Lifestyles etc**

Lifestyles, household formations and structures are further key factors for comparison, since these will have an influence on the media selection for communications with potential consumers. Comparison with competitors (domestic or international) is another key analysis that needs to be made.

(f) **Communications**

The major communications **channels** will need to be identified and compared, together with the role of advertising within the communications channel. The **Internet** is increasingly likely to be significant here. Also it is vital to identify any **restrictions** placed on the content of advertisements. Care will need to be taken to assess the impact of satellite TV on potential consumers and the more traditional communications channels.

(g) **Ability to pay**

An assessment will need to be made of customer's ability to pay for the goods. Customers will typically be members of the **distribution channel** such as distributors, stockists, wholesalers or retailers. The income distribution will give the first indication of ability to pay, but a measure or assessment of the **financial status** of the intermediaries is vital to minimise the risks. An indication of the **terms of trade** and **methods of payment** are also key factors in the comparative analysis, since these will have an impact on both the **level of risk** and the pricing, and hence competitiveness, of the products.

(h) **Barriers to entry**

An assessment of the barriers to entry is another key factor in any comparative analysis. Markets with few barriers to entry are very low in number. Hence, those countries with the **least problematic barriers** need to be identified as more attractive potential target markets.

The results of a comparative analysis should enable an organisation to expand its international marketing effort in the most effective way. In particular, organisations should be able to target those markets with the greatest potential for a **standardised approach**, in terms of both product and communications. Alternatively, the analysis may indicate that **adaptation** of product and communication is the most effective approach.

8 LEVELS OF DEVELOPMENT

> **Examiner's comments.** This was not a popular question, and the second part in particular was often misread and badly answered. Answers concentrated mainly on cultural and economic differences. Few said anything about life cycles or consumer behaviour. Some treated all LDCs as if they were completely foreign and backward. However, the choice of examples was generally quite good.

The two countries that have been selected are Germany and India. The rationale for the choice is as follows.

Germany

- Is at the same level of development as the UK
- Is a fellow member of the EU
- Has a similar industrial and commercial infrastructure to the UK
- Is relatively close to the UK physically, culturally and psychologically

India

- Is a developing country at a lower level of development
- Is a fellow member of the commonwealth
- Has a different and varied industrial and commercial infrastructure to the UK
- Is distant to the UK physically, culturally and psychologically

Differences

The differences between marketing products and/or services to Germany and India must reflect the differences between the two countries. The most important and obvious difference between the two countries is the relative **wealth**, when measured on a per capita basis, and the **literacy levels** of the populations. Other differences which must be accounted for in developing and implementing marketing programmes include the following.

- **Age** distribution of the population
- **Social** structure

  Both of these will have a bearing on **market segmentation** and **buyer behaviour**

- **Climate**, which will affect the product offering
- The stability and convertibility of the **currencies**, which will affect the payment to the supplier and also the **pricing strategy**

Cultural differences will also need to be addressed particularly with respect to promotion and the structure of the buying decision at both the channel level and at the level of the final consumer.

A marketing programme for Germany would reflect the high disposable incomes of the whole of the population, the high levels of literacy, the "cultural uniformity" of the population, and the established commercial infrastructure.

A marketing programme for India would take account of the wide disparities of income of the population, the low level of literacy of the majority of the population, the cultural diversity of the population, and the fragmented and developing commercial infrastructure.

Some products which are in the mature stage of the **life cycle** in Germany may be marketed as new or innovative in a developing country such as India.

Thus, whilst the basic marketing programmes for both Germany and India will be similar in terms of being based on business to business marketing, the detailed programmes will be very different.

9 NEW MARKET ECONOMY

> **Examiner's comments.** Not many candidates attempted this question. Those that did produced a bi-modal distribution of responses. At the poor end were emotive responses on how badly the World Bank deals with the problems of the command economies in the developing world. Responses were anecdotal rather than academic. At the better end, a clear distinction was drawn between command and market economies and how organisations need to adapt the way they do business in these markets in transition.

Context

Command economies can be characterised as those markets that are totally dominated and controlled by governmental decree, where invariably government is by a **single political party** with only token opposition. In some instances the philosophy of the governing party is communist, with no opposition and no political freedom for the electorate. State planners determine the level of output to meet the objectives of the politically created **5-year development plans,** designed to encourage growth and establish a managed equilibrium between supply and demand. Within these plans there is little or no scope for a consumer society to develop - all **consumer needs are satisfied at the basic level.** Most developing countries operate a command style of economy.

In the pre-1990 command economies of Eastern Europe and the former Soviet Union a demand existed for Western European style consumer goods (generated by the ability of consumers in some of these countries to receive German, Austrian, Italian, or Turkish TV). In spite of this latent demand there was no infrastructure in place for such goods to be made available to the ordinary people of Poland, Czechoslovakia, etc. For instance, it was common for customers in countries with car manufacturing facilities (e.g. Czechoslovakia) to have to wait several years for a new car.

In contrast, a **market economy** allows sellers and buyers to determine the equilibrium between supply and demand, with little or no intervention from government. Within the market economy **profit maximisation** is the guiding credo of business with organisations actively seeking year on year profit growth. Market economies are also characterised by **total political freedom** for the electorate, and with the governing party subject to structured opposition.

The **World Bank,** which was created in the late 1940's by the governments of the market economies to assist in the creation of an infrastructure in the developing countries, considers the market economy as the preferred economic model. Thus, World Bank aid for infrastructure development is invariably linked to conditions requiring the receiving government to change its economic philosophy from command style to market style. These changes create opportunities for the entrepreneur, but in turn they also create problems.

Opportunities

Trade between market economies and the former command economies is "freed-up" with the reduction of tariff barriers, import quotas and the general restrictions on the movement of goods. Restrictions on currency movements into and out of the country are lifted, which makes travel easier and assists the flow of foreign currency receipts. This improves the ability to pay for the goods and services from the market economies. The dominance of the public sector is reduced, which creates opportunity for direct inward investment without having to satisfy the demands of the state planners.

Problems

The most frequently encountered problems in **transition economies** are the lack of money to pay for the goods, the lack of a range of **media** to promote the goods, and the lack of market economy style **distribution** channels and **banking** facilities. However, in the early stages of transition all these problems are overcome by entrepreneurs operating outside the embryonic formal system, through the creation of a **black market**. This informal system can lead to long term problems in the transition due to organised crime taking over the black market, as in the former Soviet Union.

Due to the closed nature of command economies, domestic production is invariably of a much lower **quality** than the imported goods, which will lead to balance of payments problems and consequent currency devaluation, making market style economy goods more expensive.

Even when the quality is world class, such as the optical products from Karl Zeiss, Jena and Hasselblad in the former East Germany, the costs of production when calculated in a market economy format may be too great to be recovered by prices operating in the global market, and the companies could disappear, creating significant unemployment.

In general, transitions from command to market style economies lead to a **closure of production facilities** in the former command economies with consequent unemployment, reducing the ability to pay for the better quality goods from the market economies and sowing the seeds of unrest. **Social unrest** affects the confidence of investors and entrepreneurs that can slow down the speed of reform or transition, and has a direct impact on the demand for imported goods. The **speed of reform** also creates problems as the people, politicians, public servants and consumers all have to learn to adapt. Politicians may be tempted to divert World Bank aid money to more politically popular projects, which slows transition and market development.

Conclusion

Most, if not all, of the economies that have experienced a transition from command style to market style economy have also experienced social problems in the wake of the transition, causing the transition to take longer than anticipated.

Answer bank

10 TUTORIAL QUESTION: PRODUCT PORTFOLIO ANALYSIS

A **product portfolio analysis** is a useful tool which enables organisations to review their products relative to their **competitors**. However, there are problems involved in conducting product portfolio analysis, the primary one being **information**, with information availability, reliability, uniformity, and comparability being the major related problems.

There are two generic approaches to portfolio analysis, one an objective, quantitative approach based on **market growth** rate and **relative market share** (the **Boston Consulting Group matrix**), and the second a more subjective, qualitative, approach based on **market attractiveness** and **competitive position**.

(a) **The Boston Consulting Group (BCG) Matrix**

The Boston Consulting Group matrix demands a great deal of information if it is to be produced with any degree of accuracy. In many domestic or home markets in the developed world there is usually insufficient data available to determine market share and market growth except for a handful of products. In the less developed and developing world the lack of data makes any rigorous analysis impossible.

To overcome the difficulties of obtaining suitable information many marketing analysts will subjectively scale the axes of a BCG matrix. With the axes of the matrix defying quantification, the BCG matrix is usually created in a subjective manner for domestic markets where experience enables marketing analysts and managers to position their products against the **named quadrants** of the BCG matrix.

(i) A **cash cow** is a product with a high market share in a low growth market.

(ii) A **dog** is a product with a low market share in a low growth market (which according to BCG should be removed from product portfolios).

(iii) **Question marks** are products with low market shares in markets with high growth rates.

(iv) **Stars** are those products with high shares in high growth markets.

Any attempt to translate this subjective **domestic** approach into the **international** arena is fraught with difficulty. Many questions arise and need answers before any attempt can be made at classifying products into the categories of the BCG matrix. For instance, the position of the product in its domestic market **product life cycle** is likely to be known, as well as the domestic market life cycle for the product group, but what of each of the international markets where the product is competing or could compete? What is the state and nature of the **competition**?

(b) **Market attractiveness/competitive position matrix**

The market attractiveness/ competitive position types of product portfolio analysis, although more subjective, are less demanding than the BCG matrix in their need for quantitative data. However, they do require experience, skill and judgement in their preparation in order for them to be effective management tools. The following decision rules need to established to assess market attractiveness.

(i) Types of **barriers to entry**. A market with few tariff and non-tariff barriers will be more attractive than a market with a comprehensive range of tariff and non-tariff barriers.

(ii) **Market size**. A large market is likely to be more attractive than a small market.

(iii) **Ability to pay** by customer and consumers. A market that has a freely convertible (hard) currency, or has the ability to pay in a hard currency, will be more attractive than a market with a soft currency or one whose government exercises rigorous exchange controls.

(iv) **Market growth potential.** A market with good growth potential will be more attractive than a static or declining market. However, a potential growth market is more likely to attract competition.

(v) **Competition.** The state and nature of the competition will need to be assessed. A market with few competitors, irrespective of whether the competition is indigenous or international, will be more attractive than a market with many competitors.

Competitive position is usually assessed on the subjective scale: strong, average or weak. Considerable experience, skill and judgement is needed to assess competitive position, as well as information on which to base these subjective assessments.

The problems with this type of analytical approach are more to do with **interpretation of data** and the comparability of data between countries than identifying rigorous quantitative measures.

(c) **Appropriateness of product portfolio analysis**

Product portfolio analysis is inappropriate for some companies, some type of products, and some markets. However, it can be of use in the **strategy development** process of some global companies.

The approach to product portfolio analysis taken by the company will be dependent on the type of information available.

11 TUTORIAL QUESTION: DIFFERENCES BETWEEN DOMESTIC AND INTERNATIONAL MARKETING

The view put forward in the question is both true and false, depending upon the perspective from which it is viewed.

In the sense that the role of marketing is to **identify, anticipate and supply consumer needs efficiently and profitably,** then marketing is exactly the same internationally as domestically, using basically the same techniques and **management tools,** needing to ask the same **questions,** developing the same types of **analysis** and manipulating the same elements of the **marketing mix** to achieve good results in both cases.

Yet, marketing internationally is very different from marketing products and services in a company's domestic market. The reason for this is that the **environment** within which the marketing takes place is different. **Buyer behaviour** differs from market to market for a variety of **cultural** and social reasons, and the **rules and regulations** to which companies have to adhere can be remarkably different in the various international markets.

The SLEPT factors

Most of the differences in the marketing environments around the world can be attributed to a number of factors which are commonly referred to as the **SLEPT factors**. These are social issues, legal and economic issues, politics and technological issues.

Each of these broadly stated factors encompasses a range of issues, so, for example, the **social** factor covers not only cultural issues and social/lifestyle issues but also some of the problems associated with language. The **legal** factor covers manufacturing legislation on, say, health and safety which may affect plant location for a multinational, as well as advertising and marketing restrictions.

Answer bank

There may also be other problems, still under the legal heading, related to language, such as the requirement some countries have that export-import documentation must be completed in their language as well as one of the 'international' languages of English or French. There are, of course, very many issues subsumed under these headings, so the answer below will make reference to some key areas only.

(a) **Social**

Culture has already been referred to above, but there are many aspects to culture which may affect the processes of marketing internationally. To take a relatively simple analysis from Terpstra and Sarathy, culture comprises the major areas of material culture, language, aesthetics, education, religion and attitudes and values.

(i) **Material culture** will affect the ability of families to afford various items and may lead to a situation where a product, considered a basic need in a rich country, is seen as a luxury in a country with less spending power, with a consequent change in the marketing efforts needed to effect a sale. In this sense the elements of the marketing mix will need to be blended in a different way in different markets.

(ii) **Aesthetics** (in the sense of colour perceptions and associations) is frequently referred to in marketing texts, but, in many cases, it may be music and people's reactions to it that help to determine how the advertising messages are received in different countries. So a global product such as Levi Jeans, appealing to a reasonably homogeneous group of young people will be supported by identifiably 'young' music in all its markets, as is Coca-Cola.

Music may not, in itself, translate very well from one country to another with entirely different musical traditions. Thus, unless an American product is using the fact of its 'American-ness', to sell to a particular pro-American target market in Japan, the different musical tradition may require a Japanese musical background to television advertisements.

(iii) **Education** levels in a country will help to determine the overall literacy levels amongst that country's population. This will help to determine whether the **press media** will be a main part of the company's communication strategy.

(iv) **Language** can provide one of the most amusing and 'market-blocking' factors in the international market place. So, for example, in the UK, the English speaking telecommunications company GPT encourage their switch board operators to answer the phones 'Hello, GPT, how may I help you?'. When the company set up in France, the local switchboard operators said the same thing in French, using the company name GPT. The problem was that in France the letters were pronounced as 'Jay, Pay, Tay' - which, to a French ear sounded like 'j'ai pete' which means 'I have broken wind!'

(v) Examples also abound to demonstrate that **religion, values and attitudes**, will have an effect upon the marketing processes in the international market place.

(b) **Legal**

As well as the factors already referred to at the beginning of this answer, the **legislative framework** in countries in which our firm may be operating can have a major impact upon the marketing task. For example the German packaging ordinance, requiring certain proportions of packaging to be collected and recycled, has had an impact upon companies within the European Union, who either have to comply with the rules to ensure they can join the scheme, or face a difficult sales task to the supermarkets who would normally handle their products.

There are even non-legally binding **administrative rules**, for example advertising constraints on cigarettes in many countries, which fall under this legal heading and affect the **communications** element of the marketing mix.

(c) **Economic**

The economic performance of a country to which our firm is selling will help to determine the **material culture** of the population (which has already been referred to), as well as the extent of the **distributive infrastructure** which may affect the choice of market entry method. There may also be an effect upon payment methods in the market which will influence the company's **pricing strategy**.

Economic factors may also have a bearing upon the viability of establishing **manufacturing plants** in various countries, which will be part of the decision making process for many transnational and multinational companies.

(d) **Political**

The political system and framework of a country will influence not only the **economic success and stability** of that country but will have an effect upon many other areas (for example the education system - and, thereby, literacy levels). In some cases, where the political colour of the government changes it may mean quite extensive changes to the buying priorities of large amounts of **government expenditure**.

Multinational companies need also to be aware of the impact of political changes upon **anticipated legislation**, which may have an effect upon the marketing environment. This is, of course, true in a domestic market, but the scale of change will differ in international markets and there is a need to keep a watching brief over all the markets in which a company may be operating.

(e) **Technological**

The appropriateness of **product design** is one of the factors that is most often affected by differences in levels of technology from one market to another. There are a number of aspects which may come into play, the two key ones being the **training levels of the users** of a particular product and the **degree of local support** which may be available in terms of machines and/or repair skills. Thus, for example, a company selling farm equipment may be advised to sell robust machines of relatively simple technology to customers in lesser developed countries, to avoid problems of lengthy waits for repairs in a situation where access to repair facilities is very limited.

The technical requirements for a product may differ because there are **different standards** in each country. Perhaps the simplest and most obvious example of this is the variability of **electricity supply** and the electrical socket arrangements across international boundaries, which will inevitably affect product design for electrical goods.

In conclusion, then, although the **principles** remain the same between domestic and international marketing, the **practice** differs to a very great extent.

12 INTERNATIONAL FINANCE

Any marketing planning framework includes **environmental analysis** as a crucial stage in the planning process.

In discussing the environment, it is useful to categorise factors according to some suitable **framework**, such as **SLEPT** (social-cultural, legal, economic, political and technological). In practice, all these issues are interrelated: cultural changes affect political decisions,

Answer bank

which lead to changes in the law. In international marketing, we can extend this analysis to include the so-called **three Cs**: countries, currencies and competitors.

Issues of **finance** are becoming increasingly important as **trade is liberalised**. In the past, there used to be controls over the export of capital, but for the UK in particular, this is a thing of the past.

Finance as an environmental factor relates to a number of the factors in the SLEPT framework and indeed in the three Cs. Some relevant factors are outlined below.

Exchange rates are a hazard for businesses. A fluctuating exchange rate makes planning difficult. Furthermore, exchange rate fluctuations can affect a firm's **pricing strategy** in international markets or, at the very least, the **profits** on sales. For example, a firm which sells to Germany will either make higher profits, in sterling terms, or be able to lower its prices, if the deutsche mark rises against the pound. Conversely, many UK businesses were priced out of international markets by overseas competitors in the early 1980s as a result of what was perhaps an overvalued currency. The debate over the relative strength of the pound has continued recently.

However, more worrying for planners is the effect of **exchange rate volatility**, rather than any particular level. This is why banks offer sophisticated **financial instruments** such as hedging contracts, swaps and options to enable firms to minimise their exposures to exchange rate fluctuations.

Many economists believe that the exchange rate of a country relative to another is determined by relative rates of **inflation** and **interest rates**. This might well be true in the long run, but in the short run (eg one or two months hence) it may be harder to assess. This might be vexing for businesses who have to make short run decisions. For example, a country with higher inflation, or rather, where there are inflationary expectations, may require higher investment returns in order for investments to be profitable. Similarly, the speed at which a depreciating currency must be converted into some other store of value can influence profitability.

Interest rates also affect the exchange rate. They affect marketing planners in a number of ways. **Marketers of financial services** are directly affected: their product (eg loans) will have to have a higher price (the interest rate), and this element of the marketing mix is effectively out of their control. Indirectly, also, interest rates affect the volume of borrowing, in theory, and hence the volume of consumption and the effective demand in an economy.

To summarise, international financial considerations are important because the volatility of exchange rates can directly affect the **profitability** of a firm, and its **competitiveness** in relation to firms from other countries. This has an obvious impact on the international marketing decision.

13 TUTORIAL QUESTION: CULTURE

Salespeople are a unique breed. They are gregarious, but have to spend a lot of time alone. They are highly self motivated. They work to targets, but might then stop.

The salespeople under consideration have already proved themselves to be successful in the UK - hence their basic selling skills are sound. What has to be considered is taking these skills and using them effectively in a different country and environment. Hence they must undergo a thorough **training** and familiarisation procedure.

(a) **Culture appreciation and impact**

One of the most important parts of this would be to familiarise the sales people with the culture of the target country and also the cultural aspects of business to business

buying behaviour, together with its impact on **sales negotiations**. Ideally this training and familiarisation procedure should take place in the country or countries in which the salespeople will be based. Failing that, a suitable training course would need to be attended which would cover the essential cultural differences that would be encountered.

For instance, developing a patient approach to sales negotiations is essential if the target country is Japan. The Japanese take a long time to reach a decision (hence sales negotiations are protracted), but once the decision is made they are rapid implementers, requiring prompt delivery of goods which will have an impact on the whole of the organisation. This is the opposite of UK business to business buying behaviour, where decisions are taken rapidly (involving speedy sales negotiations) and implementation is protracted. After any training course, but prior to them making sales calls and getting involved in negotiations, the salespeople should spend some time travelling around their territory familiarising themselves with it, learning the culture, and business culture.

The salespeople should also be given some background **cultural information** to read and absorb and be assessed with respect to their competence regarding acceptable cultural behaviour and habits.

(b) **Language**

The salespeople should be fluent in the language(s) of their foreign territory. Obviously during the market research done prior to market entry it would have been established what the main languages are ie the every day language and the business language. For instance, in the Catalan region of Spain the everyday language is Catalan, but the majority of business is conducted in Castilian. The training and familiarisation course should be held in the business language - this would enable the salespeople to practice any technological phrases before taking up their position in the foreign country and making sales calls for real.

(c) **Selling skills**

Different selling skills (eg the patience required to successfully complete sales negotiations in Japan, referred to earlier) may be required and this should have been established in any market research. UK selling skills may not be adaptable - they may offend, or just not work. Hence any changes in selling style, selling presentations and approaches to negotiations must be included in the training programme, with the competence of the delegates being assessed.

(d) **Geography**

During their first few days in the new country the sales people must become familiar with the geography of the area. This should be done prior to any calls made, so that on their first operational day they know exactly where they are going, how long it will take them, and the accuracy of long distance road maps and local area maps. This will have the added benefit of orientating the salesperson to the territory and aid the local familiarisation process which are vital ingredients for success.

(e) **Product**

The salespeople will be familiar with all the aspects of the product, its uses, technology, features, benefits and what differentiates it from other products from the UK market perspective. This knowledge and familiarity needs to be interpreted into the features, benefits and differentiating factors in the target market. **Benefits and differentiation** are the most important, although a good salesperson should be able to turn any feature into a benefit. These skills need to be assessed during the training and familiarisation

(f) **Motivation**

The training and familiarisation course should motivate the salespeople into wanting to succeed. As they are all experienced and successful in the UK, they should be used to being the best in the UK. The training and familiarisation course should make them want to be the best in a different culture.

(g) **Customers**

Buying habits should have been established in the market research programme that preceded the market entry decision. The salespeople should be given background information and assessed with respect to their understanding of buying habits on the training and familiarisation course.

As these are successful salespeople in the UK, they will be used to **targeting** the customers with the most potential. Hence the training and familiarisation course must include the necessary techniques to target customers in their new territories to establish who their main customers are.

(h) **Conclusion**

Above are reviewed some of the training and familiarisation processes that must be addressed. An actual training and familiarisation programme would be **specific** to a particular country.

14 CULTURAL DIFFERENCES

> **Tutorial note.** The suggested answer below is based on disagreeing with the statement in the question.
>
> **Examiner's comments.** A very popular question which produced answers showing a good overview of the marketing mix. Tutors should note that the 7Ps approach is to be preferred to the 4Ps. Examples given were varied, but few answers gave business-to-business or service company examples.
>
> The main problems associated with this question were an inability to provide any underpinning concepts, and a failure to show how far candidates agreed or disagreed with the statement.

International marketing mixes need to be developed to meet the **objectives** of the overall business and its **integrated marketing strategy**. The marketing mixes must also take account of the cultural differences that will exist between the geographic/national markets in which the organisation competes. It is the cultural differences that cause the **standardisation versus adaptation** argument to be addressed in the international marketing planning process.

Standardised mixes bring with them all the advantages of **economies of scale**, but are based on the fundamental assumption that the rest of the world behaves and will respond in the same way as the country of origin. Adapted mixes are based on the assumption that the world comprises of a multitude of cultures and that business success depends on recognising and **exploiting those differences**. Thus, standardised mixes will be less costly to implement than adapted mixes, but adapted mixes are more likely to generate higher sales and profits.

Considering the elements of the marketing mixing in turn.

Product. There are very few products offered on a global scale that have no adaptation (examples would be 35mm cameras and film and camcorders). Most products have some form of adaptation to take account of **local needs, culture and climate**. Although McDonalds and Coca Cola are frequently quoted as global products, invariably the product offering is adapted to meet local tastes and in the case of McDonalds it is the service that is standardised. Thus the product element of an international marketing mix requires more than fine adjustment.

Price. Local duties, taxes and tariffs will automatically create price differences and alter the price element of the marketing mix. It is unusual to find a standardised global price, the exceptions being aircraft priced in US dollars and major food and mineral commodities also priced in US dollars. For virtually all other products and services the practice is to **adapt the price to suit local conditions**. The price adaptation will take account of the **cost of producing** the product, together with the costs associated with **getting it to the market** as well as the local **ability to pay**. In many instances the difference in price for the same product between countries can create a premium product out of a basic product.

Promotion. Promotion invariably needs some form of adaptation to take account of language differences and other differing meanings. Types of promotion allowed vary significantly around the world, from extremes such as preventing foreign products being advertised on TV, to more subtle differences regarding the allowable types of sales promotion. Literacy rates as well as language need to be accounted for in planning a promotional mix. For instance, it is quite common in the Arabic world for Western companies such as Mercedes, BMW and Nike to promote themselves exclusively through their logo.

Place. Distribution channels and their **accessibility** and **availability** differ widely from country to country. The model of single and two stage distribution channels are rarely encountered outside the UK and US. There is some movement in the countries of Europe to create out of town shopping centres and associated single and two-stage distribution channels. However, in spite of the changes most other countries have two or more stages in their distribution channels that have significant consequences for the marketing mix, particularly **pricing decisions**. The number of stages in the distribution channel also impacts on the **packaging** used for the product, again having an impact on the price that may change the perceived value of the product.

The service elements

Research is increasingly showing that it is the **service element** of the marketing mix that can be standardised around the world. Most global fast food operators, e.g. Hard Rock Café and Planet Hollywood, provide the same service package irrespective of location. The people employed as waiters are all of the same type (18 - 25 year olds, probably students) and the **processes** diners go through are uncannily similar, creating the impression that the **people** (staff) are operating to a global script, and the **physical evidence**, from the uniforms of the people to the décor of the restaurant, all suggest a standardised approach. The only concession to adaptation of the service package is the language spoken by the service providers.

15 TUTORIAL QUESTION: BUYER BEHAVIOUR

All marketing companies, whether dealing with **consumer** goods, **industrial** products or products or services aimed at **institutional** buying organisations, need to have a good grasp of factors which influence the actual and potential **buying behaviour** of their customers, in order to optimise the success of their marketing efforts.

This is, of course, no less true of organisations operating internationally than it is of organisations operating in a domestic marketing environment. The extra complexity is caused by the variability of the factors in different countries.

As indicated in the question, most models of buyer behaviour include **cultural**, **social**, **personal** and **psychological factors** as major determinants of behaviour, so we might examine these in turn to explain their significance to the international marketer. They are, inevitably, strongly interdependent and we will seek to look at their mutual effects.

(a) **Culture**

The factor with, arguably, the greatest impact upon the variability of buyer behaviour between people from different countries, is the **cultural background** from which they come. Culture is learned from family, friends, school, church, mosque or temple and society at large. There may be different **sub-cultures** based upon different sub-groups in society. Indeed, some international marketers benefit from knowledge of subcultures which cross national boundaries.

Thus, there is a wide acceptance that there is a widely spread youth culture, which has come into being largely via the electronic media of television and radio. Young people living in Europe, South America and the newly industrialising countries of Korea and Taiwan, for example, may display some similarity of tastes in music, clothes and leisure pursuits.

Despite **cultural convergence** at one level, there are probably more abiding differences at a much deeper level which will influence buyer behaviour across a wider area of purchasing. Such a difference is that between **high context** and **low context** cultures: high context being where understanding of communications depends very much upon the context within which they are made, and low context being where the words themselves convey the bulk of the meaning with little dependence upon the surrounding context.

Thus the religious freedom and tolerance that developed with the growth of the United States, has led to a low context culture, in contrast to the kind of high context culture one might associate with countries where the people share a common religious and cultural tradition. In this latter situation, there is an extensive silent, non-verbal language, which relies on a high level of context for clear understanding.

In Japan, for example, there are clear but unwritten rules about the hierarchical order in which executives and managers may drink their tea in a meeting. Such rules are, naturally, inculcated from an early age in Japan but executives from a Western company may inadvertently cause offence by being unaware of the rules. If competing for an order with a Japanese supplier, then the home team will have an advantage, all other things being equal, during negotiations. This is only one very small factor amongst many culturally driven rules of etiquette, any of which may trip up the unwary.

(b) **Social**

The way in which people interrelate in a social context will also have an effect upon buyer behaviour. **Peer group pressure** will apply differently in different countries, but will also be very different between socio-economic groups within countries, so a knowledge of such groupings will assist international marketers with their marketing planning.

By way of example, **packaging** and pack sizing will be influenced by the shopping habits apparent in different countries. In the UK, out of town shopping centres have led to joint husband and wife shopping trips, whereas other countries still may rely upon many smaller shops, where the purchaser will buy smaller quantities more frequently. Peer group pressure amongst males may also tend to discourage men from taking any involvement with their wives in this task.

Marketers of some products may take advantage of the inclusion of the male in the **household buying group**, by positioning impulse products in supermarkets to tempt the male susceptibility.

The concept of personal space will affect buyer behaviour for both industrial and institutional products and services, as well as the sale of consumer goods into their distribution channels. In many countries in the Middle East and North Africa, for example, people are used to dealing with others at much closer range than is the case in the UK or the USA. The issue is at least partly to do with the high context interpretation of non-verbal language, where the buyer may be watching for signals. Negotiators and sales people working for international marketers need to be trained to feel no discomfort when dealing with this sort of eye-to-eye contact. Empathy, or the ability to put yourself into another person's shoes, is a useful personal characteristic.

(c) **Personal**

The personal circumstances of a customer represent a major influence on buying behaviour in all buying situations, but most obviously in the purchasing of consumer goods.

Personal circumstances will be influenced in turn by **cultural, social** and other factors as well as the **economic** fortunes of the country concerned. Thus, in the US and some western European countries individuals will consume from twenty to forty times as much resources, during their lifetimes, as individuals in developing countries. This will clearly lead to widely different perceptions of such issues as **value for money**, attitudes to **packaging, frequency** of purchase and so on, all of which will affect the marketing targeted at this buyer behaviour.

On the other hand, **life cycle considerations** will play a major role in terms of perceived importance of the value of leisure goods, say, in contrast to nest-building products such as furniture and soft furnishings. A good knowledge of the most likely life-cycle categories and the numbers of people in each will lead to improved **targeting** for **market segmentation** purposes in international marketing.

Thus for India and other developing countries, very large proportions of the population are in the under 16 age group, which carries significant implications for marketing strategy decisions.

(d) **Psychology**

Psychological factors can play an important part at all stages of the buying process, not least in **interpreting** the marketing messages being put out by the selling companies. The issue of humour, for example, is a very sensitive area in the field of marketing **communications**. Frequently used in British advertising, humour is notoriously difficult to translate and will not, normally, cross international borders with ease.

The psychology of **time** is also very different in different countries. In the US, for instance, time is usually of the essence and meetings are expected to start promptly. Negotiations are also likely to begin early in a meeting. In the Latin countries of southern Europe and South America, clock watching is much less apparent and being late for a meeting is much more easily tolerated. Also meetings will be extended more readily if progress is being made. Such points need to be carefully watched by companies involved in sales negotiations between parties coming from such different backgrounds.

Some companies will seek to adopt a global marketing approach where they can identify some similarities of **psychological profiles** across national borders. Goodyear Tyre and Rubber Company is a case in point, where, after extensive research, they came up with six consumer segments based upon attitudes to three decision making variables of **brand, outlet** and **price**.

The segments were labelled as follows.

- **Prestige buyer**: puts the brand decision first, then the outlet decision
- **Comfortable conservative**: looks for outlet first and brand second
- **Value shopper**: considers brand first and price second
- **Pretender**: considers price first and brand second
- **Trusting patron**: chooses outlet first and price second
- **Bargain hunter**: shops for price first and outlet second

There are many examples of psychological profiling within markets, but they need to be considered in the context of the other factors discussed here to give any sound information about their effect upon buyer behaviour.

16 GOVERNMENT BUYER BEHAVIOUR

> **Examiner's comments.** Answers were waffly and strayed from the boundaries of the question which specifically referred to government buyer behaviour.

To: Ms Diane Rector
From: Mark E Ting

Diane,

Please find attached the briefing notes you requested concerning buyer behaviour at government level.

Mark

Briefing notes

In many countries, **government** is the biggest buyer and will be responsible for buying a wide range of **goods and services**. The way government buys is influenced by the extent to which **public accountability** for expenditure is deemed to be important - so cultural history of public service and accountability is critical.

The usual forms of buying procedure are the **open tender** and the **selective tender**. For a selective tender process, we need to be on the appropriate list. In some countries, it will take considerable persistence for us to get to that stage, since it may take several visits to appropriate government officials to establish **a good working relationship**. We may have to drink many cups of thick strong coffee, for example, to become accepted in some mid-east countries! There are other countries where gifts and/or 'agents fees' may be expected too, but we may have to discuss this with the company's ethics committee before proceeding.

In Europe we should have an opportunity to be the equal of any competitor in the European Union - and the bidding will normally be to an open tender.

Social and cultural factors

It is generally true that in dealing with governments and government departments, the significance lies, perhaps, with **who you know** rather than with **what you know**.

It is also true that buying decisions may be affected as much by a lowly departmental clerk acting as a **gatekeeper** in a **decision making unit** (DMU), as by a senior government official or even a politician acting as a **decision maker** or an **influencer** in the DMU.

A clear understanding of the **cultural** inter-relationships in government circles, **hierarchical** relationships and **political influence** may be critical in some markets and countries.

(a) For example, a different style is necessary for dealing with officials from **high context** cultures than from **low context** cultures.

(b) The officials we speak to may have formal **authority** but little actual **power**, which might be exercised elsewhere.

(c) We may suffer if relationships between our own **government** and the host country government deteriorate.

(d) Different cultures have different attitudes to **gifts**.

(e) Some cultures prefer a high degree of **legalism**, others do not.

(f) There may be **conflict** between different government departments.

(g) Governments are susceptible to pressure from **powerful interest groups**.

17 TUTORIAL QUESTION: MARKETING INFORMATION SYSTEMS FOR INTERNATIONAL MARKETS

The basic definition of marketing requires, first, the **'identification'** of **consumer needs** before they can be **'anticipated'** and **'satisfied'**. This is why it is important for a company to discover information about the markets within which it is operating, whether they are domestic or international. It is unfortunately true that many companies rely on haphazard, ad-hoc collection of information for a specific project.

Companies intent upon success will, however, devise a **marketing information system** (MkIS) to formalise and systematise the collection of appropriate information, leading to a more professional approach to the market place.

The need for a good MkIS is particularly strong in international marketing because there tend to be many more unknowns to face when marketing across national boundaries. A company which is successful in its domestic market, actually knows more about that market than may be consciously recognised. Many of the operating conditions and constraints are understood and ingrained in everyone's thinking. If a company is not to suffer from some of the more obvious flaws of using the **self-reference criterion** in international marketing, a properly constituted MkIS will formalise the collection and storage of appropriate **market data**.

The 12 C's Approach

In order to build a sound information base of the most likely markets identified in market scanning, the MkIS should develop a cost effective **communications channel** between the environment in which the company operates and its key decision makers. A useful model for such a system is the 12 Cs environmental analysis, which provides a helpful checklist of factors which need to be monitored in all markets. The 12 C framework includes the following sub-categories.

Answer bank

Factor	Elements to consider
Country	• Basic **SLEPT** data
Choices	• **Competitive offerings** to the market
Concentration	• Structure and spread of the **market segments**
Culture/consumer behaviour	• Factors and influences over **purchasing behaviour**
Consumption	• **Market shares** and growth patterns by demand sector
Capacity to pay	• Effect on **pricing** decisions
Currency	• **Stability** and restrictions
Channels	• The nature of the **distribution** function
Commitment	• **Access** to markets and **regulations** on entry
Communications	• Examining the **promotional** framework and **media** infrastructure
Contractual obligations Caveats	• **Business practices** and legal obligations

Just taking channels as an example, it is vital that a sound MkIS provides a clear view of the differences in distribution channel behaviour in the company's target international markets compared with its domestic market. Thus the **retail system** may be much more fragmented than in the domestic market, requiring a different pattern of area **sales management**. Without such knowledge a company's effectiveness to respond to market conditions may be seriously impaired.

Sources of information

In building an MkIS, companies would utilise a variety of information services and sources. It is logical for **cost** reasons to start with **internal** data, which may have been collected from customers and suppliers over a period of time.

The next stage is to target **secondary data** sources, many of which are freely available in libraries and databanks, eg the DTI (Department of Trade and Industry) export library will provide a wealth of data about the economic and historical political background of most markets in the world. Most developed nations have a similar government-backed information source.

Other **institutions** offering free, or low cost, secondary data include Chambers of Commerce, banks, trade associations, universities, foreign trade organisations, OECD, the World Bank, and so on.

Overseas distributors, sales subsidiaries and freight forwarders may also provide a wealth of information of a secondary nature, more specific to the company's needs. There are also a considerable number of **on-line computer data sources** available for commercial purposes including Reuters News information and details on worldwide patents.

A good MkIS also requires **primary** information to keep the system up to date and appropriate for the company's requirements. Contact networks include trade associations, agents and distributors. More task specific data may be available through multi-client studies, omnibus research projects and consortium studies.

Answer bank

The final, most expensive, stage of providing information to an MkIS is the collection and transmission of company, product or service specific **primary market data**, collected directly by **marketing research agents** in the countries being targeted.

18 SEGMENTING INTERNATIONAL MARKETS

> **Examiner's comments.** Candidates often failed to relate their answers to the international aspect of the question. Few candidates spotted the fact that the question was hinting at 'strategically similar' segments. Few segmentation techniques or models were cited or discussed, although some candidates did embellish their answers with very detailed and time-wasting diagrams.

A **segment** is a homogeneous grouping of consumers who, ideally, share the same or very similar characteristics. No consumer is exactly the same as the next but it is widely recognised that many share similar **values, beliefs** and **wants**. By clustering these together the marketer is able to **target** products efficiently and effectively that will be attractive to members of particular segments. The key to segmentation is the clear understanding, through detailed research, of the **characteristics of the population**.

In international markets this task is difficult due to a number of factors, such as culture, language, religion, literacy levels and the role and position of women in society. It is the skill of the international marketer in identifying where similarities exist that enables segments to be created. In order to do this a number of tasks need to be completed.

The primary task is to classify the **stage of need** in the selected countries as **existing, latent** or **incipient**, (Gilligan & Hird) in order to assess the most likely potential demand patterns. This helps with establishing the **target market sectors** and informs the tasks of identifying:

- Who the customers are
- Where the customers are
- Identification of secondary segments by:
  - age
  - gender
  - lifestyle
- Potential market size
- What similarities exist between the markets in the regions or countries

The results of these tasks is the formation of **strategically equivalent segments**.

Secondary research is a cost effective way of using published marketing research and other published information to enable initial segments to be formed. Governments of all countries publish **economic** and **demographic** data that can help in the segmentation process. **Market research companies** such as the Economist Intelligence Unit (EIU) in the UK regularly publish reports on the developments taking place in every country in the world. This is an invaluable source of initial data.

However, in spite of the extraordinary lengths taken by organisations such as EIU to compile and publish their research findings, the research is unlikely to have been undertaken for the **purpose** of segmentation. Therefore most secondary research will need to be complemented with **primary research** to obtain the details necessary to establish whether the segments generated by the secondary research are commercially viable.

Primary research, which can be expensive, will be undertaken to determine the details of **consumer behaviour** within the segments with respect to consumption levels and patterns.

Answer bank

Analyses of the potential performance of the segments can be undertaken using a variety of **analytical tools** such as comparative analysis, regression analysis and multi-factor analysis.

Segmentation informs the development of **marketing mixes** and determines whether **differentiation strategies** are required.

There are a number of international segmentation packages in existence such as **ACORN** (A Classification of Residential Neighbourhoods) from US based CACI, and **Mosaic** from Experian in the UK. Both packages can be customised for particular geographic markets, subject to suitable information being available. For organisations with **web sites**, and suitable software to identify visitors to the site, this data can be used for constructing segments.

19 MARKET RESEARCH IN DEVELOPING COUNTRIES

> **Tutorial note.** This looks like a straightforward question. The problems of research in developing countries are well documented. Researchers need to make extra efforts to overcome a lack of knowledge of the market. The 'foreign factor' will show itself, for example, in customer preferences and beliefs.
>
> **Examiner's comments.** The first part of the question was reasonably well covered, but many did not understand the second part of the question at all and attempted to cover up their lack of knowledge with irrelevant answers. There were also very few examples given.

Typical problems encountered in conducting market research in developing countries are as follows:

(a) Lack of reliable basic demographic and economic **statistics** upon which to develop a workable database

(b) A general lack of up to date **secondary market intelligence** information, including that which is provided by organisations such as the Economist Intelligence Unit

(c) When data, or information, is found it may be out of date, **inaccurate** or **irrelevant** for the purpose for which is required.

(d) The **units of measurement** may differ from what is usually expected in the developed world.

(e) Primary data can be difficult to obtain due to **cultural differences**, which in many developing countries do not encourage the disclosure of personal information.

(f) There is a lack of **marketing research agencies** in developing countries.

(g) Lack of telephones, poor transport **infrastructure** and problems of accessibility to respondents all hinder the primary research process.

The absence of reliable and appropriate secondary data presents significant management problems regarding the obtaining of primary data. The problems extend to all aspects of collection, analysis, and interpretation of data, as well as the training and supervision of interviewers.

Information gaps may be filled by the following analytical techniques:

(a) Analysis of **international trade statistics** between the developed world and the target developing countries can be used as a proxy measure to establish the pattern of trade, and give a first order approximation of market size

(b) Multiple factor indices using **proxy measures,** for example, estimating literacy levels from the number of schools, or government estimates of the number of school age children

(c) **Cross-country comparisons** in which the trade development patterns of an existing developing country are used to estimate the likely development of the target country

(d) **Time series** approaches with estimates of the rate of product (or service) demand growth, based on the stage of development of the target developing country

(e) **Regression analysis** looking for relationships between major variables, for example, examining the relationship between the vehicle population, estimates of GDP per head of population and population of a country to estimate annual demand for cars.

If these analytical techniques do not produce meaningful results then a **visit** to the target developing countries and gathering information from **first hand investigation** is the remaining option.

20 INTERNET AND SEGMENTATION

Creating and opening a **website** automatically gives its owner a global presence, and every site owner is most likely to be interested in where his/her **visitors** have originated, which is the start of the **market research** process. Currently, most of the **software** available for creating and managing web-sites gives site operators the ability to identify the source of every visitor to a site, (i.e. org, gov, .com etc.). In some cases it is possible to identify the particular visitor (i.e. Mark.ETing@freeserve.co.uk). Analysis of this data enables the website owner to create segments for all visitors that will differ from the conventional segments based on socio-economic groupings or lifestyle. From these analyses **new segments** will start to emerge, which describe the nature of the visitors.

For instance, the student segment visiting a site from a college campus will be identifiable from the '.ac' or '.edu' address forms. **Navigational software** within the site will show what the particular attractions of the site are for the student segment. Analysis of the navigation patterns will enable the student segment to be refined, or sub segmented, to a very fine degree. A segment of one can be achieved, which is the goal of **micro marketing** and the movement towards removing the waste from the marketing process.

Segmentation of visitors by **country of origin** becomes easy from an analysis of the final part of the address (.uk, for instance). From the navigation pattern of the visitors around the site globally similar segments can start to be created. If the site is an active trading site, e.g. Amazon.com, then the global segments of Visa and other credit card users can be created. This information can then be used for piggyback or joint **promotions** for books, credit card use and electronic commerce with Visa or Mastercard, or any other credit card provider.

Using visitor information allows very closely **targeted promotion** at the user who may or may not be an Internet shopper, but the promotion is not wasted as the company will know that all credit card users are its potential customers and it wants more of them at minimum cost.

Amazon.com uses the automatic, and continuous market research capability of their site management software as a sales promotion and selling aid. An inquiry about the availability of any title in the Amazon.com catalogue will result in the expected review of the contents and any other critique found on book covers in conventional bookstores. However, on selecting their chosen title, irrespective of whether the selection is for browsing or purchasing, the visitor/browser is also given the titles and authors of the books other site visitors/browsers have either shown an interest in during their visit or have bought. Thus, the on-line, real time, **automatic market research** process identifies the particular segment to which the visitor belongs and gives the visitor the option of extending their purchase choice and purchase, contributing to higher sales for Amazon. This application of micro marketing has yet to generate a profit for Amazon, since its year ending 1999 accounts showed a turnover of US$760 million produced a US$162 million loss.

Thus the Internet enables market research to become a **real time** continuous process, rather than a single point in time activity using conventional techniques. The market research process has been simplified, due to the management software of the site automatically **collecting** the data and performing pre-programmed **analyses** to give the site operator the information required. In time, and with the appropriate management commitment, each web-site operator will have created their own customised equivalent of ACORN (from CACI in the US) or MOSAIC (from Experian in the UK) from the information gathered from the visitors to their sites.

It is interesting to note and speculate that all this information about our behaviour when using the Internet is collected and analysed without us knowing or without us being asked whether we want to divulge the information.

21 PRIORITIES FOR MARKET ENTRY

> **Examiner's comments**. Candidates often limited their answers to generalisations about market research plans that had little direct relevance to the specifics of the question.

It is important for a company not yet marketing in **underdeveloped country markets** to prepare very carefully for **market entry**, since the process can be expensive and is not necessarily going to bring immediate rewards. The information collection and review should lead to an estimate of the **speed of payback** for each market, the eventual **size** of the market and the **synergy** that may be generated by looking at the juxtaposition of markets, if entry to more than one is anticipated.

It is clearly of importance to be sure of the markets the company is prepared to enter and the amount of product and marketing development or alteration the company can invest in new markets, before any commitment is made.

The first part of the process is to **scan** the markets thoroughly to ensure the greatest overlap between the company's current offering and the offering a particular market would find acceptable. In terms of market scanning the three requirements are that the market under review should be **accessible**, secondly that there should be a **market size** appropriate to the company's longer term plans, and that the price product market relationship should lead to **profitability** in the foreseeable future.

Accessible

Can we get our products to the market with reasonable **ease** and without excessive extra **costs**? Are there any **barriers to entry**, either from competitors or from government restrictions or tariffs, or some combination of all three?

Market size

Not only do we need to check that the market is of sufficient size to introduce the product, but we must ask how the market is progressing, what the **forecasts** are for the market in future years and what **technological developments** may have an effect upon the development of the market.

Profitability

It is important to consider all the costs of entering a particular market. This includes the costs of **logistics** to enter the market as well as the **marketing** costs, **promotional** costs, **channel management** costs and so on. Is there any reason why the company can charge a

Answer bank

skimming price in this market for any length of time? We may perhaps have some advantage over the competition which allows us to charge a price which acts as a barrier to entry for others, giving larger market share and a longer term profitability for the overall market.

The scanning process should give information as to whether the markets are **existing markets**, where customer needs are already serviced, **incipient markets** where potential customers are currently recognised but are not being serviced, or **latent markets** where there is a foreseeable market for our products. The Gilligan and Hird model taken from Doole, Lowe and Phillips is shown below. This model shows the relationships between the **costs** and **risks** associated with such marketing opportunities.

Gilligan and Hird model

	Existing	Latent	Incipient	
Competitive			Existing brands are positioned to take advantage of possible developing needs; no direct competition, but consumers need to be found and then persuaded of the product's value to them. Risk and cost of failure may be high	Low
Improved	Superior product offers competitive advantage and eases market entry	Increasingly advanced profile offers greater benefits to the market; no direct competition		Cost and risk of launching the product
Breakthrough	Breakthrough product offers self-evident superiority and the competitive advantage is high	Breakthrough product offers significant advantages but markets need to be identified and developed. Little likelihood of competitors in the short term and medium term, but customer resistance may be high		High
	Low	Cost and risk of opening up the market	High	

(Left axis: **Type of product**)

Other ways of examining the potential of country markets in order to prioritise them include using a cross-section of **economic and social indicators** in order to build a model of the country and assess its potential against a similar, or analogous country (analogy estimation). We can also use the **Business Environment Risk Index** (BERI) to give a gauge of likely potential and risk in entering a country market.

Once all the analysis has been done it should be possible to use the information to create a model such as the matrix developed by Harrell and Keifer, which assesses **country attractiveness** and **company compatibility**, in order to give a guide to the primary, secondary and tertiary opportunities for any company tackling specific markets. It looks at market size growth regulation and political suitability, amongst other things, to provide a wide view of **potential markets** and their advantages and difficulties in marketing terms.

22 EMERGING MARKETS RESEARCH

> **Examiner's comments.** A classic case of not answering the question, and instead writing "everything I know" about international market research. The question asked how the problems could be overcome.

An organisation may decide to investigate an emerging market for a variety of reasons. Some of the more frequently encountered reasons are these.

(1) **Competitive forces** in existing markets create the need to seek and exploit new, less developed, markets.

(2) Products reach **the end of their life cycles** in existing, developed markets, but are believed by management to have potential in new, underdeveloped or emerging markets.

Reason 1 will involve **identifying** the existence, or otherwise, of any **barriers to entry** and methods to overcome them, together with developing an understanding of the **customers and competition**.

Reason 2 will involve **establishing the suitability of the products** and the existence of **distribution** and **communication** channels.

The major problems involved in researching emerging markets are centred around the **lack of data** to conduct any meaningful **secondary research**. When data is present it can be inaccurate, out of date, and possibly, irrelevant for the needs of the organisation. In some emerging markets the lack of a commercial infrastructure can be a major hindrance.

Primary research is a possibility, and apart from the cost, other problems are present. The gathering of the primary data can be a major problem due to the lack of trained researchers or interviewers in the selected market. The asking of personal questions is sometimes culturally unacceptable. As well as management being faced with a range of problems relating to the collection, such data that is available can be difficult to analyse and interpret.

Against this background a number of techniques have been developed to allow insights to be gleaned which give indications of the most likely trading environment to be encountered.

(a) An **analysis of the demand patterns** for industry sectors such as food, textiles and cars, derived from the export statistics of the developed countries can give an approximation of basic demand in the selected country.

(b) From various UN **statistical publications** it is possible to obtain approximations of literacy levels, degree of urbanisation, estimates of number of households and estimates of age distribution of the population, to give an insight into potential consumer profiles.

Analogies can be drawn from measures of the **historic development patterns** of past emerging markets which are now classed as newly industrialised, eg some of the countries of the Pacific rim. From such analogies a **time series analysis** can be used to predict the rate of growth of the emerging market, for instance predicting the rate of growth or development of Vietnam from a time series analysis of Malaysia or Thailand.

Providing the information relating to the development of the newly industrialised countries is in a suitable form, then the analysis of emerging markets can be undertaken using **regression analysis** (based on identifying the relationship between key variables) and **cluster analysis** (based on identifying those outcomes that can be expected from a given set of variables).

Thus when investigating emerging markets it is evident that one problem is common to all, namely, the availability of **reliable** and **up to date** information that can be used as a source of secondary research. Primary research can be used to overcome this problem, but this can be expensive. Should the research demonstrate that the target emerging market is not suitable for entry then the **costs of the research** cannot be recovered, and may prejudice management against investigating other emerging markets.

The use of analogy and proxy measures will produce solutions which are 'near enough to be good enough', particularly when the costs of using these measures are a fraction of the costs of primary research.

23 TUTORIAL QUESTION: FOREIGN MARKET ENTRY CRITERIA

(a) **Non-financial** criteria

The key non-financial criteria for assessing the viability of entering a foreign market can be identified as follows.

(i) **Market size**

The market must be of sufficient size to support a new entrant, either through allowing the new entrant to **attract business** from existing suppliers or allowing the new entrant to create **new segments** or **niches**.

(ii) **Growth potential**

The market should display potential for growth in demand for the range of products being offered. Growth could be assessed in terms of the number of **potential customers** or in terms of the increasing **wealth** of the market assessed by measures of disposable income.

(iii) **Few barriers to entry**

Ideally, markets with no barriers to entry, with neither tariff or non-tariff barriers, offer the greatest attraction. When barriers exist more creative entry methods need to be considered to exploit the potential offered by the market.

(iv) **Price attraction**

The potential for obtaining higher prices than the home market needs to be assessed in terms of the product's uniqueness in that market and the **customer needs** that it satisfies.

(v) **Competition**

The level of indigenous competition needs to be assessed with particular reference to **competitor reaction** which can be anticipated. Also, the level of competition from existing importers into the market will need assessment.

(vi) **Communications**

Access to **media channels** and the type and form of **promotion** allowed will require careful evaluation. Many countries restrict access to the media for promotional purposes for foreign suppliers, hence the availability of, and access to, media channels may influence the market entry strategy.

(vii) **Distribution channels**

Many countries protect their distribution channels from entry by foreign competitors (a form of non-tariff barrier). Careful evaluation of distribution channel access is essential.

Answer bank

(viii) **Time**

The time it takes to **enter a market** and to **generate sales** is often grossly underestimated. Customer needs in most markets are usually satisfied by indigenous suppliers or other importers. This raises the key question of "why should customers satisfy their needs from a new entrant?" The time taken to convince customers that the new entrant can satisfy the needs better can be quite protracted.

(b) **Financial criteria**

The key financial criteria for assessing the viability of entering a foreign market can be identified as follows.

(i) **Investment in 'people'**

(1) The cost of **selecting and appointing** agents together with their **training** costs. The question of where to provide the training needs to be resolved, since this will have a significant impact on costs. **Commission** levels will need to be assessed.

(2) The cost of selecting and appointing **distributors** together with their training costs. The type of distributor appointed needs careful consideration. If the distributor is to **purchase his stock** then what will be the impact of discounts on price? If the distributor is to be appointed on the basis of him holding **consignment stock**, then what will be the level of investment in stock held by the principal? The company will need to be clear in its thinking regarding the level of discount given to distributors, particularly with respect to the promotional activity and costs to be undertaken by the distributor.

(ii) **Profit**

Expected profit levels from the market will need to be assessed after taking into account **terms of delivery** (how the goods are shipped to the market and who is responsible for the costs associated with shipping activities), methods of **payment** (open account, bill of exchange, documentary credit), **exchange risks** etc.

(iii) **Market entry investment**

If some form of **direct investment** is required to enter a particular market, then each entry method will have its own set of financial criteria to be assessed.

(iv) **Own sales office**

This will require investment in **facilities** and **people**. The facilities could be obtained on a short term renewable lease basis to minimise exposure but the people investment will require further consideration. Should the sales office be staffed by **expatriates** or nationals? If expatriates then some investment will be needed for **language and culture training**. If nationals then investment will be needed in **product training**.

(v) **Manufacture under licence**

A licence agreement can be an effective entry method to a market which is attractive but difficult to enter. However, it is not without its costs. The **technology transfer** costs need to be established and **payment methods** for the transfer costs agreed (this could involve lengthy and costly negotiations). Having agreed the transfer cost, **royalty payment** and controls need to be agreed. To aid control of royalty payments, it is usual for the principal to supply a vital component so that it can monitor output levels.

(vi) **Joint venture**

A joint venture will usually involve some form of technology transfer with the external party having a **share** of the business in return for the technology. The cost of the share or transfer cost needs to be established as well as the value of the share. Consideration also needs to be given to the **repatriation of profits** and the exchange risks associated with the profit transfer.

(vii) **Direct investment**

In instances where direct investment is the chosen entry strategy, the financial criteria agreed for assessing **viability** are very comprehensive. They will include all **costs**, expected **returns**, and **incentives** offered by the host government to attract inward investment. **Time** will also be a key assessment variable.

The appraisal of foreign market entry is complex with many variables to be considered, but the ultimate appraisal will be given by the customers or consumers in terms of whether they buy the product or not.

24 OVERSEAS EXPANSION

> **Examiner's comments.** This was the most popular question on the paper, and candidates appeared to be well informed of different entry strategies. There was a tendency to write out lists without any supporting commentary or explanation.

The companies we might consider here are companies that are not currently dealing with markets overseas. Whatever decision they make will shape their **corporate strategic position** with respect to these markets. The critical nature of this decision stems from this fact, and the implications it has for a company which gets the decision wrong.

The market entry decision determines the ground rules for the company's **competitive position** in any market, and how its customers and potential customers will **perceive** its stance in that market. It sets the parameters and constraints within which the company's marketing activities come into play. It establishes the boundaries for setting **marketing objectives**, corporate **goals** and future **activities** across the company functions.

Furthermore it signals to **competitors** and other market stakeholders the scale of the company's ambitions in that market, at least in the short and medium term, and therefore gives clues as to the appropriate competitive response. It is not a decision the company can make in isolation without taking these factors into account. As in chess, the first move sets the pattern for the rest of the game. If the first move is weak or otherwise inappropriate, the company can place itself in an indefensible position.

The alternatives

Broadly speaking there are three alternative modes of market entry, each with different sub-categories, which are **direct exporting, indirect exporting** and **overseas production**. The diagram below sets out the alternatives.

Answer bank

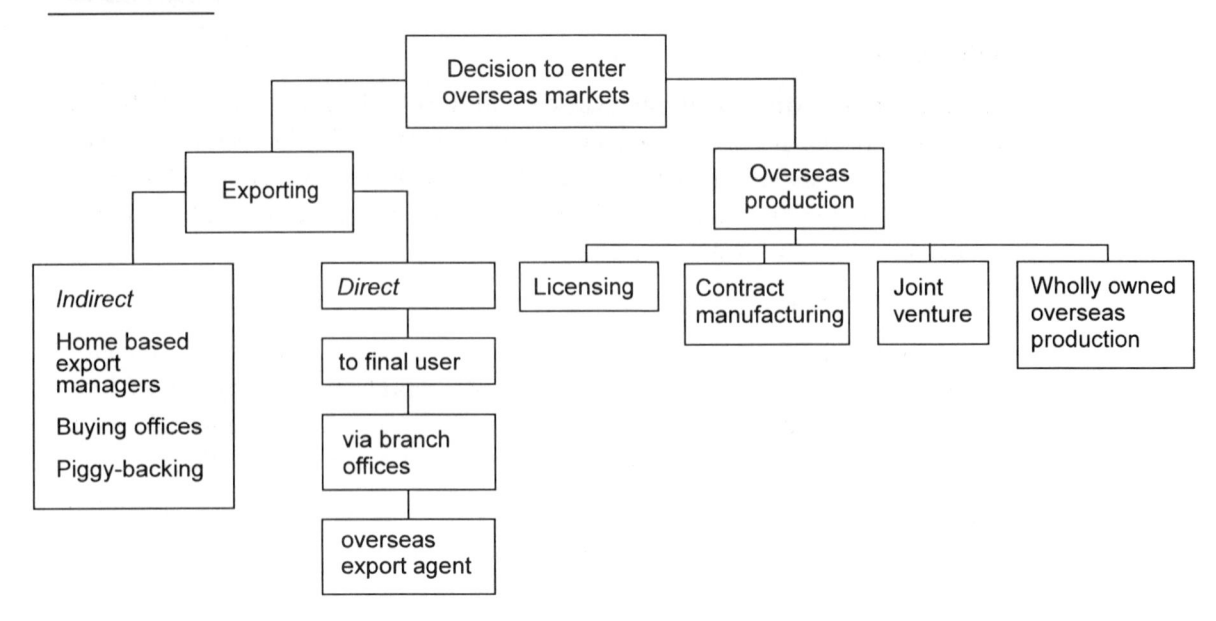

```
                    Decision to enter
                    overseas markets
                    /              \
              Exporting          Overseas
             /        \          production
                                /    |     |      \
     Indirect     Direct    Licensing Contract Joint  Wholly owned
     Home based   |                  manufacturing venture overseas
     export       to final user                           production
     managers     |
     Buying       via branch
     offices      offices
     Piggy-       |
     backing      overseas
                  export agent
```

What is important is that the company knows what its own current circumstances are and what is appropriate for those circumstances. It is vital that the company has a set of criteria against which it can measure the options before it in a logical way.

The decision criteria for market entry selection

The following criteria will form the base from which a company may start to make decisions, depending upon its own circumstances:

(a) **Strategic involvement** - What level of strategic involvement does the company want currently and what is planned for the medium and longer term? How close does it need to be to the customer?

(b) **Corporate objectives** - Where does international marketing fit into the overall corporate objectives? Will it be a central activity, is it peripheral, a growth activity or a temporary expedient? What **resources** are available and what are the company's longer term **ambitions**?

(c) **Speed of entry** - How quickly does the company need to be operating in the intended market(s)?

(d) **Nature of the market** - How **competitive** is it? How technically advanced, economically active and sophisticated are the **consumers**? What **cultural** issues pose questions for marketing activities?

(e) **Nature of the product** - How technologically advanced or complex is the product itself? What level of support does it need?

(f) **Human resources** - What does the organisation have by way of human resource support for manufacturing, operations, distribution, sales in the various markets it wishes to enter? How human resource intensive is the business and that of competitors? What **service levels** are necessary and desirable?

(g) **Administration** - What level of administrative support does the marketing/sales operation need? Is the accounting process simple or complex?

(h) **Costs, payback period** - What are the costs associated with each method of entry, what is available in resources and what payback period is required?

(i) **Control** - What level of control is needed for the markets being considered, and will these needs change over time? What level of **risk** can be tolerated in these new markets and what degree of **flexibility** is there?

It is important to realise that there is never any one right answer. It depends on the current **circumstances** of the company under consideration and its availability of **resources**. What may be right for one market may be wrong for the next.

25 MARKET ENTRY

> **Tutorial note.** This question asks about market entry methods and their application, following the familiar question pattern of 'describe first, and then show how it can be put into practise'.
>
> **Examiner's comments.** Yet again, the second part of the question proved more problematic than the first. Candidates were good at listing market entry methods but less able to apply them in a thoughtful way and come up with selection criteria. No answer provided alternatives to the standard market entry methods described in the textbooks. There is obviously a general lack of reading around the topic area.

The principle methods of market entry are **indirect exporting**, **direct exporting**, **direct inward investment** and **co-operation** through the formation of alliances, partnerships and joint ventures.

Indirect exporting involves the company in very **low risk** since it will be selling its products to a domestic organisation who will then export the product to the final destination. These domestic intermediaries are either classified as **export houses/trading companies** or export management companies.

Piggy-backing is another indirect exporting method which involves another company acting as the carrier for the product.

Indirect exporting offers the exporter little or no **control** over market development, and although it is often used by many small companies to get started in the international market place it will not lead to a global corporation.

Direct exporting involves a higher level of risk and can result in a company having a global presence if properly managed. Direct exporting is relatively low cost and, subject to no **entry barriers** being present and the company having adequate **resources**, it can allow a **rapid entry** into many markets. The most usual form of direct exporting is either through the appointment of **agents** who will be paid a **commission**, or by appointing **distributors** who will hold stock but may or may not own it, depending on the terms of the distributorship.

For certain types of business, **franchising** is the equivalent of direct exporting. An overseas organisation will pay for the **rights** to use the business concept. As with direct exporting through agents or distributors, franchising would allow a company to operate globally in a very short space of time, providing it had the necessary human resources to support it.

An arrangement whereby a company has its products **manufactured under license** could be seen as similar to franchising. The issuing of licenses to have products made on a global scale will be constrained by the human resources of the organisation.

Direct inward investment is a high risk strategy since it is subject to the acceptance of the host government. Examples of direct inward investment are the setting up of own **facilities**, or the **acquisition** of or **merger** with existing businesses in the host country. The advantages of direct inward investment are **total control** of market development and (because of the higher risks) **greater profits** can be expected. Due to the investment required, direct inward investment as a means of becoming global is **expensive** and usually takes a long time. It took Nissan 30 years to establish 24 plants in 18 countries. It took Ford and General Motors up to 40 years to establish their global presence.

Answer bank

Co-operation strategies can either involve direct inward investment such as the formation of **joint ventures** (which usually require the incoming partner to share the costs of establishing the new entity), or no inward investment as with **strategic alliances**. Globalisation via joint ventures can be expensive and slow due to the constraints of limited financial resources and possibly limited targets, whereas strategic alliances can lead to a fairly rapid global presence.

Decision criteria

These are likely to be based on any or all of the following:

- Company **resources**
- Company expectations and **objectives**
- Management **expertise**
- **Existing involvement** overseas
- The nature and features of the **product**
- Nature of the **target markets**
- Nature and size of **competition** in the target markets
- **Barriers to entry**

26 MODES OF ENTRY

> **Examiner's comments.** A very popular question: over 80% attempted it but many did so badly. The heart of the question was the financial implications of each entry mode. Market entry establishes limitations in terms of the company's strategic level of involvement, thus determining future sales and profitability.

There is **no single ideal market entry method** for an organisation contemplating international marketing. Methods range from an almost zero involvement in international marketing, to a situation where only a small proportion of a company's income is generated by its home market.

The main methods range from **simple exporting**, (using distributors and agents, local trading companies, export management companies or the company's own sales force plus a shipping agent) through to more involved methods such as licensing, franchising, contract manufacture, joint venture or strategic alliance and also situations where the company must **invest a lot of resources**, such as assembly operations, acquiring a foreign company or establishing a wholly owned subsidiary.

Risk and control

The methods shown above, with the lowest levels of involvement by the company, will probably also have the lowest levels of risk, particularly **financial risk**. On the other hand the potential for **rewards** is probably also **limited** in the same degree. The converse it true when it comes to control of the company's operations in the market place. In other words, the methods with the **least levels of involvement** also have the **lowest levels of control**.

Thus, if a company is simply manufacturing in its home market and delegates all of the marketing effort and responsibility to a distributor, with a local shipping company taking responsibility for physical distribution, the exporter will have only a modest level of financial risk. There may only be modest profit potential and a low level of control in the market place.

Financial implications

In order to contrast the financial implications of different methods of market entry, we can look in more detail at the use of **distributors** in the market place of the company's choice and compare this with the costs associated with creating its own manufacturing and marketing **subsidiary**.

Let us examine the two options in terms of the **capital required**, the **financial risk** and the possibility of **repatriation of profit**.

Capital required

In the case of using a distributor overseas, the level of **investment capital** is going to be very small. If we think of a motor manufacturer, it may be that there would be some need to support our distributors with finance to bring the quality of showrooms to an acceptable minimum level, but for very many other manufacturers the expectation would be that the distributor bears most of the financial responsibility for premises, showrooms, warehousing and the like. Similarly the distributor, who will usually buy the goods we are exporting to sell on his own behalf and, thereby, make a profit, will also, therefore, be committed to providing the finances which will cover most of the costs of the **working capital**.

In the case of our own manufacturing and marketing subsidiary, we will have to take on a substantial amount of **investment capital**, either if we are building a new plant from scratch or if we are buying out a pre-existing company. If it is a case of building a new plant, the investment capital will be at **risk** for a long period of time until the plant comes into operation and starts delivering a **return**.

There will also be a considerable need for **working capital** even when the plant is complete and this will be a **continuing commitment**.

Financial risk

There are a number of factors to be taken into account here, the two key issues being the risk of **currency fluctuations** and any **political risks** contingent upon the country within which we are operating. If we are using distributors, the risk is limited to the amount of goods in the pipeline which have yet to be paid for. The level of this risk is dependent upon the **terms of trading** we have agreed with our distributors and we can offset this risk by buying sterling forward from the bank and allowing our bankers to take the **currency risk**.

A wholly owned subsidiary may well have a lesser risk associated with currency fluctuations for goods, but it is likely to have a much higher risk associated with the **political situation** in the country of operation. At the extreme, there may even be a small risk of **appropriation of assets** if the local government lurches strongly to the left or the population becomes concerned about the disturbing effects of inward investment.

Repatriation of profits

Using a distributor will not bring a high level of risk under this heading because the profit is made at the **point of sale** which is likely to be in the home country. The profit will therefore be in the home currency.

For a company with a subsidiary, it may have to face **local taxation** of its profits in the country of operation, unless it is providing assembled parts from its home market at internally derived pricing levels. If this practice is too obvious, however, there may be more political factors to contend with, depending upon the rigour with which the host government monitors **transfer pricing** deals.

Conclusion

Having outlined some of the financial implications associated with different methods of entry, it should be clearly understood that there will inevitably be a whole range of factors to take into account which might make one or other of these possible methods more, or less, appealing. There is never one right answer. It depends, amongst other factors, on the **stage of development** of a company and its **experience** of international marketing.

27 RISK AND REVENUE

> **Examiner's comments**. Of the handful of students who attempted this question the overwhelming majority guessed at what R & R and consequently gave a very general, and unspecific account of what they understood by global partnering.

Risk and revenue sharing agreements are a relatively new form of partnership pioneered by the **aero engine manufacturers**. A risk and revenue sharing agreement is based on the principle that all the major component suppliers to the engine builder will undertake (and pay for) all **R & D** relating to engine upgrades or totally new engines.

Thus, every significant member of the **aero engine supply chain** is taking a risk, in terms of the investment of effort and money incurred in developing their particular element of the engine, in the expectation that the **returns** from this investment will flow from the sale of the completed engines.

In general terms, risk and revenue sharing agreements are simple arrangements as there are no third, jointly owned, companies as in conventional joint ventures. There are no technology transfers, so one partner cannot dominate the other. There are no cross share holdings or other form of joint, or shared, investments.

Risk and revenue sharing agreements **spread the risk** of complex product development amongst every member of the supply chain in proportion to the **contribution** each member's element makes to the **finished product**. The returns are also in proportion to the contribution each element makes to the final product. It is a form of **strategic alliance** based on total **trust** and intimate **knowledge** of the industry.

For instance, if your total business is based on the supply of parts for aero engines then you have very few customers and, probably even **fewer competitors**. So developing a part for Rolls Royce or Pratt & Whitney is a fairly safe bet given that these companies also have few customers (Boeing, Airbus) and many end users, namely the airlines of the world.

The supplying companies will know their customers (engine builders) in great detail. They will also know their customer's customer (aircraft builders) in detail and will have a very good knowledge of the end user (the airlines). Risk is also minimised by undertaking development (albeit at your expense) in your **particular area of expertise**. If your expertise is the design, development and manufacture of combustion chambers, then your risk and revenue sharing agreement will focus on improving the existing, or developing the next, generation of combustion chambers.

The disadvantages are very similar to other forms of strategic alliance, notably, **change of management** or change of ownership at either partner resulting in a loss of empathy with the products and their continual development. The final customer may change their mind and stay with existing products, or go out of business, so that all the effort and money in development is wasted.

Significant changes in the **environment** could affect the use of the final product, e.g. a risk and revenue sharing agreement between a sail maker and a clipper ship builder would have floundered with the introduction of steam ships earlier this century. Similarly risk and revenue sharing agreements in the steam railway engine supply chain would have ended due to environmental changes caused by the introduction of diesel engines.

28 CO-OPERATION BETWEEN FIRMS

> **Examiner's comments.** A popular question, with disappointing answers as few wrote much on strategic alliances: many identified them with joint ventures.

The common feature of licensing, joint ventures and strategic alliances as **methods of market entry** is that the multinational works in concert with another organisation to a greater or lesser degree in order to effect its entry into the desired market.

Licensing

A **licensing agreement** is an arrangement where the licenser (ie our multinational company in this instance) gives something of value - such as **patent rights** or **trademark** rights or **know how** on products or production processes - to the licensee in the country market, in exchange for certain **performance and payments** from the licensee.

These rights may be given for just one market or a whole range of markets, depending upon the relative positions of the two parties in the markets concerned. There is a clear assumption that the licensee takes on a much greater role than a manufacturer who produces a product under contract, and there is usually an assumption by the multinational that for that market the licensee is in a better position to tackle the market than the MNE itself. This may be to do with the capital costs of building a plant in the market or there may be positive **marketing advantages** in using a local partner.

(a) The key benefits associated with this method of entry are that there is a **low level of investment by the MNE** and, as noted above, low capital costs of entry. Usually there will be a rapid multi-market penetration for the products if the license has been granted to several licensees at the same time. This is, of course, important if we are dealing with a fashion item such as garments, films, computer games and the like.

Licensing will usually give rapid access to local **distribution channels** without the associated costs. Payment is by results.

(b) **Control**

To be effective and safe as a method of entry the multinational needs to be very careful over selection of its partner(s), viewing **quality issues** as paramount and establishing **legal agreements** with care and forethought. Since one of the dangers associated with licensing is the possibility of **training your future competitors**, there should be full control of key components to the licensing company. Where appropriate **geographic coverage** of the license should be clearly agreed and stated to avoid later problems of **market definition**. Any and all **trademarks** and **patents** should be **registered** in the appropriate countries/areas.

Joint venture

As with licensing, a joint venture (JV) is a way to acquire **manufacturing capacity** in the market of choice without paying the full cost of investment in plant. The difference is that the MNE will have some level of **joint ownership** and, therefore, capital investment. This is normally of the order of between 25% to 75%. The key is that the international firm has enough of an investment to acquire a degree of **management control** in the market place. As international operations have become increasingly important over time, so has the practice of entering JVs.

(a) The **benefits of a JV operation** to an international firm are chiefly that product and **market development costs can be shared** and therefore the risk of **market entry can be reduced**. Again, because less is committed than in a full market entry with a subsidiary operation, **rapid internationalisation** can be achieved. Complementary

Answer bank

management skills can be brought to bear on a particular market to the advantage of both parties and in some circumstances it may allow a multinational company entry to what otherwise might be a closed market.

(b) In terms of the issues of **control and strategic management**, it is important that JV partners are seen to share their problems without apportioning blame to the other party for market setbacks. It is likely that the JV will develop its **own management culture** different from either of the partner companies, but there should be open access to both sets of partner managements.

Strategic alliances

A strategic alliance is a much more broadly based approach of equals to the issue of tackling entry into particular markets, where each party brings **complementary resources and skills** to the operation. It is somewhat less likely that one of the parties will necessarily be based in the market of interest. It may be that one party gains distribution in markets of interest to it by offering distribution facilities to its partner in markets where it has good channels already open.

(a) It may also be based on complementarily of **technological** skills as well as **marketing** skills and resources, or some judicious mixture of these. Before Rover was taken over by BMW it had a strategic alliance with Honda in terms of product development as well as market access to European and Japanese car markets. In a shrinking world where firms have to be large to tackle some key market areas, the practice of initiating strategic alliances is now growing very quickly.

This is affected very much by the sheer pace of **innovation diffusion,** where smaller companies find it hard to keep up. As a **market protection** strategy and as a way to provide **access** to new markets it can be very successful, but it may also lay one of the partners open to **takeover** by the other as weaknesses become apparent.

(b) **Control.** The control issues are largely similar to those experienced in a joint venture situation, based upon **stability** and **objectives** shared by both parties.

29 TUTORIAL QUESTION: STANDARDISED APPROACH TO INTERNATIONAL MARKETING

Any international marketing textbook will point out that there are many factors pushing companies towards **differentiation** of marketing approach to cope with the great variety of **consumer needs** apparent in different markets around the world and, if that were all there was to solving the problems of international marketing, then every company would follow that route.

There are, however, considerable sources of advantage and possible benefits to a company which adopts a **standardised approach** to international marketing. It is important at the outset to establish that there will be, almost inevitably, some **adaptation** required by a company - perhaps to translate a set of pack instructions, for example - but even this activity could be dealt with using a standardised approach to international marketing. Thus, by keeping the instructions brief and simple and in just three key languages, say, English, French and German, a company could satisfy customer needs in very many countries around the world.

What, then, are the key advantages of such a standardised approach? Terpstra and Sarathy suggest that **economies of scale** feature very strongly, leading to lowered costs, improved market position and sales. Standardisation of the product element of the marketing mix is the most common and is normally a pre-requisite for other types of standardisation of approach.

(a) **Economies of scale in production**

If a product has only one source of production and, therefore, long production runs are possible, there will inevitably be economic efficiencies to benefit the company, from raw material sourcing through to operational savings on machine time. Such an advantage would be reduced as a company finds the need to multiply production facilities or where the optimum size of plant reduces as a proportion of world demand.

(b) **Research and development (R&D) and new product development (NPD)**

The economic benefit of both R & D and NPD are enhanced in a situation where the company is able to offer an identical product round the world - since adaptation costs time and duplication of effort.

(c) **Marketing economies**

With a standardised product offering there are benefits available in several other areas of marketing effort. Spare parts requirements for **after-sales service**, for example, may be minimised by being able to keep stocks low and relatively mobile across national boundaries. Equally, the photography necessary for sales force **support literature** can be minimised when the products or, at least, the packs, have been standardised.

A standardised approach to **advertising** becomes possible with a standard product and brand image. Thus, the Mars corporation felt that the benefits of standardisation across Europe were sufficient to invest millions of pounds sterling to change the name of a major brand of chocolate in the UK market from Marathon to Snickers to bring it into line with the name elsewhere.

(d) **Consumer mobility**

Many consumers **travel** on either holidays or business across national boundaries. An example of consumers opting for the comfortable purchase in this respect would be the yellow pack of Kodak film.

(e) **'Country-of-origin' image**

It may be that in some circumstances the **cultural associations** of the country of origin of the product provide more advantage to the product offering than if it were changed to meet differentiated needs of a local market. For example, the Frenchness of French perfume provides a stronger motivation for keeping the image standard rather than attempting to differentiate the product for the specific market in which it is being offered for sale.

Summary

The key benefits discussed above are available to a company seeking to achieve a **standardised** approach, but should not be used to excuse a situation where it can be shown that a better market position could be achieved by **differentiation**.

30 STANDARDISATION

> **Tutorial note.** Make sure you understand the term 'standardisation' and try to bring some examples into your answer. The second part of the question needs a bit more thought. Standardisation may be hampered by variations in factors such as culture and laws, or financial considerations.
>
> **Examiner's comments.** Answers to the first part of the question were quite good, but some candidates need to be aware that 'standardisation' and 'globalisation' are not the same thing. Global communications do indeed support standardisation, but many answers fell into the trap of describing the criteria for globalisation and would have earned few marks. Answers to the second part of the question tended to be inadequate.

The factors encouraging and supporting standardisation of products are, principally, **economies of scale** in production, **research and development** and **marketing communications**. With standardised products, and a belief that an **ethnocentric approach** to the markets of the world is appropriate, then standardised marketing plans can be used in all markets.

Standardised marketing communications enable single images to be created, and for some products competitive advantage can be extracted from **country of origin affect**. With standardised products produced in a number of plants around the world, production can be shared amongst the plants and markets supplied from any or all of the plants to take advantage of prevailing favourable conditions.

The use of satellite broadcasting by advertisers encourages the use of **standardised advertising** due to the very large footprints of the satellite transmissions. Thus in the medium term, developments in global **communications technology** could give greater impetus to standardisation. In the recent past Ford announced that their Mondeo was to be their first 'world car', and historically a number of product such as 35mm film, blank VHS tapes and certain designer goods have become standardised throughout the world.

The circumstances that prevent or hinder standardisation are legion. Differing **usage conditions**, for example due to differing climates, make standardisation of some products difficult. Differences in **taste**, **income** and **level of sophistication** will also impact on standardisation.

Intervention by government in the form of tariffs and non-tariff barriers together with pressure from **regulatory bodies** can prevent a standardisation strategy being effective. Markets will vary dramatically in their **development cycles**, and correspondingly, products will be at a different stage of their **life cycles** in differing markets. For instance, bicycles are leisure products in the developed world but vital transport products in the developing world. This demonstrates that the global standardisation of bicycles will be difficult, but regional standardisation may be practical.

Technology differences will also hinder standardisation. Computer users in the developed world are more likely to operate with the latest versions of micro processors in their PC's. Users in the developing world will invariably use the older technology. It is in the interests of both the micro processor manufacturers and the PC manufacturers to maintain these differentials, in order to fully re-coup their investment in the respective technologies.

The standardisation of **global brands** is a far more frequently encountered phenomenon, for instance Nike and Reebok. These companies appear to be exploiting the global communication of sport and the desire of young people to be associated with the brands worn by their sporting heroes.

Global communications are also helping to establish English as the **global language**. This helps to develop global brands since there can be universal transmission of the values associated with the brand, and universal understanding of those values.

31 MARKETING AND FINANCIAL IMPLICATIONS OF A MOVE FROM DIFFERENTIATED TO STANDARDISED MARKETING

Our company's change in strategy, to standardised marketing from differentiation and market adaptation, is generally in line with the moves being made by many other companies operating in the international market place.

This trend is increasing as the world tends to became a smaller place with faster **global communications**, greater **cross-cultural exchange** and better **access to resources** (both financial and operational) across national boundaries.

Answer bank

In order to assess fully the key financial and marketing implications of such a change we will have to decide the extent of the move towards standardisation. This may range from straightforward product standardisation to the standardisation of all the elements of the marketing mix. Inevitably, whatever the final extent of commonality there will still be some differences to accommodate.

The key points I would make are given below, starting with the main **marketing implications**, followed by the probable **financial implications**.

(a) **Marketing implications** can be examined by marketing mix element.

   (i) Firstly, as far as the **product** is concerned there will need to be a concerted effort to reduce our **product range** to a smaller number of standard products. This will require market research to determine the optimum mix of products, the characteristics and benefits of our products giving widest satisfaction across all our markets and the possible gaps left by our consolidation programme. We may need to speed up our **new product development** programme to fill such gaps and replace the weakest of our products in the range.

   It would also make sense to centralise our **research and development** process, which would not only bring greater control but will bring together talent that is currently spread throughout our main markets.

   Work will need to be done to standardise **packaging** options and **brand** names in a way that will not lose **goodwill** for our products, at least in our main markets. The process of standardisation may take several years to complete successfully and careful **planning** will be needed to retain our competitive positions.

   (ii) As far as the **price** element of the mix is concerned we will need to standardise our strategy to give us the optimum **return** from all our markets. This may entail putting prices up in some markets and reducing prices in others. Here, again, we may need to undertake such change in phases over time, in order not to weaken our market position.

   (iii) The **place** element, deciding on the logistics and **channels of distribution**, may be one of the more difficult areas to standardise, since distribution channels do **differ quite markedly** in different markets, more so for consumer products like ours than for industrial products.

   Ideally, we should take greater **control** of the largest proportion of our distribution process, in order to be able to effect the greatest standardisation across the product range. The more we delegate the distribution function, the less will be our control of the presentation to the final consumer.

   (iv) Finally, the **promotion** element of the mix may be the most difficult in which to achieve a standardised approach, not least for the **linguistic** difficulties we will need to overcome. Also, the **cultural** differences we will encounter in our different markets may militate against a totally common approach, unless we can say that our product clearly appeals to an **identical market segment** across all markets, in the same way as Kodak film appears to in many of its world markets.

   We will be able to make a common approach to the **sales support material** for our sales forces if we have a standardised strategy. We may also benefit from a common **training approach** for our sales staff - although this will depend to some extent on the standardisation possible in the distribution channels.

   As for **sales promotions**, we can attempt a standard approach provided **legal** barriers or differing **cultural** backgrounds do not prevent it.

Answer bank

(b) **Financial implications**

(i) The bad news is that, in the short to medium term, there are going to be new and extra **costs** to be taken into account. For example, rationalising the research and development programme may well incur expenditure on new premises and equipment, in addition to removal expenses.

Also, there will be additional costs of **training** and staff development to attain common approaches to our marketing programmes internationally.

(ii) The good news is that there will be potential **savings** in a number of areas as the benefits of a standardised approach feed into the system. To stick with the research and development example, we may be able to reduce and or re-deploy the numbers of people involved across all our markets and we can cut down on **duplication of effort**.

There may well be a number of general savings to be made from **economies of scale**, for example origination of advertising material, production operations and so on, which will enable our company to make extra profits. Our market position might become more favourable, leading to **market share** improvements from making our prices more competitive.

In summary, further analysis will be needed to determine the net benefits across all our markets, as far as both our market position and our financial position is concerned.

32 GLOBALISATION

> **Tutorial note.** Ensure that you can define 'globalisation'. The question provides an opportunity to display some up to date knowledge.
>
> **Examiner's comments.** The question was usually well answered, with many candidates gaining a distinction mark. Few answers contained any reference to macro developments such as the role of international bodies. Knowledge beyond that contained in the standard texts was rarely displayed. The definitions of 'globalisation' were usually off the mark.

If a definition of globalisation is accepted as being:

'the process by which the world becomes more homogeneous with regard to the products and services demanded'

then the forces driving its development are as follows.

(a) Developments in **global telecommunications** using satellite broadcasting are helping to establish English as the international language for interpersonal and business communications.

(b) Global telecommunications are helping to establish global brands that are killing off local brands in certain product categories.

(c) The emergence of a **global consumer,** particularly amongst young people, is a reality exploited by many multinationals who have developed both a global **product range** and a global **brand** and **image**.

(d) **Multinational** car companies (GM and Ford) are exploiting developments in transportation systems to source components for their assembly plants in the US and Europe from suppliers all over the world. This is improving the wealth creating (**value adding**) activities of the developing world, and creating consumers with discretionary money to spend in places where previously no spare money existed.

(e) Developments in **transportation systems**, particularly air transport, have brought global **travel** within the reach of increasing numbers of people. Increased travel brings increased **demand** for goods to be available in places visited by the travellers.

(f) Increasing **affluence** of consumers, as the global economy grows due to the relaxation of trade barriers through agreements negotiated by WTO and the actions of the multinational companies, encourages spending on travel. This fuels the need for more homogeneous products and services. For instance, airports around the world are beginning to look the same, with similar check-in and baggage processing facilities, retail outlets, and restaurants. This reflects the **convergence** of consumer needs.

(g) The **convergence of consumer needs** on a global scale re-defines concepts of **economies of scale** and the **competitive** and **absolute advantages** these can generate. The car companies, led by Ford with its Mondeo, are designing and building cars with a global consumer in mind.

(h) The **acquisition and merger activities** of companies to ensure profit growth contributes significantly to the process of globalisation, as management teams are forced to abandon their ethnocentric 'comfort zones' and adopt **regio-centric, geo-centric** or **poly-centric** approaches to managing increasingly global businesses.

For many companies in an increasing number of industries, survival will be dependent upon them taking a **global perspective**. There are many ways to achieve the objective of being a global company with the right way for any particular company being the way which achieves the **objectives** set for globalisation.

33 EVOLVING OPERATIONS

> **Examiner's comments.** This was the most popular question on the paper with most candidates having a reasonable stab at the evolution from domestic to global. Fewer candidates chose to focus on the first part of the question and discuss the changes in organisation, resources and operations, and only a handful answered the question as set and considered the impact on the host country.

It has been demonstrated that most companies that engage in international trade proceed through a **four-stage process**. This process takes them from being totally focused on the **home market**, through **experimental involvement** due to receiving unsolicited orders from overseas customers, to **active involvement** in which the company seeks out overseas customers, and on towards a **committed involvement** in which the company will have active assets in other countries.

The changes that take place within the company will be dependent on the size and type of business of the firm. For instance, the changes for a motor manufacturer or a fast food operator will be much more visible in the host country than a clothing manufacturer or bank.

Changes to the organisational structure, resources and operations will all be dependent on the following.

(a) The **level of involvement**, with experimental involvement requiring little change, active involvement requiring some change, and committed involvement requiring considerable change.

(b) The **number of countries** the company chooses to operate in will have a wide impact, and one country will have far less impact than 10 or 12. Also, the size and location of the target country(ies) will have a wide impact.

Answer bank

(c) The **value and variety** of products will impact the changes – starting a car plant anywhere in the world requires massive organisational change for a single, very expensive, site development and supply chain. Introducing a fast food chain needs many, much less expensive, site developments and a fairly complex supply chain.

Companies may choose to evolve through an **export department** to an international division and on to an **overseas subsidiary**. Overseas subsidiaries raise the debate regarding the type of **control**. Should control be **centralised** in the home country, or should control be decentralised, with overseas subsidiaries given **autonomy** for operational and tactical matters?

Other issues that surface throughout the internationalisation process involve the **focus** of the company. Should it be **country** focused, **product** focused or **brand** focused? Will a **matrix structure** be the best compromise?

In terms of **resources**, management needs to decide whether to use **expatriate staff** or local nationals. This decision is closely linked to the type of control chosen. Centralised control may favour the use of local nationals operating under an expatriate as country manager, whereas decentralised control may favour a much larger expatriate management team supported by local nationals.

Finance will need arranging. Decisions need to be made regarding the source and management of money in terms of whether it is under the control of the headquarters (centralised) or controlled by the management in the host country (decentralised). **Physical resource requirements** will also need addressing and the type of ownership, eg lease or outright purchase.

Operations will need to change from the **domestic ethnocentric style** to one that is appropriate to the host country. Management will need to be sensitive and sympathetic to local **culture and customs**, and not expect the home country style of operations to translate unchanged to the host country. Forms of **strategic alliance** or partnership may be an appropriate style of operations for some companies in some territories.

The development of international trade with more and more companies having a global presence has a significant impact on host countries. **Social patterns** change and there is an almost unstoppable movement from rural societies to urban societies. **Economic effects** can be dramatic with direct inward investment creating employment, adding value, raising living standards, and improving the economic and social situation of the host country population.

On the downside, host countries may have objections to their traditional way of life being changed. Not all countries see benefits from what has been popularly referred to as the Americanisation of the world. Certainly from a UK perspective one does not have to look too far back into the 20th century to see that the positive views once held by the British people towards the empire were not shared universally.

34 GOING GLOBAL

> **Tutorial note.** The answer below focuses on the risk and reward (finance) aspects. An answer could have been constructed concentrating on the organisational factors of type and structure of organisation, and the impact these factors would have on the other factors for going global. Similarly, answers could focus on resources - finance complemented by a review of HR and operations.
>
> **Examiner's comments.** A very popular question, but many answers described external factors, which were not required. The use of examples was quite good, but few chose obvious ones such as commodities or raw materials.

There is no single ideal method for an organisation contemplating international marketing or going global. Similarly there is no single list of factors an organisation should consider to help them make the decision.

The main methods of market entry range from simple **exporting**, (using distributors and agents, local trading companies, export management companies or the company's own sales force plus a shipping agent) through to **more involved methods** such as licensing, franchising, contract manufacture, joint venture, strategic alliance, acquiring a foreign company or establishing a wholly owned subsidiary. Each of these approaches has its own risk profile and will require its own list of internal factors to be considered.

Risk and control

The market entry methods with the lowest levels of involvement by the company will probably have the lowest levels of **risk**, particularly financial risk, and tend to offer the lowest potential for **rewards** (profits). Similarly, when it comes to control of the company's operations in the market place, the methods with the least levels of involvement have the lowest levels of control.

Thus, if a company is manufacturing in its home market and delegates all of the marketing effort and responsibility to a distributor, with a local shipping company taking responsibility for physical distribution, the company will have only a modest level of financial risk. There may only be modest profit potential and the company will have a low level of control in the market place.

Financial implications

In order to contrast the financial implications of the different methods of market entry, the use of distributors can be compared with the costs associated with creating a manufacturing and marketing subsidiary.

Consideration will need to be given to the internal factors of **capital** required, the **financial risk** and the ease of **repatriation of profits**.

Capital required

In the case of **using a distributor** overseas, the level of **investment capital** is going to be very small. For a motor manufacturer, it may be that there would be some need to support the distributors with finance to bring the quality of showrooms to an acceptable level. For many other manufacturers, the expectation would be that the distributor would undertake the financial responsibility for premises, showrooms, warehousing etc. Similarly the distributor will be committed to providing the finance with which to cover the costs of the **working capital** for purchasing the goods and holding and maintaining the stock.

In the case of creating a manufacturing and marketing **subsidiary**, the company will have to take on a substantial amount of investment capital, either for building a new plant from scratch or for buying out an existing company. If it is a case of building a **new plant**, the investment capital will be at risk for a long period of time until the plant comes into operation and starts delivering a **return**.

There will also be a considerable need for working capital even when the plant is complete, and this will be a continuing commitment.

Financial risk

There are a number of factors to be taken into account here, the two key issues being the risk of **currency fluctuations** and any **political risks** contingent upon the country within which we are operating. If we are using distributors, the risk is limited to the amount of goods in the pipeline which have yet to be paid for. The level of this risk is dependent upon the terms of trading agreed with the distributor and this can be offset by buying sterling forward from the bank.

The more involved entry method of a wholly owned subsidiary may well have a lesser risk associated with currency fluctuations for goods but it is likely to have a much higher risk associated with the political situation in the country of operation. At the extreme, there may even be a small risk of **appropriation of assets** if the local government lurches strongly to the left or the population becomes seriously concerned about the effects of inward investment. This has happened previously in India and some South American countries.

Repatriation of profits

Using a distributor will not bring a high level of risk under this heading because the profit is made at the **point of sale**, which is likely to be in the home country. The profit will therefore be in the home currency, given that the bills get paid promptly.

For a company with a subsidiary, it may have to face **local taxation** of its profits in the country of operation, unless it is providing assembled parts from its home market at internally derived pricing levels. If this practice is too obvious, however, there may be more political factors to contend with, depending upon the rigour with which the host government monitors **transfer pricing** deals.

Conclusion

Having outlined some of the financial implications associated with different methods of entry, it should be clearly understood that there will inevitably be a whole range of factors to take into account which might make one or other of these possible methods more, or less, appealing. It depends, amongst other factors, on the stage of development of a company and its experience of international marketing.

35 TRANSNATIONAL VERSUS MULTINATIONAL MARKETING

Transnational companies seek **global scale efficiency** and **competitiveness**, through recognising **opportunities and risks** across national boundaries in the external environment, and across functional boundaries in the internal environment. They aim for worldwide **resource and asset utilisation**.

(a) **Transnational marketing**

A transnational's approach to marketing is not one of selecting a particular strategy but one of taking a **strategic perspective**. This perspective allows for product policies that may be either adapted for each market, or interdependent and standardised. Similarly, marketing **communications** strategies and plans may be independent (ie adapted for each market,) or may be interdependent and standardised for the set of markets covered. **Customer segments** may be unique and specific to a particular market or may be transnational.

For instance, a company active in the German speaking regions of Europe may identify particular segments in Germany, Austria and Switzerland and treat each of these segments in a unique manner (eg specifically tailored packaging). Alternatively, the company could identify similar customer segments in each of the three countries and treat them all the same.

Control of the marketing effort will reside in the country or area covered by the transnational, with profits remaining in the area for business and market development.

(b) **Multinational marketing**

In contrast, the multinational enterprise (MNE) approach to marketing is invariably one of control from outside the country in which the operations are located. MNEs will attempt to apply a standardised approach to marketing through both product offering and marketing communications.

(c) **Making the transition**

Organisations make the transition from MNE to transnational activities through a number of approaches, although most are aimed at achieving **scale economies of marketing effort**. Products invariably need some adaptation to enable successful and profitable sales levels to be achieved. Hence, this leads to a 'trade-off' between production economies of scale and marketing economies of scale, since **providing customers with what they want takes precedent** over selling customers what the organisation offers.

The development of **communications** across national boundaries is starting to provide scale economies for **product advertising** in a number of neighbouring markets. These scale economies in communications will need to be matched by scale economies in the provision of a variety of goods to satisfy the needs generated.

The transnational recognises that it will be dealing with organisations that are customers, suppliers, competitors and partners. Hence the marketing approach taken by transnationals is one of **building relationships** in the total **supply chain**.

In contrast, the MNE can regard itself as a simple entity with operations in many markets satisfying local customer needs with policies determined by headquarters.

(d) **Conclusion**

Transnational companies tend to be more **marketing orientated**, that is, more customer focused, offering products adapted to a particular market, more flexible in their approach to markets and more **adaptable** in their approach to **organisation and management**.

Multinational companies tend to be more **product orientated**, that is, offering standard products in all markets with minimal adaptation, **less flexible** in their approach to markets, and more rigid in their approach to organisation and management.

36 TUTORIAL QUESTION: STRATEGY DEVELOPMENT

> **Examiner's comments.** This was an easy question for those who understood the stages of internationalisation. You could have included management organisation, timescales and building on the learning curve.

There are various **models** which describe the stages companies go through in the development of their **international marketing strategies**. All are portrayed as a **sequential chain of events** which start with no involvement and end with the development of long term international strategy. The main difference between the models is the number of **links** in the chain and how the links are defined and described.

Interest in international marketing usually starts with an **unsolicited request** to satisfy an order from a previously unknown overseas customer. The customer will have taken the initiative to identify possible suppliers from a variety of sources: directors, attendance at exhibitions or referrals to enable him to select a particular company with which he has had no previous contact. Fortunately at this point in the journey towards becoming an international operator, management has no idea of the impact on the organisation

Answer bank

structure or the **timescale** involved. However, the management of most companies will be aware of the horror stories surrounding **exporting**, particularly **documentation** and **payment** problems and that many are deterred from rising to the challenge offered by the unsolicited order.

For those that take the plunge the first step to international activities is the selection of **target markets**. The countries of Europe are always high on every manager's list as is the USA. However, wise researchers ignore physical and time differences and consider the countries of South East Asia and the Pacific Rim, which have significantly higher growth rates than the countries of Europe and North America. Once targets have been selected using **secondary research**, these targets need to be visited to obtain **primary information**.

Initial entry into a foreign market is usually through an **agent**, who has been recruited either from a visit to the market or by the company presence at an international trade fair. At this stage, since the agent will be paid on a **commission** basis, the additional costs to the company will be minimal. The management will need to decide how it will do business with its foreign clients particularly in terms of **methods of payment**, since this will have a bearing on the personnel they will need to recruit and **train** to handle the **documentation**.

As activities in target markets increase, **distributors** may be appointed, and other markets will be considered to maintain the growth momentum. Other markets may require different **entry methods**. Tariff barriers may be so great that a **manufacturing licence** will have to be negotiated with a local contractor to effect entry. In this case, a different **organisation** would be required, and a key component in the manufacturing process would need to be supplied to ensure that the terms of the licence agreement were not abused.

The negotiating and granting of manufacturing licences is usually the first step on the path to **direct investment** in the target country. With direct investment the **risks** are high but the **rewards and control** are in the hands of the headquarters staff.

The challenges encountered on the path from fulfilling the first unsolicited export order to a direct investment in a foreign market are many, varied, exciting and constantly changing. Some of the **issues** management must confront on this path are the following.

(a) Should the product be **standardised** with the same product being sold in all markets?

(b) Should the product be **adapted** to meet the needs of each market?

These are the extremes of the **ethnocentric-polycentric spectrum** of organisation culture.

(a) Should the product be **standardised where appropriate** and **adapted where essential** on a regional scale (regiocentricity) or a global scale (geocentricity)?

(b) Should the **management structure** be of a macropyramid type with all the essential services and functions, such as marketing, centralised?

(c) Should the management structure be an **umbrella structure** with key services and functions devolved to the overseas operating companies?

(d) Should an **inter-conglomerate** structure be used, with the centre providing broad strategic direction?

The **design of the business** in terms of organisation structure, culture, and management roles will evolve as the company develops its international marketing strategies. Typical of this chain of events are the appointment of an export sales manager, followed by a creation of an **export sales department**, which usually evolves into an **international division** with a director at its head. Further expansion internationally will involve either a global **product division** structure or a global **geographic division structure**.

37 PLANNING INTERNATIONAL MARKETING

> **Examiner's comments.** Answers often consisted of vague generalisations. Application of knowledge is essential to success and candidates were required to concentrate on the management issues.

This question goes to the root of the difference between domestic and international marketing. Although the process stays the same we have to deal with many different **cultural backgrounds** in addressing **customer needs and wants**, and in handling the many different **communication issues** which are affected by differing cultural values in the markets with which the company is involved. There are different approaches to **organisational** issues too, which will inevitably affect the planning process.

The **self reference criterion** acknowledges that we grow up in our own society absorbing that society's norms and values, and when marketing domestically it is safe to assume that most of our customers share broadly the same values. This is not a safe assumption when dealing with country markets different from our own. Many of the key differences are summed up in the following table, which looks at domestic planning and international planning in parallel. It has to be said that the table takes a broadly UK or US standpoint, when referring to domestic markets.

Domestic planning	International Planning
Normally a single nationality and language	Multi-lingual, multi-cultural, multi-national
Relatively homogeneous market	Fragmented diverse markets
Market data easily available and easily assimilated	Data collection a formidable task and need to be wary in interpreting data
Political factors normally fairly unimportant	Political factors often impinge on marketing decisions
Financial climate usually stable and reasonably predictable	Economic and financial factors can be very volatile
'Rules of the game' in business sectors generally understood and followed	Rules not always clear, often changeable and affected by cultural values sometimes dimly perceived
Business management usually a shared responsibility with basic financial controls	Business management perhaps less rigorously controlled, more autonomous

Just taking one of the issues above, in order to highlight the problems of planning for the international markets more clearly, a company has to be very careful in collecting, analysing and acting upon **marketing research data**. For one thing, for political reasons the secondary data in a market may not be comparable or as accurate as data available in the domestic market.

For social and cultural reasons it may not be possible to design an exactly equivalent research survey for primary research, or it may not be possible to ask the questions of a comparable sample of people. The **socio-economic groups** in market A or B may be totally different from the socio-economic groups in our domestic market. Having acquired the raw data, it still may not be possible to arrive at a comparable interpretation.

There may also be problems recruiting trained researchers, or holding equivalent focus groups, because of differing expectations amongst potential respondents about marketing research techniques.

This brief skim over the surface of potentially difficult issues of marketing research does not really do justice to the **potential for misinterpretation** associated with cultural factors.

Answer bank

We also need to spend some time reviewing the other problems associated with the **organisational issues** affecting international marketing planning, and causing difficulties not seen in domestic marketing. These too are affected by cultural factors and the self reference criteria, although perhaps a more significant factor is the relationship between **head office management** and **subsidiary management**.

HQ and local managers fail to see eye to eye

There is tension when head office believes there is unclear **allocation of responsibilities** as far as the subsidiaries are concerned and the subsidiaries think that head office offers resistance to planning and their **involvement** in it. This is a reflection of each party seeing the world only from their own reference point.

Head office personnel tend to think of managers in subsidiaries as having a lack of **multinational orientation** and unrealistic expectations, whilst the local managers resent HQ involvement and believe they misinterpret local information. There is also a genuine likelihood that HQ managers do have a lack of awareness of foreign markets and are **insensitive to local decisions**. At the same time local managers may have a lack of **strategic thinking** and perhaps also a lack of **marketing expertise**.

Management processes

There is also likely to be a difference with respect to the **marketing processes** carried out centrally and locally. Some of the common faults include a lack of a standardised base for **evaluation**, and often poor IT **systems and support** and poor **feedback and control** systems. Local companies may also suffer from poorly developed procedures or incomplete or outdated internal and market information. There may also be too little **communication** with HQ and insufficient use of multinational marketing expertise.

Many of the problems identified above stem from having **too localised** a view of the world. The ideal situation is one where each individual manager is prepared to take responsibility for the process of **strategic thinking**, rather than it being restricted to a separate strategic planning department. The **planning process** should also be regularly reviewed and refined in order to improve its **relevance and effectiveness**.

38 ELECTRONIC COMMERCE

> **Examiner's comments.** Too many candidates answered this question without reading it! It was very difficult to assess a candidate's knowledge of the impact of e-commerce on the marketing strategy of a global consulting firm when they chose to write about Amazon.com, Sainsbury's and consumer shopping!

The creation of a **web-site** on the **Internet** by any individual or organisation automatically creates a global presence. Ideally, all organisations with web-sites should have an international marketing strategy in place that recognises the **global communications media** they are using, and have **processes** in place that will respond sympathetically to random responses from enquirers around the world.

If organisations are intending to use their web-sites for **processing orders**, including payment, (electronic commerce) then consideration will need to be given to how this information is accessed by **non-domestic customers**. Electronic commerce using the Internet, and international issues, are difficult to separate.

In a domestic market the creation of **call centres**, in any location in the world, is another form of electronic commerce. Thus, in principle, providing there are suitable English speakers in Hong Kong, there is nothing to stop HSBC having a global call centre in Hong Kong that its customers in the UK believe is a UK call centre accessed by a local number.

Answer bank

This type of approach to call centres could be extended to the global consulting organisations.

Impact and opportunity

Electronic commerce allows global consultants the opportunity to offer their clients, irrespective of where they are in the world, a 24-hour service without the expense of offices and infrastructure in each of the countries in which they operate. It offers a **low cost market entry opportunity**, in the sense that all contact with potential clients anywhere in the world can be developed to such a level through the real-time interchange of information. Personal contact, with its associated costs of travel, accommodation and subsistence is minimised. The Internet allows for:-

(a) **Cost effective** global communications between headquarters and the satellite offices around the world

(b) **Communications with clients** for the delivery of services and advice

(c) **Promotional or prospective** communications with potential clients

All the above communication systems need to be protected and as **secure** as possible.

Dangers

The major issue with the Internet, and consequently electronic commerce using the Internet, is **data security**. For certain types of information and communication, **data protection** is a key issue. For instance, a global consulting organisation working with Ford in the US would need to protect any information conducted by e-commerce from by Peugeot in Europe. System corruption could be as big a danger as security and data protection issues.

System failure is another major issue that could wreck relationships between client and consultant if the failure resulted in loss of information and the necessity to rework the project.

Overload of the Internet system, in terms of the number of consultants competing for client attention and causing confusion, could result in them choosing a local consultant they know rather than a global player they do not know.

39 THREE YEAR PLAN

Marketing plan - objectives and background

A three year international marketing plan must be based around clear **marketing objectives**. These will be specific and clearly defined for each product/market by country for the first year. There must be clear targets for Year 2 and there must be a sound and realistic expectation of the company's likely market position in the third year.

These objectives will be set in the context of **information and assumptions** about the world economy, trading patterns and any changes in the regions and markets in which the company is operating. Moreover, they will be set in relation to the **historical performance** of the company, covering details of sales by market/country, costs, profit levels and so on. They should also be placed into the context of a general **forecast** of future potential beyond the three year planning cycle.

Overall strategy

The company's overall strategy in relation to its products and markets should be included, with reference to the key **opportunities and threats** identified and the key **strengths** which

Answer bank

will be utilised and developed, and any **weaknesses** which need to be corrected or compensated for.

Appropriate marketing strategies by market and by country should be identified, with indications of the **operations** and **financial requirements** necessary to achieve these targets.

Detailed tactical and operational plans

Cascading down from the overall strategy, should be detailed plans for each of the markets, country by country, including **budgets**, brand and communication **objectives**, **distribution** and logistics planning, sales and other human **resource requirements**.

A clear indication should be given about the co-ordination and **integration of marketing activities** across national boundaries, working to organisational strengths and resources - who does what, where, when and how.

These plans should cover all the controllable aspects of the company's operations. These include the **product** and its packaging, **promotion** (including sales function and sales promotion as well as advertising), the **distribution** channels and the relevant financial aspects **(price)**.

Control and evaluation

These plans should also include a clear process of **evaluation** against month by month targets, and criteria for success. Budgets for achievement as well as budgets of costs and expenses should be developed and included so that appropriate control may be maintained.

Contingency plans should also be prepared, so that **variations** from budget can be accounted for and accommodated or corrected without panic. A plan should be a true guideline for action and kept under continual review as a working document, rather than appear as a one-off paper that may be just put into a drawer after a single reading or approval.

Planning process

It is important that a three year plan is part of a **continuing planning process**, which is itself kept under review. Responsibility for implementation of the plan should become part of the responsibility of all managers in the organisation Ownership of the plan should be company-wide, not just seen as the preserve of the international marketing manager.

40 GLOBAL WORKFORCE

> **Examiner's comments.** Few candidates noted the need for the following as motivating factors:
> - Involvement in planning
> - Need for good communication
> - Clearly defined procedures and responsibilities
> - Clarity of reporting
> - Organisational clarity
>
> Most candidates took the question to be primarily about reward systems. Few challenged the assertion made in the question that processes and systems were relatively unimportant.

In any **value adding system** it is **people** that make the **processes** work. Different cultures have differing approaches to work and differing motivations. However, as **Hertzberg** noted in the 1960's the universals of motivation hinge around **hygiene factors** such as the working environment and reward (pay) packages and the **motivational factors** of recognition and personal development and enhancement.

As many UK companies are finding as they move their production to the low cost production areas of the world, certain cultures (particularly Muslim) do not respond in the same way as European cultures, due to the dominance of the eldest male of the family. Thus, whilst many UK clothing manufactures have moved production to the countries of North Africa and are employing local female labour they are finding that irrespective of the financial incentives offered the productivity does not alter. Research is indicating that since the pay is handed over to the eldest male of the household there is no incentive for the female worker to work any harder or more effectively. The research is unclear regarding the motivation of the employees, although reviewing the evidence with a UK mindset indicates that personal motivation is likely to be low, as the female employee will receive no more recognition in the workplace and no more money for her personal use.

To ensure high levels of motivation the organisation must create a positive image to its employees. **Training and development** of individuals needs to be seen as relevant to them and their personal development and esteem in society. For instance in the Oriental cultures it is more important to have experienced a programme of education, training or development than to receive an award. This is in contrast to the European culture, in which the gaining of the qualification or the award is of major motivational significance.

Most of the literature on world class performance highlights the Japanese practice of implementing employee suggestions to improve operational process, and then recognising and rewarding the employees in a small way. Illustrative statistics show that each employee will make between 30 - 50 suggestions per year and that 95% of all suggestions will be implemented, with each implemented suggestion receiving typically a $10 award plus recognition in the company communications. In contrast, UK/US organisations receive very few suggestions per year, implement around 5% of them and offer enormous rewards for the successful suggestions.

Most European cultures can handle significant levels of organisational ambiguity. Virtually all other cultures require **clear structures** and clear lines of **responsibility** and **authority**. **Reporting** and **communications** within organisations need to take account of cultural preferences. The UK/US approach of managing to budgets and the variances from **budgets** is not a universal practice. It has been recognised that this practice has demotivating effects on UK/US employees.

Appraisal schemes are widely used as a motivator in UK/US organisations. Most other cultures, including some European cultures, are not comfortable with appraisal processes, particularly those involving two way or 360 degree feedback. Many cultures prefer the **command and control** style of management with senior management being seen as omniscient, and all communication flowing **downwards** from the top of the organisation to the lower levels. Criticism of those in authority is an alien concept and encouraging the practice in overseas subsidiaries in the UK/US style does little to increase motivation.

The UK and the US use **promotion** (usually based on merit) as a motivator, while many other cultures prefer promotion based on seniority.

Clearly, motivating a global workforce is a complex process. Current management literature is focusing on **corporate visions**, with all employees believing in the vision and wanting to make it work. However, at the operational level much cynicism remains as to its durability and long term effectiveness.

Answer bank

41 EXPATRIATE STAFF

> **Examiner's comments**: This question was often misinterpreted. Too many candidates embarked on very detailed analyses of the strengths and weaknesses of expatriate versus home-based staff, which was not what was required. The training procedures were sometimes well thought out, but answers were often too general and without consideration of costs and timings.

The choice between using **expatriates** and **local sales staff** highlights the inherent dilemma in the **personal selling** element of the promotion mix in international marketing.

Comparing expatriate with local sales staff

The strength of using expatriates is that these are people with a thorough **knowledge** of the company and its **organisation structure** and **management**, its culture, brands, and products and how they are used. These people will fully understand the **objectives** and **performance criteria** set and the performance measures used.

However, unless they have had considerable exposure to a given region or country they are unlikely to fully understand the **local culture and language**, and as such may not be operating optimally. This could have a detrimental impact on the development of sales in the region or country.

The strengths of using local sales people is that they fully understand the culture and language of the country/market in which they operate and should be able, in principle, to generate optimum levels of sales.

However, the local sales person may see the position as a job being done for a **distant management** which works to totally different principles and which uses motivational techniques which appear totally inappropriate. This lack of understanding and empathy with the overseas principal could have a detrimental impact on the development of sales in the region or country.

Expatriate sales training programme

The following training programme is proposed:

(a) Six months before confirming the appointment of the expatriate, start **language training** in both everyday conversational language and technical and commercial language.

(b) Three months before confirmation, and whilst continuing with the general language training, start developing skills in the **idiomatic language**.

(c) Two months before departure send the expatriate for a one week pre-appointment acclimatisation visit to the target country, to gain a first hand impression of the local culture.

(d) Following this visit, and with the language training continuing, commence a detailed **culture awareness** programme in which the expatriate can develop the necessary social skills to operate effectively in the target market.

(e) One month before appointment send the expatriate to the target country for a two week **sales development period** to enable him/her to test out skills and knowledge in the field.

Conclusion

An organisation may consider it appropriate to train 2 or 3 sales people as home based expatriate sales staff, to allow exposure of a larger number of interested sales staff as part of a company wide sales **staff development** programme. A benefit of this approach is that the company always has appropriately trained and experienced staff available for sales development in regions with common languages and similar cultures.

42 KNOWLEDGE BASED ORGANISATIONS

> **Examiner's comments.** This was not a popular question, testing the ability of candidates to discuss 'knowledge asset management', for example through the use of company Intranets or the release of knowledge to gain competitive advantage.

Knowledge based organisations have invested heavily in creating and maintaining extensive **information systems** regarding their products and processes, customers, competitors, and the business environments in which they operate. Every action is considered to be a **learning activity** irrespective of whether the outcome is successful or unsuccessful, and the results of the actions update the information systems.

Knowledge based companies tend not to have a **blame culture** and encourage all staff to take modest **risks** so that what is being done can be challenged and improved. The learning gained from taking modest risks and experimenting with what is done contributes to the knowledge within the organisation - but only if it is **captured** in an appropriate information system.

On an international scale knowledge based companies are starting to exploit the potential of the **Internet** to enable them to trade anywhere in the world, with knowledge of who they are dealing with extracted from the click trails of visitors to their Internet sites.

Knowledge based organisations gain **competitive advantage** through the following channels.

(a) Understanding the **knowledge assets of their employees**, such as personal skills and competencies (e.g. language skills, creative skills) and using these in the most effective way to give job/career satisfaction to the employee and competitive advantage to the organisation

(b) Linking these **human assets** to **technology** through the creation of information systems based on **database** and Internet technology. The human skills of critical enquiry and **evaluation** are of particular significance in this regard, since to be successful the organisation needs to be continually asking itself why it is doing activities in a particular way and are there alternative/more competitive ways of doing such activities

(c) Using the above to continuously improve strategies and plans

   (i) **Targeting** markets and customers within them more effectively

   (ii) Obtaining and processing product/service **ideas** more quickly

   (iii) Sharpening the **prospecting process** for sales, potential customers and information on customers (both existing and potential)

   (iv) Developing more appropriate **market segments** based on customer profiles and more responsive segmentation processes based on changes in customers buying habits

An enduring example of a knowledge based organisation is IBM which has continuously re-invented itself in its 80 year history. Skandia is a more recent example of an organisation re-inventing itself to exploit the knowledge it possesses about its customers and markets. The global consulting firms such as Arthur Andersen and Price Waterhouse Coopers are all good examples of knowledge based companies.

Answer bank

Organisations are at risk of losing their knowledge when employees leave, hence the importance of removing a blame culture approach to management and replacing it with a more open **recognition and reward** approach.

43 DATABASES

> **Examiner's comments.** This was quite well answered. Many candidates gave the example of the Internet and database marketing, but basing an answer solely on the Internet was not enough. Little reference was made to using information technology to gain competitive advantage through effective segmentation and customer relationships.

Databases, particularly those linked to **EPOS** systems through **loyalty schemes** allow marketers to understand and segment their customers with levels of **precision** not achieved in the past. Marketing databases enable organisations to develop marketing plans that more closely meet the needs of customers. In particular, **marketing objectives** can be set which reflect the potential customer's individual characteristics and thus gain significant competitive advantage by removing waste from the marketing process.

EPOS systems, which were once considered to be database **stock control systems**, are now providing data about consumer **buying behaviour**, which is giving them a value to marketers way beyond the designers' original specifications.

Many retailers have linked their EPOS systems with their **loyalty schemes** into a common database and use this data for highly targeted **marketing communications campaigns**, such as information regarding special offers and forthcoming new product launches. This is highly targeted and waste minimising promotional activity. The EPOS system will have tracked a customer's purchases over a period of time and will know that, for instance, that customer has a propensity for responding to special offers or for trying new products.

A number of companies have become major marketing names on the basis of their marketing segmentation databases, namely, **Experian** of the UK, with its Mosaic software, and **CACI** of the United States with its Acorn software. MOSAIC and ACORN databases are designed to assist in the market segmentation process and are derived from comprehensive **geographic** (location) and **demographic** data (e.g. electoral rolls, type of property etc.).

Both of these software shells have been adapted to suit the data available for many of the countries of the world and provide international marketers with geo-demographic databases. Hence, UK and US marketers going global can use familiar software to present information in a format they understand on the characteristics of their target markets.

As the UK and US retailers start going **global**, (such as Walmart of the US and Tesco of the UK), and take their EPOS and loyalty scheme information technology with them, then not only will they gain significant competitive advantage over their local rivals but they will have processes and information on a global scale from which they can lever competitive advantage through selling the knowledge to other organisations. Thus, the established providers of marketing databases for segmentation could find themselves with new competitors with even more detailed data and information about customers and their buying habits.

Implementation and control of marketing programmes is more easily undertaken with real-time data. For instance, the **effectiveness of promotional programmes** can be easily measured at the point of sale from the EPOS data. If the customer is using a loyalty card and has received a promotional mail-shot then the response to the mail-shot can be accurately assessed and its effectiveness measured. **Customer response** to new product launches is also very easily evaluated using EPOS data.

In summary, marketing databases allow companies to benefit from reduced **time and effort** (and ultimately **cost**) involved in preparing marketing strategies and plans, through the use of **continuously updated information** that can add significantly to competitive advantage. The benefits for companies from using marketing databases for planning and control purposes are derived from improved **accuracy** of data and information, **rapid access** to the right information, and the opportunity to work from **real-time data**. All of these benefits **reduce waste** and can lead to competitive advantage and improved profits.

44 TUTORIAL QUESTION: EFFECTS OF ORGANISATION STRUCTURE ON PRODUCT STANDARDISATION

The degree to which the elements of marketing should be **standardised** or **differentiated** is one of the perennial issues in international marketing. In order to have a standardised marketing mix, it is imperative to have a standardised product. On the other hand a standardised product does not necessarily imply that a company has a standardised mix.

It is also likely that different **organisational structures** will bring different views to bear upon the management of this process.

(a) **Organisational structures**

There are various ways of viewing the types of organisational structures that exist in international marketing. One approach is that taken by Simon Majaro, who likens a business organisation to a **pyramid**, with a large base of people performing the fundamental operations of a business.

Above them, there is a middle layer of supervisors and managers translating **strategic messages** from above into day-to-day operational decisions needed by those below. At the top of the pyramid is a small apex of strategic managers, setting the long term agenda for the organisation.

Majaro poses three broad categories of structure for international activities. In the **interglomerate** there is a central financial control, but the rest of the organisation operates freely under its own discretion, provided that it meets the financial objectives.

The second is the **umbrella** organisation, perhaps typified by Unilever at the larger end of the scale, where there is a fair degree of autonomy for local companies, but where central services and committees try to ensure efficient running and the cross-fertilisation of ideas.

Finally, there is the **macropyramid** organisation structure, where there exists a strong centralised strategic management pyramid, with truncated pyramids in the various market places, which merely have the function of putting into operation decisions taken centrally.

(b) **Standardisation**

It will generally be the case that the more **centralised** the organisation, the greater the likelihood of standardisation being an important factor, since this will ease the implementation of centralised control. In an interglomerate type of organisation there will be very little attempt to centralise or standardise and it is not uncommon for companies in the same group to compete without the managers realising they are even part of the same organisation.

In an umbrella type of organisation there may be some pressure from central services to find **economies of scale** by attempting to standardise product offerings. The degree to which such pressure will have an effect upon the **new product development** function will depend upon how NPD is managed in the group's companies. NPD is an

Answer bank

integrated part of the marketing structure with clear lines of responsibility in each of the companies, it will probably be easier to impose a central control to the process internationally. This may involve concentrating physical research and development into one location.

New product development may be seen by some companies in an umbrella type multinational as a separate function spanning more than one departmental are. It may be more difficult to impose a central control on NPD.

The most centralised form of organisational structure proposed by Majaro is the macropyramid, where the majority of strategic decisions are taken centrally in the group's headquarters. In order to ensure tight central control there will inevitably be a tendency to attempt a highly standardised marketing mix, certainly where the product element is standardised as much as possible.

(c) **New product development**

The role of NPD in an organisation will depend upon the breadth and complexity of the organisation and the number of markets in which it is operating. The role of NPD is:

- To make sure the product mix matches **market needs**
- To enable the organisation to **compete** effectively
- To reduce the organisation's **dependence** upon vulnerable market segments
- To match **competitors'** moves
- To help achieve long term **profit and growth**

NPD may be driven by **technological** or scientific discoveries or by a recognition of the **needs** of consumers in the market place.

Where a multinational organisation has very good **internal communications** it is more likely that the NPD process is centralised. Where internal communications are slower it is more probable that NPD is conducted in several locations, the results of the work being disseminated through the company when managers have greater confidence in success. This will depend to some extent upon the history of success of product development as a part of company strategy.

A **consumer driven** NPD strategy will be more likely to be centralised if the organisation is highly **market orientated** and has a history of responding rapidly to changes in the market place.

45 RETAILING DIFFERENCES

> **Tutorial note.** This question is open to misinterpretation, and you may be tempted to write about the obvious differences displayed between retailers in developed and developing countries, such as the quantity of goods on shelves. From the point of view of international marketing, the question is really asking about those environmental factors which differentiate the two and affect their respective marketing strategies, such as access to distribution networks or capital.
>
> **Examiner's comments.** Those who attempted the question tended to totally misinterpret it and gain few marks. Most references to the respective marketing plans concentrated on communications aspects only and contained few examples. Very few candidates referred to a particular product in their answers, despite this being a requirement of the question.

The factors that differentiate between retailers in developed and developing countries can be classified as either **environmental** (which affects the way the retailers are structured), or **logistic** (which affects the process by which they satisfy the needs of their customers).

Factors which differentiate the **structure of retailing** are as follows.

(a) **Shopping and buying habits** will influence the development of a retailing sector.
 In the developed world, shopping is not a daily necessity and the retailing sector is continually responding to changing buying habits. In the developing world shopping is a daily ritual and buying habits are relatively static.

(b) The stage of **economic and market development** will determine income levels and the spending power of customers within a given market. It will also influence the concentration of retailing and the development of distribution channels.

(c) The **location of customers** will range from the large, established conurbation's in the developed world to the widely dispersed populations in the developing world (complemented by scattered large conurbation's).

(d) The availability of, and access to, **technology** by both retailers and consumers will influence the manner by which transactions occur - 'electronic money' either by EFTPOS or credit/debit card is common in the developed world, whereas transactions are principally for cash in the developing world.

(e) **Cultural differences** will influence the product and services offered.

The factors which will influence **logistics** are as follows.

(a) **Technology** that is available for transporting and storing products to the retail premises will vary. For example, frozen food is accepted in the developed world, with householders having freezers to store frozen food supplied from cold stores operated by both the retailers and food processors. This pattern is unlikely to be encountered in the developing countries with little or no freezing facilities at any stage of the distribution channel. Thus, customers' needs in the developing world are satisfied by what is available rather than what can be made available using technology.

(b) The **transport infrastructure** will have a significant impact on the development of retailing. The US and the UK, together with an increasing number of EU countries, have developed out of town retail parks, allegedly in response to consumers' changing buying habits. These developments have yet to be implemented in the developing world. Good road systems and car ownership are key environmental factors which will affect this.

(c) The **size and dispersion of the market** will significantly affect the development of retailing, particularly with respect to the **service level** offered and expected. Consumers in the developed world expect instant satisfaction and are highly critical when this cannot be provided. This puts high pressure on the **supply chain** to perform to high standards. For example, in the UK the major food retailers (who account for around 80% of all food purchases) expect a 99% accurate delivery performance from their suppliers. As yet there is no evidence of these performance levels being expected in the developing world.

It is evident from the above that the marketing plans of retailers in the developed world will need significant modification to be operated effectively in the developing world.

The main **modifications** will include:

(a) Interpreting and assessing the **SLEPT factors** very critically to establish the impact they will have on the marketing plan.

(b) Taking account of the **context** of the market place will invariably involve all aspects of the marketing mix, as well as the **environment** in which the consumers live. The self reference criterion can have no place in a marketing plan for a retailer in the

Answer bank

developing world, although they may achieve the level of the developed world as their economies grow.

(c) Critically assessing the **costs and risks** of the significantly different distribution channels and the impact on **pricing strategies** and hence **competitiveness**.

It is highly unlikely that a marketing plan prepared for the retailing sector of the developed world could be used in the developing world without significant modification. The most appropriate and effective modifications are likely to be made after a detailed fact finding visit has been made.

46 TUTORIAL QUESTION: CRITERIA FOR SELECTION OF INTERNATIONAL PRODUCTS

The expression **overseas operation** may refer to either the **export** to or the **manufacture** of products in one or more foreign markets. The criteria discussed below may be applied to either situation.

(a) **Product range**

Consider the **breadth and depth of the company's product range** in its domestic market and the way it has developed there. There may be specific reasons relating to the home market which would militate **against** the marketability of certain aspects of the range in a foreign market. For example, products might have been designed for use in conjunction with another manufacturer's products which are only available in the domestic market.

(b) **Nature and size of overseas market**

The scope of the overseas market must be assessed to see how much of the company's range could be presented with a reasonable expectation of success. This may also be associated with (c) below.

(c) **Experience in the overseas market(s)**

The greater the company's experience of the market or markets under consideration, the greater may be the choice of products within the range which may be viable.

(d) **Level of investment**

The amount of investment (both **operational** and **marketing**) the company is prepared to make in these markets will constrain the choice of products for consideration. A new introduction to a new market or into a competitive situation may well require a greater marketing investment than would the maintenance of the same product in a particular market position in its home market.

(e) **Product complexity/technology**

The degree of complexity and/or the level of technology in the product will determine whether it is added to the company's list of products to be considered in this market. This factor will clearly need to be assessed against the technical competence of the consumers. This may be associated with a country's **educational system**.

(f) **Channel of distribution infrastructure**

Some or all of the company's product range might need a greater degree of technical support or after sales service than may be easily available in the channel(s) of distribution in some markets. This may be associated with the stage of **economic development** in the country concerned.

(g) **Stage in product life cycle (PLC)**

A product well into the maturity, or even decline, stage of its product life cycle in its home market may still be a relative **innovation** in the target market and would need different marketing support.

(h) **Nature of the marketing task**

The precise nature of the marketing task for each product in the range may help to determine the choice of products for the market.

(i) **Product modification**

Dependent to a large extent upon the nature of the product itself, the degree to which a product needs to be modified for a specific market will help to determine whether it is feasible to introduce it to that market.

It may be that no single one of the above points would decide the fate of any one product. Nevertheless, a **systematic analysis** of all of these points for all products within the range should give a good guide to the relative merits of selecting one product against another for inclusion.

Last but not least, in this evaluation exercise, would be the analysis of the **financial contribution** likely to be made by the inclusion of a particular product. It may not need to be profitable in its own right to make it worthwhile including, if the contribution it makes to overheads were to make all other sales more profitable.

47 NEW PRODUCTS AND INTERNATIONAL INPUTS

> **Examiner's comments**. A lot was written on NPD but little about possible international inputs or the NPD issues facing companies at various stages of international development.

The need for **new product development** is continually increasing. This is due to the following.

- Shortening product life cycles
- Speed of innovation
- The application of new technology to product design, development and manufacture
- The rate of new product introduction on a global scale.

A constant stream of new product introductions is required to minimise the **risk** to the company of not having a suitable product for consumption at the right time. Also, as the **cost** of product development rises and the subsequent investment in **production facilities** rises, a stream of ideas to exploit these investments is vital, since there is no evidence to suggest that the proportion of ideas that succeed in the market place has increased significantly from the 5% success rate identified in the 1960's.

Potential sources of ideas for new products can be employees, customers or competitors. Obtaining international **inputs** for new product development demands that the organisation has a fairly comprehensive **international marketing information system**. This does not mean the organisation has to be a major player in the international market place but it does mean that the organisation scans the world for ideas to screen, and subsequently appraise, develop, test and exploit.

A company that only exports, unless it has a comprehensive international marketing information system, will be reliant on its agents, distributors and other **intermediaries** for its supply of ideas. This supply of ideas will highly dependent on the relationship between the company and its intermediaries. It is always possible that the intermediaries could give

Answer bank

the same ideas to other companies they represent, thus creating competition before the product is developed.

If the company relies solely on its **domestic** customers and employees for ideas for new product development, then the resulting products will have an **ethnocentric** feel to them which may not suit customers in export markets. Thus, the exporting company will need to have wide ranging sources of new product ideas to avoid any of the problems that can be caused by trying to sell products designed for a domestic market to an international market.

A company that has several wholly owned foreign plants has a distinct advantage in obtaining ideas for new product development.

(a) It can obtain ideas directly from employees, who will have knowledge of the needs of the consumers in the areas in which the plant is located.

(b) The organisation can obtain ideas directly from its customers and competitor activity. These ideas can be for the exclusive use of the company. Such a company has the opportunity for a greater number of product ideas as well as the potential to develop products for distinctive customer groupings.

The company with several wholly owned foreign plants must be at an advantage in new product development over a company that operates on an export only basis. However, irrespective of the type of company, **management attitude** towards new product development and the associated risk will be of considerable significance.

48 NEW PRODUCT DEVELOPMENT

> **Examiner's comment**. Candidates were required to express the international dimension of NPD, not just add on a few lines to answers taken from the Planning and Control exam.

For the majority of companies in the world there is no choice. They either **innovate** (actively engage in new product development) or they cease to exist. This stark choice - **innovate or die** - faces all organisations irrespective of whether they compete on a global scale, or serve a local niche market. The shortest **time required** to bring a new product to market usually gives the company capable of managing the high speed of development a significant **competitive advantage**.

Critical issues in speeding up the product development process

1. The development of an **international orientation to innovation** recognises that competition from a new product can come from anywhere in the world at any time. Such an orientation must come from senior management.

2. **Build obsolescence into the product,** such that the life cycle of the generic product can be managed by the organisation rather than be established by the customers. This will require a detailed understanding of customers' needs. For example, Japanese consumer electronic companies practice this approach. The generic product is the hi-fi system, but the 'shelf life' of a particular model of hi-fi is very short, typically months.

3. **Organise the company to undertake R & D in a number of countries,** thus creating an infrastructure that can rapidly transfer any breakthrough from country to country.

4. **Track competitors' activities** as rigorously as is practical, and monitor their activities through the creation and maintenance of an effective and efficient **marketing management information system.**

5. **Take risks and spread the risks geographically,** if necessary through creating strategic alliances which co-operate on research and innovation to the benefit of all

parties. Aircraft engines are developed this way, through competitors co-operating and including suppliers of major components in the R & D process.

6 **Building flexibility into the R & D process** such that parallel processing or simultaneous engineering principles can be applied.

7 **Using computer technology**, such as databases for information management and the Internet for intelligence, to assist in the overall management of the R & D process

The most important factor in speeding up the new product development process is the **commitment of senior management** towards innovation and its rapid diffusion throughout the organisation.

49 ECONOMIC DEVELOPMENT AND PRODUCT DESIGN

A whole range of factors will have an impact upon the **design** of a product for any market in which it may be targeted. The **technology** acceptable in the market, the **distribution channels** available, **cultural** factors, **buyer behaviour** and **product usage** factors, for example, will all play a part in influencing design.

Some, or all, of these factors may be affected in turn by the overall level of **economic development** in the target markets.

As an example, we can look at the design issues associated with a range of office furniture: desks, chairs, cabinets, and cupboards, etc. For the sake of clarity, we will do this using a three stage model of economic development, considering countries either as **lesser developed countries** (LDCs), **newly industrialised countries** (NICs) or **advanced industrialised countries** (AICs). This is a fairly simplistic model of what may better be seen as a continuum of economic development, but should provide a basis of reference with which to associate product design issues. By way of example, we will consider utility and style.

(a) **Utility**

To a large extent it may be said that virtually all office furniture is primarily functional, although for the Chief Executive of a large company, the primary function may be to impress visitors. Nevertheless, it is most likely that potential purchasers of office equipment in LDCs will be seeking very basic **utilitarian values** in the product - to the extent that the prime competitors for our company's office desk would be locally made tables constructed from locally available materials. Value for money and, therefore price and basic construction, may be the most critical factor here.

In NICs the utility of the product will, of course, still be important but this may be overlaid to some extent by additional benefits sought such as **style** and **fashion**, which will affect design, extent of the range offered and, possibly, the addition of specialist desks for reception areas or for use with computers. One factor here is that, since NICs are by definition newly industrialised, there may well be large orders to be had for newly built and purpose built factories and office premises.

(b) **Style**

The issue of style has already been touched upon above but merits separate comment in terms of the brief which may be given to the design department.

Even LDCs will have some businesses and organisations which may have access to sufficient funds to pay for additional style benefits in their office furniture. However the overall size of the top end of this market may not make it feasible to have too many competing companies offering too wide a range of styles, so our product range designs may be limited for these countries.

Answer bank

This may be especially true if the company has decided to **manufacture locally**. The range of manufacturing and assembly skills in LDCs may be limited, granted the **educational infrastructure and skills** training, availability of technicians to install and or maintain computer controlled machinery, and so on.

Moving through to NICs, the market for office furniture may be sufficient to support a very much wider range of styles, perhaps for customers for whom style has become much more important than mere utility.

This factor will become even more significant in the AICs. There will be much more **competition** to provide for customers in the top segment of the market which is likely also to be the most profitable per unit sold with higher **margins** and less **price sensitivity**.

Also towards the top end of the market, it may not be necessary for the furniture to last so long since fashion may dictate change before the product has reached the end of its useful life.

50 PACKAGING DECISIONS

It is important, first of all, to establish that packaging may be taken to refer to the immediate product (or brand) pack or to the outer packaging for transportation purposes. The **functions of packaging** are many and varied, so it may be helpful to identify some of these key functions before proceeding.

(a) **The brand pack**

From the customer's point of view, the key functions of the brand pack are to provide a convenient, safe and appropriate way of transporting the product from the point of purchase to the point of use or consumption. Depending upon the physical nature of the product, the pack must **contain, protect** and **allow storage** and/or continuous access in use (eg a large domestic detergent pack), or it may simply protect briefly until early consumption (eg crisp packet or chocolate bar wrapper).

The brand pack will also provide **recognition** which is of benefit to both buyer and seller. It will also facilitate **display** for the retailer/distributor at the point of sale.

(b) **Outer packaging**

The outer packaging may consist of a display outer contained in a larger transit pack, sturdy enough to protect the contents on their journey from factory to the point of sale. The key functions here are **ease of transport** and **product protection**, functions which will be of primary benefit to the manufacturer and members of the channel(s) of distribution.

(c) **International marketing**

The various demands of international marketing may influence the packaging decisions in a number of ways.

(i) Depending upon the **number and geographic location** of the international markets, it may be that the **distribution channels are considerably longer** than for domestic markets, perhaps involving more handling and intermediate storage. The packaging may need to be more robust and protective.

Manufacturers must also be aware of the potentially different **climatic conditions** through which the product may travel. For example, one UK adhesives manufacturer ran into a problem with its products boiling over when delayed at customs controls in Turkey for a week.

Answer bank

This problem was overcome, at least partly, by changing the packaging specification - although it was also necessary to change the product specification to cope with a wider variation in temperatures than in the domestic market.

(ii) The **language** of the buyers will also have some effect upon at least the 'brand' pack. Depending upon the nature and complexity of the product itself, and therefore the need for instructions or information, the number of languages and extent of instruction may vary considerably. For example, a camera will normally be accompanied by an instruction booklet translated into many languages, whereas a shampoo may have up to three languages briefly describing its method of use. It may alternatively be targeted at each market in which it is being sold with the instructions translated into the appropriate language for that market.

(iii) The **cultural context** of the buyers will also have a bearing on the packaging decision. Thus, for example, differing **perceptions** of colour in different cultures may require different approaches to pack **design and presentation**.

In a 'throwaway' culture such as the UK or the USA, the pack may be quickly disposed of as waste, whereas in many areas of the developing world the pack itself may have a **secondary value** for storage, or some other conversion usage. Equally such added value to the packaging may be 'built-in', as part of a sales promotion. One successful sales promotion idea in the UK market a few years ago was a brand of coffee offered for sale in a specially designed storage jar.

In some countries where a 'throwaway' culture may once have prevailed, the pendulum is now moving back. In Germany, for example, where the law is moving towards greater **environmental awareness** and responsibility, pack designers need to cater specifically for **recycling** requirements both in design and in materials use.

(iv) Finally the relationship of the **cost of packaging** to the cost, value and final price of the delivered product needs to be borne in mind when considering the packaging decisions within the international marketing strategy.

This applies both to brand packaging and transit packaging. If the total cost of the packaging element of the mix represents a very small proportion of the final price of a high value but vulnerable product, it is clearly worth building in a safety margin to avoid having to write off or write down the value of damaged products.

For low value, large volume products the level of risk of damage in transit must be offset against the potential loss of profit from over-packaging a non-vulnerable product - or of making such a product overpriced and uncompetitive in a foreign market.

51 MARKETING SERVICES

> **Examiner's comment**. Only the better candidates successfully related the characteristics of services to their international dimensions.

The distinguishing features of **services** are as follows.

(a) **Intangibility** - they cannot be handled in any way

(b) **Perishability** - they cannot be stored

(c) **Heterogeneity** - they are not easy to standardise

Answer bank

(d) **Inseparability** - the simultaneous production, or provision, and consumption of services

(e) **Absence of ownership** - no goods change hands

Services are the fastest growing sector of world trade, and in the mature markets of the developed world account for around 70% of GNP, and frequently 75% plus of the workforce.

Principal difficulties of marketing services

(a) **Cultural differences**, particularly with reference to the degree of **customer involvement** and the **relationship** between the buyer and seller, are critical factors in the marketing of services. Customers purchase services from local providers. For instance, the major accountancy firms such as Price Waterhouse Coopers operate on a global scale through a network of local offices, in virtually every country of the world. This approach recognises differing approaches to accountancy, and also that customers are not going to travel to a world headquarters for accountancy services.

(b) Due to the need for close customer contact and the local nature of the service provision, services can be the target of political hostility from foreign governments. This hostility can extend to **legislation** being created to favour indigenous providers of services, and **restriction of access** to the market to outsiders. The regime in Iran banned all things Western and went back to the basics of Islamic life, to the point of making it illegal to own satellite TV aerials.

(c) Most consumers are very locally focused in their purchase of services, particularly financial services. Some financial service companies have overcome this by acquiring well respected brand names, for instance the Hong Kong and Shanghai Banking Corporation acquired the Midland Bank (as was) in the UK. UK customers are quite comfortable dealing with the what is now known as 'HSBC' irrespective of its ownership.

(d) Thus, it is the **characteristics of services** which makes them difficult to market in foreign markets, particularly the inseparability between provision and consumption. Many of the difficulties associated with the marketing of services can be overcome with a **local presence.** However, it is almost impossible to market services in those countries which display political hostility towards the country of origin of the service provider.

52 STRATEGIC MARKETING COMMUNICATIONS

> **Examiner's comments**. Quite a few candidates misinterpreted this question and wrote answers in general terms. The question was very rarely viewed in a strategic sense, with candidates seemingly unable to think from a managerial perspective.

Our day to day lives are centred around how we communicate with each other and this is closely influenced by our **cultural** background. To succeed in a market which is not the company's home market requires a high level of understanding of the target market. Failure, more often than not, shows through in the form of mistakes, failures and omissions in the **planning and control** of the **marketing communication** programme.

Culture may be loosely defined as 'the way we do things around here' and is reflected in religion, schooling, aesthetics, peer groups, legal framework, language and so on. It is usually the area which provides the greatest opportunity for companies to make mistakes.

Planning

If a company is to avoid the many pitfalls awaiting the unwary in terms of marketing communications, the key is sound planning which will allow sound decisions to be made. There are several key issues which must be considered, which are outlined below.

(a) **Standardisation/adaptation**: whether or not the **product or service** is standardised internationally, there will be a separate decision as to whether the **communications** should be standardised or adapted to local markets. There are efficiencies to be had by standardising, especially where there is a globally similar target customer group.

For example the analgesic Panadol was seen by its brand management team to be able to benefit from a **global brand recognition**, using the UK packaging pattern and logo as the ideal. The UK packaging was blue and the logo was circular and easy to recognise. Different European markets had, for a variety of reasons, acquired different packaging - some packs were green and had a different logo. The Scandinavian market, different again, had a mainly white pack because customers expected medicines to appear in white packs. Other countries used the brand name Panodol, with yet another logo.

In the event the company standardised the logo shape (still using both names, however) and also co-ordinated the pack shape, leaving the different colours for continued recognition within each of the markets. Thus, some international branding was possible but different cultural background forces were catered for. The company had to hope that a reasonable **balance** was struck between the **pressures for standardisation** and the **necessary local specialisation** in the packaging.

(b) **Push and pull strategies**: differing **channel pressures and conditions** may also lead to communication difficulties which need to be recognised and planned for. Companies do not always get the planning correct, despite detailed marketing research and forethought. The Boots company introduced one of its leading over-the-counter products into one European country with a significant advertising budget (ie using a primarily 'pull'-type communications strategy) only to discover that there was a tradition of consumers being closely advised by the pharmacist, which they had not picked up from their research.

The pharmacists were found to be advising their customers that there was a cheaper alternative product available. In this case the marketing communications should have been directed towards the pharmacy distribution channels, providing good reasons for them to support Boots' product. (This would have been a 'push'-type of communications strategy).

(c) **Media availability**: it is significant that different country markets have a different balance of media available for advertising support - so that, **even if a company wished to have exactly the same communications strategy in each market**, it would not necessarily always be possible. TV advertising may be relatively restricted, as in Germany in comparison to the UK, for example - or magazines may not be so specialist or so widely circulated.

(d) **Political and legal factors**: may be different in each of the markets in which the company operates and this will provide very different ground rules.

(e) **Management**: multi-country marketing communications may require significantly different management approaches, depending upon the degree of standardisation of the message and the medium.

(f) **Centralisation**: as with the standardisation issue there is a balance to be struck between pressures to centralise decision making in the communications field and the pressures to decentralise.

Answer bank

Control

Planning should not be done without also putting into place the means whereby the marketing communications effort is effectively controlled. Control issues in international marketing invariably revolve around the following factors.

(a) **Objectives**: Clear communications objectives must be established which provide a **benchmark** against which the success of an international communications campaign may be measured.

(b) **Standards**: Clear standards must be set across international markets for the delivery of the communications message in a way that is appealing and satisfactory. This may be associated with **media quality** standards, or with **creative** campaign planning standards.

(c) **Management issues**: multi-country delivery of communication messages must be tightly controlled to achieve the best effect and to deliver the best **value for money**. This inevitably raises issues associated with the management of **resources** across international borders. Here again a balance must be managed between **clarity of control** and the benefits associated with **local market knowledge.**

A multinational company may also be using more than one advertising or promotions agency. A clear set of guidelines needs to be established to ensure **accountable reporting lines** between client and agencies.

53 GLOBAL POSITIONING

> **Examiner's comments.** This was an unpopular question. There was little evidence in the answers that candidates understood what 'positioning' is and the implications for international planning and control. Too many answers referred to the globalisation v standardisation issues, and few candidates knew how to relate the question to the examples cited.

Levi, Nike, McDonalds, and Virgin are just a few of the company names that are familiar world-wide for their company **logos, products and services,** and corporate and brand **images.** For instance:

(a) Levi's jeans are a fashion symbol for people throughout the world, although they now suffer competition from companies such as Gap and Diesel. Wearing Levi's conveys a message about the person wearing them and acts as a status (or differentiation) symbol.

(b) Nike sports and leisure wear conveys association with sporting excellence and achievement, and allows the wearer the potential to emulate sporting heroes

(c) McDonalds is the most recognisable place for fast food world wide. Research has shown that the golden arches are the most recognised corporate symbol in the world. McDonalds sets the standard to which other fast food operators aspire.

(d) Virgin is seen as a company that provides products and services for people world wide. Much of Virgin's position in the global marketplace is due to the charisma of its founder and owner, Richard Branson.

Developments in Global Positioning

Slide 1 Segmentation

- The **definition and refinement** of segments within target markets on a global scale eg the creation of **strategically equivalent segments.**

- Understanding the **expectations of consumers** within the strategically equivalent segments

Answer bank

- The **focusing of communications effort** on closely defined segments eg world student population

Slide 2 Marketing Mix Development

- **Developing products services** that meet the expectations of the target segments

- Developing **pricing policies**, products and services to ensure **affordability** by all members of the strategically equivalent segment and **profitability** for the company - **differential pricing** between markets may be necessary to achieve a **global position**

- **Distribution channels** must be in place to ensure the effective delivery of the expectations of the target segment

- **Communications** must be developed which create the same image world wide

Slide 3 Global Positioning Developments

- The creation of **strategically equivalent segments**

- Universal methods of **identifying and defining segments** through the use of **ACORN** (a US developed segmentation system), or Mosaic (a UK developed segmentation system)

- The exploitation of **global telecommunications systems** to enable one image and message to reach a world audience at the same time through, for instance, the global broadcasting of major sporting events such as football or Formula 1 motor racing

- The adoption of the 'think global, act local' mindset amongst an increasing number of managers throughout the world

- The adoption of **particular strategic positions**, eg lowest cost producer or differentiator

Slide 4 Implications for Planning and Control

- Setting corporate and marketing **objectives** which reflect operation on a global scale

- Establishing **standards and performance criteria** against those standards that are applicable and workable on a global scale

- Creating **control systems** that can collect the performance data and information

- Creating systems that can accommodate fluctuating **exchange rates** between markets and **interest rates** within markets, and assess their impact on sales and profitability

- Creating **operating procedures** that take account of differing commercial practices in differing countries, and the degrees of risk that accompany trading on a global scale

Global positioning is a relatively simple concept to understand (identify a target segment, create an image for the product or service, and communicate that image to the target segment whilst ensuring the product or service is available for the target segment to purchase) but it is difficult to achieve in practice.

Most of the products or services with a clearly recognised global position have taken many years to achieve this status. At one extreme Levi's has been developing its global brand and position for over 100 years. Nike is a phenomenon of the last 20 years, the period of the development of satellite broadcasting and the world youth culture.

Answer bank

54 PAN-REGIONAL ADVERTISING

> **Examiner's comments**. A popular and well answered question. The best examples identified the control element and related them to a specific example.

This answer will consider the situation in the European Union (EU). **Pan-regional advertising** in this instance means the adoption of an advertising strategy for an organisation which treats the whole of the EU as a unified market in terms of the advertising communications for that product.

Advantages

The key advantages of adopting such an approach rest with the comparative ease of management required (in theory, at least) for pan-European advertising. This implies cost savings as well as economies of scale, in areas such as of advertising production costs.

Such a strategy would also allow for clearer **brand positioning** across the European market, with a unified advertising message and the associated benefits of being able to create Eurobrands and better added value for the customers. All of this is clearly dependent upon a large degree of **standardisation** of product across these markets and an identifiable **European customer profile**. It should be noted that this is only likely to apply to larger **FMCG** brands, or **industrial products** which have a common customer base.

Pan-European **positioning** is on the increase, but genuine pan-European **communications approaches** are not (perhaps because of the many disadvantages touched upon below!)

Disadvantages

Aside from the issue of **control and co-ordination** (discussed in more depth below) the main disadvantages are chiefly associated with **cultural** factors. The key to successful communications is the generation of a clear understanding. The different cultural bases across Europe militate against a common approach.

This is because the different European cultures are characterised by differences in language, religious customs, value systems, education, legal systems, aesthetic values and taboos, all of which lead to different **perceptions** of both message and medium. Both Terpstra and Jeannet and Hennessy provide useful cultural models.

Control

The issue of control and co-ordination of a pan-European strategy, as applied for example to the market for cars, is an important and difficult task which perplexes and sometimes escapes many companies.

(a) **Agency choice**. Given a central point of control of the communications process within the car manufacturer (an issue which may itself be problematical!) an early problem for the company is to make the correct choice of agency. Do we have a **global agency** already handling the company's affairs which can operate on a pan-European basis? Have we already appointed a pan-European agency? Do we rely upon the management of a disparate set of national agencies to deliver a common advertising approach? How do we manage the control process in personnel terms? Even with a common advertising platform, there will have to be translations made for most markets within the EU.

(b) **Media execution**. Assuming a common advertising message can be achieved, despite different buying habits in the different markets, (for example, the decision making unit, DMU, for a small car in the UK market may be biased towards women, while the DMU in Italy is more likely to be male dominated, even if the intended driver may be the woman of the household), there may still be problems over media choice.

Answer bank

Availability of television advertising time is somewhat restricted in Germany, for example, so the balance of TV time to print media space may have to be adjusted across the various markets. Any pan-European campaign must have a degree of **flexibility of media execution** built in to be manageable.

(c) **Management expertise**. The success of a pan-European campaign is very much dependent upon the depth and quality of management expertise in both the agency(ies) and in the company and its various subsidiaries across the European market. It must be capable of translating a **common strategy** into some very different country markets and picking up on cultural situations where the common approach may not work.

55 INTELLIGENCE BASES

> **Examiner's comments.** Students are strongly advised to read the answer to the mini case on McDonalds and globalisation from the December 1997 paper (see page 141) for additional insights into McDonalds.

Current **technology**, both hardware and software, enables organisations to create **databases** that are dynamic due their ability to be updated, in some instances in real time, rapidly and cost effectively. It is the up to the minute information held by dynamic databases, along with the ability of the **interrogation** software to extract information in any form the inquirer chooses, that gives them their intelligence status.

The **intelligence bases** of companies should contain all the known facts about the individual and collective **buying behaviour** of all its customers. These databases should reveal who their customers are, what they buy, how frequently they buy, why they buy (the value or benefit sought from the product or service), and what they expect in terms of product and/or service quality.

In the UK the loyalty cards issued by the major retailers give the issuers all the details of shopping visits to the issuer's store. This information can be used to establish those customers that always include a new product in their shopping basket, and can inform store management decisions on the location of new product offerings. It should be noted that Safeway in the UK recently abandoned its loyalty card scheme in favour of more price-led promotions in-store.

McDonalds has achieved its global position using all the elements of the marketing mix in a highly creative and coherent way, which will have led to the development of a very comprehensive intelligence base relating to worldwide eating out habits, including the fast food segment. This intelligence base will have been instrumental in informing the McDonalds **product strategy of standardisation**, unless it has had to adapt the product range to conform to local cultures as in India, for instance, where it introduced the lamb burger. Any traveller from one part of the world to another knows precisely what will be on offer at McDonalds. The "Golden Arches" logo has become a universal symbol for fast food, delivered in the same format (**people, processes** and **physical evidence**) everywhere. The intelligence base of McDonalds will contain the results of its **marketing research activities** into consumer behaviour as well as all the **SLEPT** and **12C factors** that will have a potential impact on its business.

Levi's with the 501 created a global, premium priced product aimed at a particular global segment, and promoted the 501 range with **standardised images** based on music, and real people doing real things in an urban setting. This was a much subtler approach to creating a global position, since most of the action took place in the mind. The global position of 501's was achieved through catching the spirit of the time, mid 80's onwards, through the use of advertising based on what people wanted to see and emulate. It is highly likely that

Answer bank

Levi's intelligence base was created around the desire to understand the **lifestyle aspiration** of the target customers.

Nike exploited the global interest in sport to create the impression in the minds of potential wearers of Nike products that they could 'Just do It'. Similar to Levi's it is highly likely the Nike intelligence base was created to assist in the understanding of the lifestyle aspirations of its target customers.

All the above companies have been either the first, or one of the **early entrants**, into the market places that they now dominate. Each of these companies will have had to create their own intelligence bases from **first principles**.

Currently, published case study evidence is suggesting that the founders of these companies took enormous leaps of faith in the first instance to get their products to market. Now each of these companies will have databases that know more about each one of us that uses their products.

> **Note**: Reflect on your response to a question about whether you would be interested in and willing to buy a pair of spectacles that receive and display 3D television pictures together with stereo sound. Now, reflect on your likely responses 30 years ago to a McDonalds research question regarding interest and potential buying patterns of fast food.

In contrast, Virgin has always been a late entrant into the markets in which it now competes, and has done something different to give customers improved choice and improved service, all at lower prices than the established competition. Its rail services have been less successful, as they inherited significant problems, but management promises to improve its image and service. Virgin usually has the advantage of joining a market in which buying patterns have been established and can use this intelligence to create the position of its choice against known competition.

The implication for international marketing planning can be summarised as:-

(a) Setting corporate and marketing **objectives** which reflect the knowledge that is obtained from operating on a global scale

(b) Establishing **standards and performance criteria** that are applicable and workable based on up-to the minute information gained from operating on a global scale

(c) Creating **control systems** that can collect effectively the performance data and information

(d) Creating systems that can accommodate fluctuating **exchange rates** between markets and **interest rates** within markets and their impact on sales and profitability

(e) Creating **operating procedures** that take account of differing commercial practices in differing countries and the degrees of risk that accompany trading on a global scale

Global positioning is a relatively simple concept to understand after it has been achieved, namely:

- Identify a target segment
- Create an image for the product or service
- Communicate that image to the target segment

Most of the products or services with a clearly recognised global position have taken many years to achieve this status. At one extreme Levi's has been developing its global brand and position for over 100 years, at the other extreme Nike is a phenomenon of the last 20 years, the period of the development of satellite broadcasting and a global youth culture.

Answer bank

56 PLANNING AN INTERNATIONAL ADVERTISING CAMPAIGN

> **Tutorial note.** This question has a wide coverage. Split it down into the three campaign issues of planning, executing and controlling to ensure that your answer stays focused. Management issues are at the true heart of the question, rather than the operational detail of the advertising campaign.
>
> **Examiner's comments.** This was one of the least popular questions on the paper. The main problem encountered was an inability to manage the answer in the given time. Some candidates failed to make a choice as specified in the question.

Planning an advertising campaign that covers all the countries of European Union (EU) must start with a consideration of whether a **standardised** approach is to adopted, or an **adapted** approach. To some extent the **objectives of the campaign** will settle the standardised versus adapting debate.

If the objectives of the campaign are to increase **awareness** of a brand that is already familiar across the whole of Europe, for example Nescafe, then a standardised campaign is likely to be highly effective. If the objective of the campaign is to **launch** a new product then an adapted campaign is likely to be more effective.

The planning process will need to take account of the **environmental** issues of language and culture, which will have an impact on the content of the campaign. The advertising **regulations** in each of the countries of the EU will have an impact on the content, and this will need attention at the planning stage. **Availability of media** will need to be addressed.

If a standardised campaign is to be planned then the images, descriptions and transference of key themes between the **media channels** (eg TV, newspapers, magazines, billboards throughout Europe) will need to be considered. The plans will need to address the **availability** of the different forms of media and the **audience habits**, with regard to the **scheduling** and **frequency** of the message.

If an adapted campaign is to be planned then similar issues will need to be taken into account, but this time for each of the target countries.

Execution of the campaign may start with the selection and appointment of the **agency** to handle the campaign. Some organisations may see this as part of the planning process. In executing the campaign, management attention will be focused on the scheduling of the messages and images, and assessing the credibility of the media being used against the objectives of the campaign. The **management** of the key players including agencies, media and audience during the execution of the campaign will be vital to its success.

Execution and **control** can go hand in hand to form a **feedback loop** to control the campaign. The results of the **advertising research** should inform the direction of the campaign, and enable adjustments to schedules or frequency of message (and occasionally content) to be made, to ensure the campaign is achieving the objectives set. In extreme cases, where the campaign is a long way from achieving the objectives set, the execution and control loop should stop the campaign and prevent resources being wasted.

Planning and executing a pan-European campaign is not easy. In spite of the EU single market concept, each of the member states still has considerable control over what is acceptable advertising, with many differences remaining between the countries.

Careful planning of both standardised and adapted campaigns is essential to avoid problems with **regulatory bodies** and other **interest groups**.

The success of a campaign will be as much a function of the choice of **agency**, its creative team and resulting **campaign content** as it will be due to the **execution** and **control** of the campaign.

Answer bank

57 GLOBAL COMMUNICATIONS

> **Examiner's comments.** There were some exceptionally good answers to this question from candidates who clearly understood the implications of culture, economies of scale, the standard vs. adapted debate and the emerging world cultures around sport, music, fashion and the use of English as the global language. However, there were also far too many drab answers that appeared as recollections from news items read in local papers rather than evidence of having read any management journals

Strategic review of satellite broadcasting

Satellite broadcasting enables a cost effective **international communications strategy** to be developed as a fundamental part of the international marketing strategy of an organisation. However, any consideration of the use of satellite broadcasting for advertising must immediately open the **standardised vs. adapted debate**.

Any advertisement used on a satellite channel presents the same message to all viewers, irrespective of where they are located under the broadcast footprint of the satellite. Thus satellite broadcasting is encouraging standardisation and the identification of **strategically equivalent segments** of consumers.

Standardised advertisement provides opportunities for **economies of scale** to be achieved from the production costs of advertising, possibly also from the air-time costs, resulting in lower **costs per hit**.

To effect economies of scale in production, advertisements are produced with strong **visual images** and **musical themes** so that they can be effective in delivering their messages in a **language free** way. For instance, Unilever, owner of the Magnum brand of ice cream, uses the same TV advertisement, based on the delights of eating an ice cream, across Europe on the satellite channels. Unilever gains all the benefits of both economies of scale in production and low cost hits to its target segment of premium ice cream eaters in each of the countries, through its bulk purchase of airtime from the satellite broadcasters. Similarly, De Beers use a single advertisement for diamonds globally, both terrestrial and satellite broadcast, with changes to the final frames containing text being the sole concession to region. A standardised TV advertising campaign using strong images and little language allows for standardised **supporting campaigns** in other media.

Adaptation is essential when **cultural sensitivity** needs to be addressed, which would indicate that satellite broadcasting should not be the preferred choice, irrespective of the attractions of economies of scale. With adapted campaigns, using terrestrial broadcasting to target particularly sensitive areas, the advertiser has more freedom and ability to link with other media, maybe using radio, newspapers and billboards to effect an **integrated campaign** that takes into account the cultural sensitivity of the area.

Unless the particular area under the footprint of the satellite is culturally the same or culturally neutral, such as USA or Australia, then the opportunity for an integrated campaign is very limited. In fact in some particularly culturally sensitive regions the use of standardised advertisements on satellite TV could ruin an acceptable integrated terrestrial campaign.

Tactical review of satellite broadcasting

Satellite broadcasting gives the ability to communicate with segments of customers at any time. Thus, **tactical segments** begin to emerge, such as news viewing segments, or speciality sports viewing segments, which have little in common other than shared viewing preferences.

In instances when adaptation is needed, (e.g. financial services) a freephone number for each of the countries covered by the footprint is shown as an overlay on the last few frames of the advertisement. This technique allows both the strategically equivalent segments (potential credit card users) and the tactical segments of particular target viewers in a selected country or region to be reached simultaneously.

In spite of the large number of communication satellites, some countries do not have reception facilities. Also, differing groupings of countries both within and between regions are within different satellite broadcast footprints.

The satellite broadcasting of advertisements which will create **awareness** of products not usually available in the country where the advertisement is viewed will lead to a **demand** being created for that product. Thus, the communication strategy based on satellite broadcasting needs a **complementary distribution strategy** in place so that the fundamental question of "where do I get ......?" can be answered for consumers.

58 ADAPTING GLOBAL BRANDS

> **Examiner's comments.** Most candidates answered this question and did a good job. Good marks were earned by interpretative depth and good examples.

The **creation of global brands** is a phenomenon of international trade. Ford with its car manufacturing plants, sales offices and dealerships in most countries of the world must rank as the pioneer in the creation of the global brand. Global brands are legion, and the logos associated with these brands now head the list of **world symbol recognition**. The combination of developments in **communications** (satellite TV and the Internet) and in travel together with the use of **sponsorship** for major world events, such as the Olympic Games, the World Cup and Formula 1 motor racing have helped to make Coca Cola, McDonalds, Nike, and Marlboro leading global brands.

Although the brand, its logo and associated livery remains constant around the world, there are **adaptations to the products** to take account of local/regional needs and tastes. For example: Ford designs and builds cars to suit regional markets, and cars designed and built in Europe are significantly different from the cars designed and built in the USA; Coca Cola adjusts the sweetness of its drinks to satisfy local tastes. McDonalds alters its menus to take account of regional religious sensitivities.

The reasons for companies adapting their brands are numerous with the underlying principle being the achievement of **profit**. There is no point in pursuing the creation of a **global brand with no adaptation** if no one wants to buy a standard product with standard imagery. Thus, **customer preferences** with respect to name, colour, design, size, taste, etc, are of paramount importance when decisions are taken to go global with a successful local brand. Of equal importance in the decision to go global is the need to be aware of the **competitive environment** created by existing global brands and the impact this will have on the success of the decision.

Adaptation of brands will be necessary to conform to **local/regional legislation** which will affect all aspects of the marketing mix and in extreme instances can block the creation of a global brand. Similarly, the level of **economic development** will have a significant impact on the development of a global brand.

The level of **market sophistication** and infrastructure particularly with respect to **communications and distribution**, the level of **technological development**, and **after sales service** capabilities (where required) together with consumer **ability to pay** are all

Answer bank

dependent on the level of economic development and will directly influence the adaptation required to the proposed global brand.

Climate and geographic considerations favour adaptation of both the product and the brand. For instance, in hot climates the brand values associated with a particular range of cars may concentrate on the air conditioning system, whereas in cold climates the brand values may reflect other properties such as ruggedness or ability to start first time.

Demographic considerations favour the adaptation of brands. Brand adaptations to appeal to the young would be required if the population distribution of the target market is biased towards the young.

The **nature of the target markets** (mass or multiple niche) and the product will determine whether the brand needs adapting. For many global brands which satisfy both mass and niche markets the values associated with the brand do not change. For example, McDonalds provides the same level of service in every outlet reinforcing its global brand value, although the menu changes slightly from country to country.

59 TUTORIAL QUESTION: SELECTING DISTRIBUTORS AND AGENTS

(a) The **selection of representatives** in a foreign market is a critical process. Selection of the wrong representative can have disastrous consequences for the firm. Representatives must be selected on the basis of their **business competence**, including their experience of the territory and the **knowledge of customer needs** and the manner by which their needs can be met.

Of equal importance, the representative must have empathy with the company and its products. Ideally the representative needs to treat the product as if it were his own such that **price/value** relationships and **price/quality** perceptions can be properly reinforced with customers. Empathy with the senior managers of the company is an essential ingredient in the selection process of representatives so that **goals** can be shared and **attitudes to quality** in terms of customer service and customer care can be mutually developed. The representative must be totally trustworthy and made to feel part of the company.

It needs to be recognised from the outset that the representative in the foreign market is the eyes, ears and image of the company, which may be based thousands of miles away. Thus, the investment of management time in the selection process of representatives will pay dividends in the future. However, the time to select suitable representatives can be protracted and requires significant management commitment.

(i) **Selection procedure**

A typical selection procedure for a foreign distributor would include the following.

(1) A **visit** to the market by a senior manager to inspect and assess potential distribution premises. The visit should also include calls on customers of the distributors.

(2) Assessment of competence of potential distributors will be **subjective** and based on the **knowledge and skills** of the management of the distributorship, their existing **product portfolio**, how well the company's product fits into the portfolio and so on. The knowledge and skills of the sales staff, their experience, length of service, territory covered, knowledge and skills of service personnel and the administration staff are also relevant.

Answer bank

(3) Following the assessment visit and depending on the complexity of the product, the most likely potential distributors could be invited to the company for in-depth product knowledge assessment and visits to the home company's customers.

(4) A **scoring model** may be used for the final selection which could include any or all of the following criteria.

- Ownership of distributor
- Career history of owners and managers
- Past and present success with other firms
- Past and present success with other products
- Market coverage
- Type of customer covered
- Frequency of customer calls
- Number of sales persons
- Quality of sales persons
- Distributor's market knowledge
- Distributor's product knowledge
- Distributor's marketing competence
- Distributor's servicing facilities
- Distributor's enthusiasm and empathy for the product
- Distributor's enthusiasm and empathy for the company
- Financial status of distributor
- Business reputation of distributor

If such a screening procedure was used, then each criteria would be weighted with respect to its importance to the company, and each potential distributor would be rated on each criteria.

(ii) **Conclusion**

The time and care required to select and appoint representatives can never be overstated. All screening and scoring processes can be affected by bias, therefore most representatives are appointed on the basis of the subjective judgement.

(b) Effective use of agents requires the deployment of agents in situations where they are appropriate and superior to other forms of market entry. Agents are effective when:

(i) They provide **adequate coverage** of the market in question and have suitable connections

(ii) The goods in question require only **selling** and no local stocking, maintenance or after sales support

(iii) The exporter is prepared to take the **responsibility and risk** associated with the logistical operations involved.

Efficiency is concerned with the way agents act on behalf of their principals. Efficiency may be improved by:

(i) Suitable **rewards and motivation** schemes, such as **commission** based systems

(ii) Appropriate **training** in the product and organisation of the company, to give the required knowledge to carry out the task

(iii) **Monitoring and control** of the agent's activities, for instance requiring regular reports on sales and calls, measuring performance against target, checking expenses

Answer bank

(iv) Providing suitable **promotional support**, such as samples, trade exhibitions, fairs where appropriate, and promotional materials.

60 LOGISTICS AND DISTRIBUTION

> **Examiner's comments**. The examiner was looking for an understanding of how channel management can be used as a competitive advantage.

The key to long term success in international marketing is a company's ability to recognise and meet **customer needs**. Prime amongst those needs is to have the appropriate product **available** to customers where they expect to see them and buy them. This, of course, is the role of distribution and logistics.

In a shrinking world, with larger and larger companies becoming more and more competitive, **distribution** and its effective and efficient management can actually provide the competitive edge a company needs for success.

It may be a function of the logistics strategy of an organisation to inform the company when it may need to consider manufacturing or holding inventory in a country rather than merely delivering goods when they are ready.

With competitive pressures applying to distribution channels members of any distribution channel are becoming increasingly demanding upon their suppliers: in many cases the balance of power now lays with the distributors. This means that to be successful in many market places, key considerations for manufacturers include the following points.

(a) **Channel efficiency**. Levels of inventory-holding must be carefully worked out to provide an appropriate service to customers without over-burdening the distribution channel. This also requires very careful **delivery scheduling**, especially where international transport by sea is concerned, with due allowance for possible delays. Simplification of procedures in delivery processes will always help.

(b) **Channel needs/demands**. Just in time delivery has been a major requirement in many industries for some time, and together with proper scheduling mentioned above will provide good service for the company's customers, minimising **out of stock** situations. In industry to industry marketing the requirement is now for **zero defect** deliveries.

Companies with global brands have further considerations to which they must pay attention when organising their logistics and distribution strategies. The distribution solutions they seek must fit with the brand positioning assumptions.

It may alternatively be the case that the company's leading **competitors** in its domestic market are themselves moving into international markets (as international retailers like Marks and Spencers and many others are doing) and it may be worthwhile to follow where they lead, if the company itself had not yet made the decision to go international.

Consideration may also be given to the changes in **technology** which lead to the possibility of **international direct marketing** and **electronic marketing** on the **world wide web**.

Finally it is necessary for the company to remember that its basic distribution strategy is constrained by the distribution cost structure which may be represented by the following function:

$$D = T + W + I + O + P + S$$

where
D = total distribution cost
T = total transport costs
W = warehousing cost

I = inventory costs
O = order processing and documentation cost
P = packaging cost
S = total cost of sales for not meeting standards set

As some of these cost functions increase, others will decrease. So, for example, larger deliveries to a holding warehouse in your main market may reduce total transport costs through efficiencies or discounts with the freight forwarders. This may be achieved at the expense of increased warehousing and inventory costs. It is, of course important to keep the correct balance and this will depend upon many of the other factors previously discussed.

61 DEVELOPMENTS IN DISTRIBUTION AND LOGISTICS

> **Examiner's comments**: Those who chose this question concentrated far too much on distribution and ignored the logistics element. Very few candidates expanded their discussion beyond e-commerce, or articulated how the developments they identified could give companies a competitive edge. There were very few examples cited, showing the need for wider reading.

With the increase in competitive forces and the trend towards **global business, distribution and logistics** are developing as one of the major sources of competitive advantage for multi-national companies. This report looks at recent developments and what is being done to take advantage of the changes and stay ahead of the competition.

Key driving forces

There are several key changes in the global economy which are changing distribution and logistics. These are as follows.

(a) The growth of the **global consumer** has meant that many consumers recognise and buy products which originate from many different parts of the world. More and more brands are global.

(b) Companies are becoming more **international** and operate in several countries.

(c) New **telecommunications technology**, including the continual expansion and development of the Internet, has contributed to the speeding up of all forms of communications.

(d) **Transport communications** are shrinking the world. Air travel has made moving people and goods around the world faster and cheaper.

(e) Certain **types of product** are becoming standardised across the world, and concentrated on particular **brands** eg Kodak and Fuji 35mm film, Sony Walkman, Intel Micro-Processors.

(f) The desire to hold **less inventory** by manufacturers and retailers has arisen due to uncertainty about the length of time consumers will demand particular products.

(g) Changes in **patterns of retailing** have seen greater concentration of retailer power in the developed world.

(h) Developments in **home shopping** using dedicated TV channels or the Internet have completely changed the distribution of some goods.

Changes in the activities of multinationals

Multinationals in general, and the vehicle manufacturers in particular, are developing **integrated supply chain management systems** to gain competitive advantage and improve profitability.

Answer bank

For instance, companies such as General Motors already manufacture different parts of their cars for assembly in different parts of the world, with the final product being sold world-wide. These activities are driven by the **cost savings** that can be made through concentrating production of particular parts at specific locations, and exploiting **transport systems** to ship the parts to where they are needed for final assembly. This allows **significant economies of scale** to be achieved, resulting in standardised parts being produced at the lowest possible cost.

Lowest cost component production facilities operating to **zero defect standards**, complemented by the exploitation of cost effective transport systems, enable significant competitive advantage to be derived from waste free final assembly operations, producing finished goods that exactly meet customer requirements. This is the Toyota formula for both the supply of new vehicle and parts for the vehicles after-market world-wide.

The impact of the emergence of global consumers - grey markets

Levi's is a global brand targeted at a global consumer and priced differently in different parts of the world. Without an integrated and logistic system **grey markets** of cheaper Levis products would emerge which would undermine Levi's pricing policies. Therefore, Levis must exploit all the advantages offered by modern distribution systems to ensure that there is minimum stock in the supply chain. The supermarkets in the UK try to exploit this grey market (for example Tesco at one time stocked Adidas products).

Information systems and management

All of the developments in distribution and logistics have been made practical through the use of information technology, enabling continual improvements to be made to the information in the **control systems**.

62 RETAILERS AND INTERNATIONAL ACTIVITIES

> **Tutorial note.** This is clearly intended as a general knowledge question, to enable candidates to demonstrate an awareness of the issues. There is scope to include other factors as well as those discussed below.
>
> **Examiner's comments.** The examiner was disappointed by the lack of examples and 'the lack of awareness that retailing is a largely ethnocentric business with relatively few international companies - but matters are beginning to change'.

There has been an increasing move by a wide range of retailers to establish themselves as **international organisations** in order to take advantage of a world where there is more movement of people between countries and a growing **cultural cross-fertilisation** between peoples. Sometimes, these moves towards internationalisation have proved to be generally successful, as with McDonald's and Pizza Hut. Sometimes they have been less than successful, as with the experiences of Marks and Spencer or Thorntons in the USA.

Retailers are close to the final end consumer, and the primary motivation for this kind of internationalisation is often a recognition of the wide **overlap** between **consumer needs** in many countries. Retailers normally target a specific, restricted segment of the population of any one country, and their perception is that such a **segment** may be replicated in another country.

There are many marketing factors which may have an influence on retailers in this process and include the following.

(a) Development of the '**global consumer**' and identifiable world segments.

(b) **Information technology** has led to rapid transference of news, images, cross-cultural awareness and better communication within companies.

(c) Development of **world brands**

(d) The development of the **European Union** has created a single market in Europe, which has increased incoming competition for retailers, who then may seek to expand elsewhere to compensate for pressure on the home market.

(e) The **urbanisation** of populations of the world has continued apace, which means that growing numbers of people can more easily converge on single retail sites rather than having to rely on local shops in their immediate localities.

The opening up of the former eastern bloc countries has also provided **new opportunities** for retailers prepared to expand into new and uncharted marketing territory (eg McDonald's early venture in Moscow).

The growth of **franchising** as a retail marketing tool has made it much easier for strong branded retail outlets to cross national boundaries without high risk capital expenditure, as local entrepreneurs take up a significant part of the risk.

On the other hand, one should recognise that the internationalisation of retailers, such as Tesco expansion into Eastern Europe, may not be as speedy as that of **branded products**, which may be able to make use of existing **local distribution networks**.

Government regulations may restrict the growth of retailing on a significant scale. For example in Japan, existing retailers have a legal right to veto the establishment of any new large scale retailers. The US government had to intervene to enable Toys'R'Us to gain entry to Japan.

63 DISTRIBUTION IN THE GLOBAL VILLAGE

> **Examiner's comment**. This question was not done well. The term 'global village' was obviously new to some candidates, and they were similarly ignorant of the importance of distribution in the development of the global market. Candidates must make sure that they read quality newspapers and journals to make themselves aware of world trade developments.

The very expression **global village**, coined to describe a world in which **communications** across huge distances are as quick as they once were in a small village, and consumer needs are **converging**, is both evocative of the way international marketing planning and logistics may be viewed, and suggestive of ways in which distribution methods are seen to be easier.

There are many factors that have contributed to this process of change. The list includes the following.

(i) The increasing **dominance of multinationals** in some aspects of trade and marketing and the consequent reduction in numbers of companies in some industry areas (automobiles for example)

(ii) Vast **technological change** in the area of communications, telecommunications, internet and intranet, television and radio links

(iii) Rapid development of **technology** in many other areas, where international and global co-operation has played a part in speeding **research and development**

(iv) Huge **population increases** world-wide

(v) Globalisation of marketing and the development of **world brands**

Answer bank

(vi) Increasing **affluence** in many areas of the world and the linked demand for manufactured goods

(vii) The rapid **industrialisation** of Pacific Rim and other countries, changing the location of manufacture of many goods.

Taking four of these as major factors, let us have a look at how they have influenced distribution methods in companies involved in international marketing.

- Change in communications
- Multinational growth and supply chain change
- Rapid industrialisation of lesser developed countries
- Technology development world-wide.

Communications

Both the **speed** and the **quality** of communications has improved, almost beyond recognition, over recent years. This means that **control issues** within companies, and **communications** between companies and their customers, is very much better and faster. Virtually no business of any consequence is without its own fax or email service, and written confirmation can be almost instantaneous.

In terms of distribution methods this has had the consequence that deliveries and planning for deliveries has been made more efficient. Companies can now use services of more than one company to help track their products as they journey from factory to customer. Geographic location systems can be put in place in a consignment of goods which can be tracked by satellite systems.

Multinationals and supply chains

Multinational enterprises (MNEs) have been getting larger and **merging**. Leading writers are arguing that the trend will continue - so that for many sectors there will be fewer players of world class dominating the field. We have seen this in the automobile industry, with many European companies merging to be able to compete effectively with US and Japanese giants.

There have been, at the same time, much closer links with companies in the **supply chains** in order to extract best value for money and reduce **stockholding**. This has had major consequences on distribution methods with companies delivering to their customers on a **just in time** (JIT) basis. This may mean more frequent deliveries of a smaller size, and a change in the place and ownership of the stocks needed to keep the supply chain operating fluidly.

Some suppliers in this sector keep members of staff on their customers' premises to help **manage** the process. This is the case for paint suppliers in the car industry particularly.

The kind of close relationship is one of the outcomes of the global village where **links** are very close despite long distances between companies. The change in supply chain linkage is demonstrated in the following model taken from Monczka.

Answer bank

Supply chain model

Traditional

Tier 2 supplier → Tier 1 supplier → OEM → Tier 1 customer → Ultimate customer

Integrated supply chain

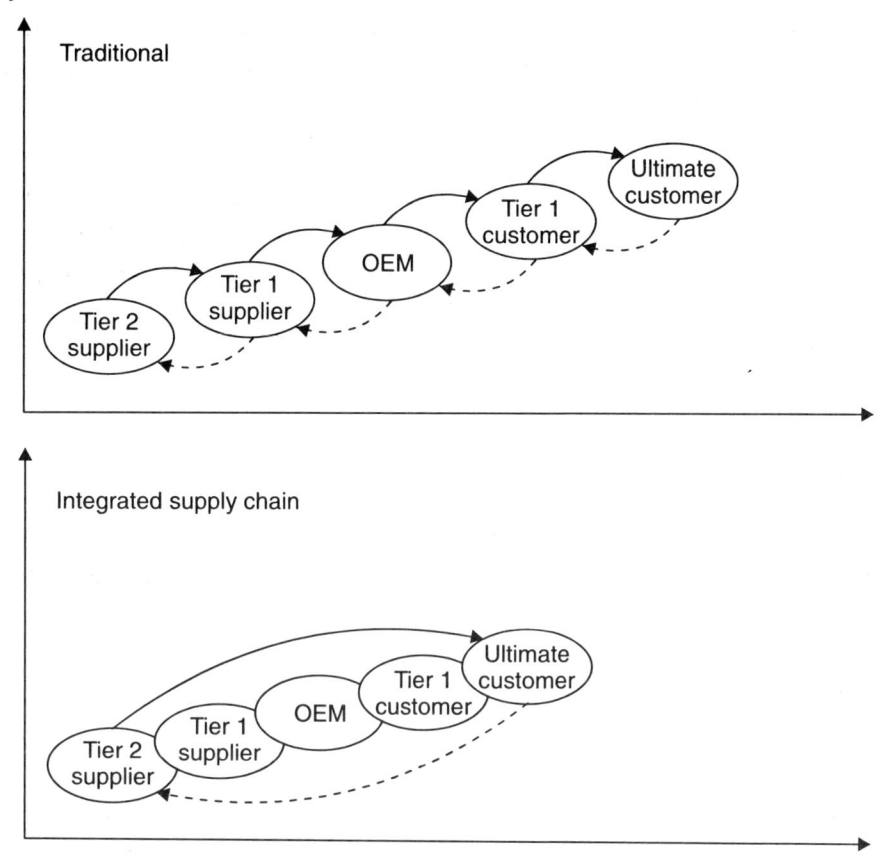

Tier 2 supplier → Tier 1 supplier → OEM → Tier 1 customer → Ultimate customer

Historically, businesses in the supply chain have operated relatively independently of one another to create value for an ultimate customer. Independence was maintained by buffers of material, capacity and lead-times. This is represented in the **traditional model** shown above.

Market and competitive demands are now, however, compressing **lead times** and businesses are reducing inventories and excess capacity. Linkages between businesses in the supply chain must therefore become much tighter. This new condition is shown in the **integrated supply chain model**.

Monczka further claims that there seems to be increasing recognition that, in the future, it will be **whole supply chains** which will compete and not just individual firms.

Rapid industrialisation

Rapid industrialisation in recent years has changed the pattern of distribution and the flows of materials around the world. This again has been a feature of the rapid spread of know-how and manufacturing expertise - partly a function of **education** revolutions in developing countries, led by better access to **information** and **knowledge based** resources.

Many multinational and international players are **sourcing** components from the cheapest sources world-wide, and bringing them together to be assembled in low cost labour areas, perhaps with additional access to high technology assembly resources. This kind of operation is only possible with extremely good control **databases and procedures** to ensure that components and assembled parts are in the right place at the right time.

Technology development world-wide

Close ties in the global village have meant a rapid **spread of technology and understanding**. Some of the impacts of this are seen in the changes in manufacturing base in the world, and the growth of the eastern economies in the last twenty or thirty years. Much of this success has been due to the development of technological excellence, through

Answer bank

the application of **research and development** funded for the longer term by banks in Japan, Korea and other Pacific Rim countries. Recent events have, however, cast some doubt over the solidity of this largesse, with banks suffering from over-exposure of funds and collapses and difficulties in the region.

One of the consequences of rapid technological advance is the increasing **miniaturisation** of high-tech equipment and the impact this has had on the weight of many products. This has led to a situation where it is quite justifiable to consider moving stocks of products by air, rather than by sea, when they are high in value and not heavy - thus requiring a lower proportion of the sales revenue to be allocated to transport costs.

This has also benefited the **time element** in the logistics equation, allowing consistency of delivery, inventory stability, flexibility and reliability.

64 TUTORIAL QUESTION: EXPORT PRICES

A company can have a standard approach to **pricing** in all export markets which may be **demand based** (a market and external influence approach), **cost based** (an internal influenced approach), or **competition based** (an external and market influenced approach).

A pricing policy based on market and external influences, either demand or competition based, is a sound approach as it enables the company to exploit the **unique selling points** and benefits of its products. A cost based approach to pricing, whilst having the advantage of ensuring the company recovers all its costs and ensuring that each product sold makes a **contribution** to profit, has the disadvantage of not fully exploiting **market opportunities** that may be present.

Alternatively, a company can adopt a policy to charge a **standard price** in all markets, such that the product price in sterling is the same as the equivalent price in dollars.

The advantages of a **standardised pricing policy** in all export markets are fairly limited since **economic, legal** and **competitive** factors in each market make it a difficult policy to implement. Price standardisation can usually be adopted for certain **high technology** products with **limited competition**, which would give the innovator the opportunity to recoup the R & D investment fairly rapidly. Such an advantage may be short lived as the technology becomes more freely available and competition starts to reduce prices.

(a) **Some examples of products sold with a standard price**

Crude oil is traded on world markets at a standard but fluctuating price - a price that does not necessarily reflect the ease of extraction - but the refined products (petrol, kerosene etc) are priced on a market-led basis. Few, if any, advantages are obtained by the oil companies from the standard world price of crude, except possibly in times of conflict when crude oil prices rise rapidly and 'windfall' profits can be made.

Civilian aircraft makers tend to adopt a standard pricing policy, with all civilian aircraft priced in US dollars. This is due in part to limited competition and the high technology content of the products - an advantage which allows R & D expenditure to be recouped and re-invested in further product development.

(b) **Disadvantages of a standard price**

(i) No account is taken of **local market conditions** in which a higher price can be achieved.

(ii) No account is taken of the **price and profit advantage** that may be gained from **adapting or customising** the product for customers and consumers in the target market.

(iii) No account is taken of customers' and consumers' **perceptions of value**.

(iv) No account is taken of the possible **uniqueness of the product** in a particular market, where customers and consumers are likely to be **less price conscious** due to the unavailability of alternatives and substitutes for comparison.

(v) No account is taken of the degree of **fashion or status** associated with a product and the price/quality relationships which could be exploited.

(vi) No account is taken of the **frequency of purchase** of the product. Frequently purchased products are more price sensitive than less frequently purchased products.

Whilst a standardised pricing policy may be conceptually attractive, the advantages of operating with an adapted pricing strategy far outweigh the advantage of a standardised approach.

65 PRICING CONSIDERATIONS

> **Examiner's comments.** This was another badly answered question, with far too many candidates focussing on the collapse of the S E Asian economies rather than on pricing and methods of protection against currency collapse. Bare pass candidates were either competent at pricing considerations, or competent on payment methods. Very few candidates were sufficiently competent at both to produce good answers.

In general the fall in value of any currency disturbs the **trading equilibrium**. The fall in value of many of the currencies of South East Asian countries made imported goods into these countries more expensive. This would have **reduced demand levels** and, in some instances, notably Malaysia, resulted in **exchange controls** being applied.

Pricing decisions are invariably a balance between financial, marketing, operational, and competitive considerations. Hence, **pricing objectives** could be set in one of the following ways.

(a) By **financial considerations** resulting in price levels being set to achieve a specific financial measure such as ROCE (return on capital employed) or ROI (return on investment).

(b) To achieve **marketing strategies** of market **skimming** (high price) or market **penetration** (low price)

(c) To take account of the **competitive environment** being encountered by the organisation

(d) To exploit a **differentiation strategy** (price setting).

In an international context the length of the **distribution channel** and any **tariffs** and import duties imposed by the importing country will impact on pricing decisions.

Any other **government restrictions** or controls on the movement of goods into a particular country will incur costs, which in turn will impact on the price and pricing decision.

Pricing decisions will also need to take into account the **risk** associated with engaging in international trade, such as the collapse or devaluation of currency, and delayed payment. The differing price/value relationships in each country will affect the pricing decision.

Unless payment is made in the exporter's currency by a secure method (eg cash with order or irrevocable letter of credit) then there is a risk that the exporter will not obtain the full price of the goods at the time of payment due to **currency fluctuations**. Currency fluctuations can be considered as one of the natural hazards of international trade and

Answer bank

organisations can take measures to protect themselves against currency fluctuations or collapse.

The most secure method of protection is to **price in the exporter's currency**, and ask for payment with order, so that the exporter takes no risk and the importer, or customer, takes all the risk due to currency movements. This is not a customer orientated approach to pricing! Irrevocable letters of credit are another secure method of payment for normal hazards. However, in extreme instances of currency collapse and political turmoil governments have been known to impose conditions on issuing banks that cancel payment by letter of credit. The Nigerian government imposed such conditions during the 1980's.

Other measures used as contingencies against currency fluctuations include:-

(a) Pricing in a **third currency** eg US$

(b) The exporter and importer **agree an exchange rate in advance** for a fixed period with the buyer and seller equally sharing the gains or losses at the end of the period

(c) **Forward buying of currency** at an agreed future exchange rate as a **hedge** against currency fluctuation or collapse

The ultimate protection must be to use no currency as the means of exchange and engage in **countertrade**. However, countertrade always assume that somewhere there is a buyer who will pay someone in money for the goods used in countertrade agreements.

66 TRADING BLOC AND PRICING

> **Examiner's comments**. This question was not popular - perhaps pricing strategy is insufficiently covered. 'Overseas students were to the forefront'.

Trading blocs are established to assist in the **development of trade** between the member countries of the bloc. In turn this makes it easier for companies within the countries of the bloc to do business with one another. There are many types of trading bloc ranging from the rather loose alliance within a **free trade area**, through various forms of **common market** to **total economic union**.

The common feature of each of these trading blocs is that it makes trading between companies in the member states easier and can make it more difficult for companies in the countries of the rest of the world to trade with the bloc. In some cases, the creation of a trading bloc can make it more difficult for members of the bloc to trade with the rest of the world. Trading blocs can create a fortress mentality among the member states.

Prices

In general, prices of goods within the trading bloc are lower than when the same goods are traded outside the bloc with the rest of the world. This price difference will be due to the **tariffs**, where they exist, being more favourable to trade within the bloc than to trade outside the bloc.

The pricing consequences for companies within a trading bloc which chooses to harmonise tariffs to a common level of 4% will be many and varied. If customers and consumers are satisfied with the supply of products at the present prices, then the companies exporting to countries where tariffs are greater than 4% may choose to hold their prices constant. However, as it is unlikely that companies exporting to countries whose tariffs were less than 4% would want to hold their prices constant and lose money, then there is likely to be a significant **realignment of prices** within the bloc.

The establishment of a common tariff may have the impact, for companies trading with previously high tariff countries, of allowing companies to trade within the free trade area as a whole, thus introducing **new competition** created by the tariff reduction within the bloc. Companies which were trading in previously low tariff countries may have to consider switching production, providing that the cost of production is equal or less to that of the home country.

Depending on how the bloc treats its tariffs with the rest of the world, companies from outside the bloc may be attracted to invest in facilities within the bloc to take advantage of the preferential trading conditions within the bloc. Companies within the bloc may have to consider investing in facilities in other parts of the world should the external tariffs prove to be prohibitive.

For companies outside the bloc the common 4% tariff may encourage inward investment and thus increase the level of competition. In some circumstances, particularly if the level of business was marginal, the raising of a tariff from 1% to 4% may cause an externally owned company to withdraw from trading within the bloc, again altering the level of competition.

In summary, the establishment of a common tariff within a trading bloc previously operating with a range of tariff levels will create a general realignment of prices due to the changes in the level and nature of the competition. Whilst customers and consumers alike will actively seek lower prices, particularly in those countries where the tariffs have fallen, the empirical evidence suggests that a common tariff within a trading bloc **increases prices** in the medium to long term.

67 INTERNATIONAL PRICING STRATEGY

> **Examiner's comments**. A popular question, well answered, even though some answers concentrated too much on tactical issues.

Pricing strategy is part of the tactical decision associated with the marketing mix and also fulfils a corporate role for many companies in helping to define their market positioning. It can also be important in terms of the development of **global strategies** for larger companies.

In this light, then, there are many factors that must be taken into account when establishing **international pricing strategy**. They may usefully be broken into three main categories: **environmental factors**, **market** factors and internal **company and product** factors. Since the internal factors are those over which a company has most control these are the ones which will be covered first.

Company and product factors

(a) **Costs.** All pricing decisions must first take account of all costs, not just the normal fixed and variable costs but the impact upon these of moving into new markets, with the possible economies of scale that might bring and/or extra marketing costs.

(b) **Product range.** The pricing strategy must also take into account the **international product range** and the way the company intends to develop the appropriate product/markets, given **product life cycle decisions** and potential **NPD** decisions and costs.

(c) **Logistics.** International marketing can bring new requirements with respect to the level of **inventory** carried and the costs of getting the product to market.

Overarching all of these considerations are the company-wide corporate and marketing **objectives** which will influence the chosen **strategy**, not only in terms of product and brand positioning but also in terms of profitability objectives.

Answer bank

Market factors

Once the internal factors have been taken into account, **customer perceptions** in the international market place must be considered. What has been the history of the development of the relevant markets in our countries of choice?

(a) **Market structure.** The overseas market differs from the domestic market. **Distribution** channels and **communication media** and practices may vary considerably and may therefore need to be taken into account when deciding upon the pricing strategy. The company must take into account the degree of discounting practised in the market and the **margins** expected in the distribution channels.

(b) **Competition.** The level and kind of competition may well be different in non-domestic markets. Knowledge of what impact our product will have on the market must temper the pricing decision. The company needs to look not just at direct and indirect competition but also at possible substitutes in the foreign markets.

Environmental factors

Any coherent pricing strategy must also take into account the environmental factors in the intended markets. These may include the view taken by **governments** on inflation, market pricing, and economic factors such as the fiscal requirements in Germany associated with packaging recycling issues, or the higher levels of value added tax on drinks and restaurant prices in Sweden.

The company's pricing strategy should also take account of possible **currency fluctuations**. This may be particularly important where **transfer pricing** strategies are to be considered by a multinational company, as will the impact of any **taxation** legislation.

68 INCOTERMS AND THEIR USE

> **Examiner's comments.** Only 10% attempted this question on Incoterms, a basic aspect of exporting. Incoterms can be used in defining levels of service, to support a differentiation strategy.

The most frequently used **Incoterms** are: **ex works**, **FOB** (free on board), **CIF** (cost insurance and freight), and **DDP** (delivered duty paid).

In terms of **customer service** levels the **ex works** Incoterm is the most 'customer-unfriendly' as it demands that the customer is responsible for the organisation and costs of getting the goods from the supplier's premises to the customer's premises. At the other extreme, **DDP** is the most customer-friendly, since it demands that the supplier is responsible for everything until the goods are on the customer's premises. Needless to say, ex works is the cheapest method of purchasing goods and DDP is the most expensive.

The question most purchasers wrestle with is 'what is the value of the difference in price between ex works and DDP'? In practice this is extremely difficult, if not impossible, to measure. Hence, most of the world's trade is conducted on the basis of **FOB** or **CIF** contracts.

FOB contracts

In FOB contracts the supplier is responsible for the goods (and any costs associated with moving the goods) until the goods cross the rail of the ship. This means in practice that the customer can monitor the performance of the supplier in terms of the number of times the goods were presented in a manner acceptable to the carrier, and the accuracy or otherwise of the documentation.

Customers can either use the performance monitoring reports to encourage existing suppliers to improve their service in a specified way according to imposed performance criteria or they can use them to impose performance criteria on new suppliers. Smart suppliers would use the requirements of FOB contracts to monitor their own performance and improve their customer service levels accordingly.

CIF contracts

It is frequently claimed that customers find CIF contracts from competing suppliers the easiest to compare. Hence, a CIF contract can be considered to be part of the customer service package.

For the supplier, the CIF contract is more demanding since under this contract the customer is holding the supplier responsible for all sub-contractors (eg shippers, handlers etc) activities and costs. Hence, for CIF contracts, not only does the supplier need to monitor his own performance as in a FOB contract, but in addition needs to monitor the performance of his sub-contractors to ensure timely arrival of the goods at a receiving dock specific by the customer and in a condition acceptable to the customer.

Measuring and monitoring performance are essential activities to improve customer service.

Conclusions

Incoterms were introduced and have periodically been updated to reduce the uncertainties surrounding international trade, and to **standardise the language** regarding the movement of goods. In the competitive world of the late 20th century the manner by which the Incoterms are fulfilled can offer opportunities for **competitive advantage**. Also, as the world becomes more **customer orientated** and customer service levels become order-winning criteria, the **measuring and monitoring of performance** against standard terms agreed between supplier and customer is of increasing importance.

69 INTERNATIONAL FINANCIAL RISK

> **Examiner's comments**. This was a straightforward question and candidates were obviously comfortable answering it. Almost all who tried it received reasonable marks.

Any movement into the international marketing arena will involve some extra element of **financial risk**, if only because of **payment delays** or **stockholding costs** for longer supply chains. The key areas of risk are associated with the following factors.

(i) The strategic level of **involvement** in the market

(ii) The exposure to **foreign exchange** and **political risk**

(iii) The risks associated with **repatriation of profits**, such as differential inflation, taxation and other government interventions.

These risks become apparent right from the start and continue to play a part in management thinking, even of those companies very well versed in international marketing.

The following model, taken from Doole Lowe and Phillips, is useful in showing the **risk versus control** decision needs.

Answer bank

Risk versus control

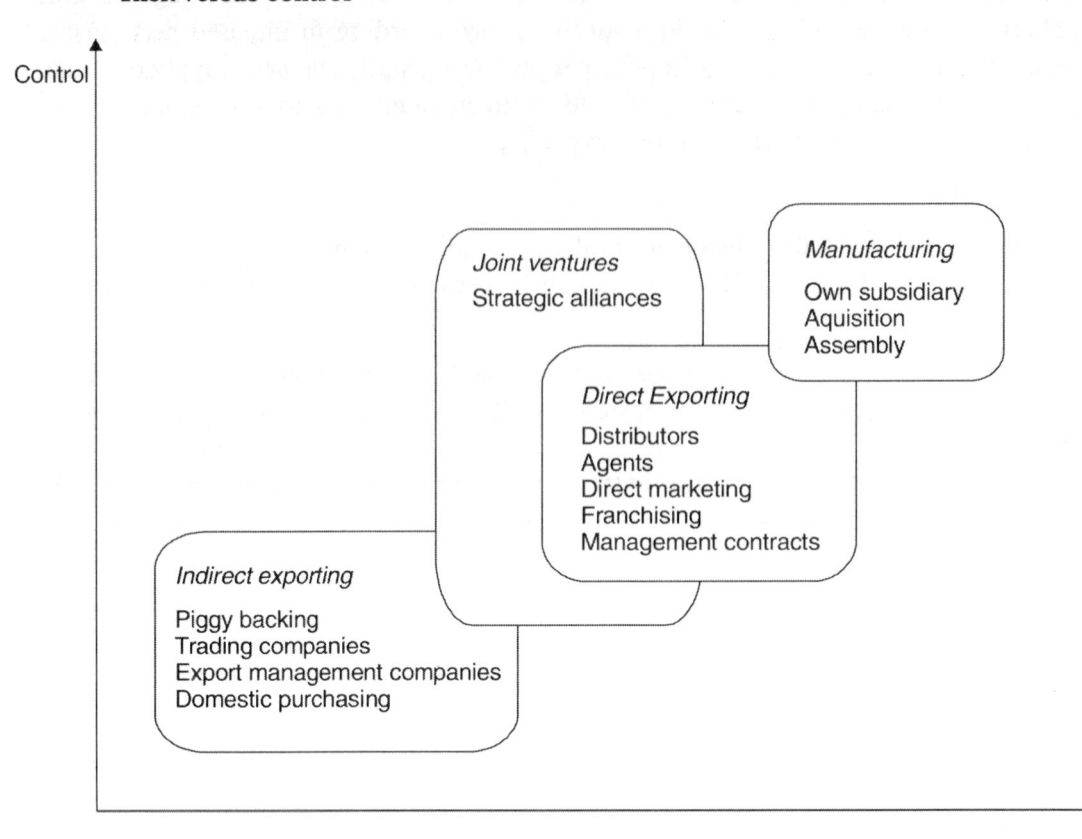

```
Control ↑
                                    ┌─────────────────┐
                                    │ Manufacturing   │
                ┌──────────────┐    │ Own subsidiary  │
                │ Joint ventures│   │ Aquisition      │
                │ Strategic alliances│ Assembly       │
                └──────┬───────┴────┴─────────────────┘
                       │  ┌─────────────────────┐
                       │  │ Direct Exporting    │
                       │  │ Distributors        │
                       │  │ Agents              │
                       │  │ Direct marketing    │
                       │  │ Franchising         │
                       │  │ Management contracts│
        ┌──────────────┴──┴─────────────────────┘
        │ Indirect exporting │
        │ Piggy backing      │
        │ Trading companies  │
        │ Export management companies │
        │ Domestic purchasing│
        └────────────────────┘
                                                        → Risk
```

As may be inferred from the model above the **greater the degree of involvement** in a foreign market with subsidiaries and factories and other financial commitments, the greater also is the **degree of risk**. Competent businesses can offset the greater risk by a **greater degree of control**. The key is to exercise that control carefully, to ensure the risk remains at manageable levels. A **monitoring process** should be put into place to give early warning of threats. **Contingency plans** should be designed.

Political/economic risk

Operations in a foreign market are always subject to political and economic risks. For example the economy may weaken and this will mean that the population has less to spend on the product area. If we have a manufacturing plant where we are assembling components bought in from other countries and the economy weakens, the exchange rate may also move against us, making the components more expensive.

Here again the essence of good management is to make sure that we have the **best information possible** at all times so that we can plan ahead for such eventualities. This might allow us, for example, to find alternate sources of supply at lower prices to ensure our continuing competitiveness.

Profit repatriation risk

Whenever a company is operating in a foreign country and seeking to repatriate profits to head office, there is always the potential for prevention of maximum repatriation.

If this is a continuing threat and the operation includes the transfer of components or raw materials from branches of the same company, it may be possible to increase the **transfer prices** of such products in order to extract more money from the subsidiary. Alternatively the parent company can charge for consultancy or other services on a **cross-charge** basis within the company.

Answer bank

Summary

The key to all of these potential risk situations is that there should always be sufficient **forethought and planning** applied to be able to counter such risks expeditiously.

70 TUTORIAL QUESTION: EVALUATION AND CONTROL IN A MULTINATIONAL

In one sense at least it is true to say that marketing **evaluation and control** is essentially the same for multinational business and domestic business. The purpose of evaluation and control is to check out how the business is doing against pre-established **objectives**, and to apply **corrective measures** where there is a variance from such objectives.

Having established this identity of purpose, however, it is also necessary to recognise that the process may well be very different, if for no other reason than the fact that **multinational** business is more **complex** and thus more subject to **variances** from objectives set.

At one extreme this may be that the objectives were incorrectly set in the first place. Business done across national boundaries is subject to the problem that market data may not be very accurate and thus **forecasting** may be difficult. One additional element of marketing evaluation in a multinational situation is to keep under review the setting of objectives.

(a) **Evaluation**

One of the key problems with respect to marketing evaluation in a multinational business is that the performance of any particular **strategic business unit** (SBU) can only be measured against its own plan, a plan determined by headquarters or against the performance of a similar SBU in the organisation.

(i) The standards expected may be **perceived** differently by managers whose experience has been acquired from very different **cultural and business backgrounds**.

(ii) **Comparing markets** may not be a case of comparing like with like, unless the markets have a high degree of commonality.

(iii) Another problem of evaluation is that the **competitive situation** in different markets may be very different and the company's success or otherwise may be strongly influenced by such differences. This is especially true if mature markets are compared with new and emerging markets. The stage of the **product life cycle** and the nature of the **marketing task** may also be different in different markets, making the task of comparison very difficult.

(b) **Control**

Phillips, Doole and Lowe identify three essential elements in the control process.

- Setting standards
- Measuring performance against standards
- Correcting deviations from the plan

Control provides the means to direct, regulate and manage business operations, requiring a significant amount of **interaction** amongst managers. A major additional problem of multinational business control procedures is the logistical difficulties they may pose across a wide number of markets. Here again, the **cultural** background of the individual managers involved is going to add complexity to the process. The control process may also need to be robust enough to withstand problems of **language** and the interpretation of **objectives**.

Answer bank

Response to control messages may sometimes be delayed due to time-zone differences across world markets. There may also be a different sense of urgency apparent in the managers in one country.

71 STRATEGY BREAKDOWN

> **Examiner's comments.** This was a classic case of students answering the question they wanted to see, rather than the one that had been set. The question was about global control and setting performance standards, and few answers really got to the heart of the problem of why strategies break down and how this may be prevented.

All strategies are dependent upon **people, processes** and **systems** working in harmony, and for any strategy to be **implemented** successfully it is essential that every person believes in the **vision** the strategy is attempting to achieve.

Control of the implementation process is effected using a "**plan-do-review**" cycle to ensure that the objectives and outcomes are being achieved and to assess whether the strategy and plans need adjustment to take account of **changes in the business environment**.

Performance standards need to be set in the plan-do-review cycle, and these can be both **quantitative** and relate to budgets or **qualitative** and relate to assessments and improvements in corporate or product/service image. Standards set within the strategy could also be **comparative standards** that are assessed using **benchmarking** processes, again which will be subjected to the plan-do-review cycle.

The principal reasons strategies break down are as follows.

(a) **Inappropriate standards** being set and then not being rigorously assessed for effectiveness in periodic plan-do-review cycles

(b) Problems with the measurement and interpretation of **variances**. This can lead to an unwillingness to change the strategy due to lack of understanding regarding the reasons for the outcomes not being achieved.

(c) On a global scale, the **differing cultures** bringing with them their own interpretation of the vision and the strategy to achieve it and deviating from the plan to suit **local conditions**. A more culturally sensitive global strategy could prevent this from happening.

(d) Management creating and building problems into the strategy through unwillingness to consider and approve variations. Gary Hamel has commented on the "genetic similarity of senior management" across industries and their fixation with "doing it their way" rather than doing things that all the evidence is suggesting should be done. Also, management's obsession with the quick win or rapid pay off leads to many problems with strategy implementation.

(e) **Communication problems** are a fertile area for strategy breakdown due to the use of language that is not universally understood. The US/UK control through budgets is a common cause of mis-understanding and communication breakdown.

(f) The lack of **monitoring operations** resulting in no remedial action being taken as a result of adverse variances being observed

(g) Inappropriate choice of **management systems** on a global scale. Standardisation of any system brings its attendant problems and adapted systems are more difficult to manage. Thus **systems design** is critical.

Answer bank

The exhortation by Kenichi Omae to **think global and act local** can prevent many strategies from breaking down. A corporate vision and strategy which is built on the vision and strategies of its subsidiaries is likely to have more chance of success than a vision and strategy handed down from head office.

Organisations need to be aware of how for they can be **polycentric** with its attendant high costs and complexities, but with a good chance of strategic success, compared with being **ethnocentric** with its much lower costs but higher risk of a strategy breakdown.

72 EVALUATING MARKETING STRATEGIES IN COUNTRIES AT DIFFERENT LEVELS OF ECONOMIC DEVELOPMENT

Evaluating international market strategies invariably requires an indirect approach using **management reports**, compared with evaluation of a domestic marketing strategy in face-to-face meetings.

In the developed world, **advanced communications**, such as video conferencing, can be used as a direct form of communication for evaluating the international marketing strategy. In the developing economies a more standardised information system based on reports will be necessary.

The primary advantages of meetings are the more intensive interchange of information and monitoring practices. However, the effectiveness of meetings can be limited due to the frequency with which they are held and the time commitment required.

To exploit the advantages **reports** can offer, particularly in less developed economies with limited communications, it will be necessary for management:

(a) To **standardise the format** of reports to allow comparison between subdivisions

(b) To use an agreed **common language** and currency

(c) To establish a **frequency for reporting** which will allow managers to manage efficiently and effectively

Reports also have their limitations in that they can generate too much information for corporate management to handle, resulting in difficulties with decision-making and control. The late arrival of reports can impede the effectiveness of management action. The management of subsidiaries can resent the imposition of reports due to the **information requirement** being too great, a perception held of **undue interference** by headquarters, an inadequate level of **delegation** given to the subsidiary and a lack of understanding of **local conditions** by corporate management.

Irrespective of the level of economic development of markets, information systems need to be defined that:

(a) Provide **only the information required** for decision making

(b) Are **updated** sufficiently frequently to enable corrective action to be taken

(c) Provide **feedback** to the subsidiary

Thus, the key differences in evaluating the performance of the marketing strategy for the USA and Uganda would be as follows.

(a) For the USA, a direct form of evaluation would be used, either through meetings or video conferences, in which all the relevant information would be reviewed in person by the senior management, with the potential to have immediate contact with the local marketing management kent team to clarify any misunderstandings.

Answer bank

(b) For Uganda an indirect form of evaluation would be used based on reports submitted by the management team in Uganda to a format and content specified by headquarters.

The key difficulties in evaluating the performance of the marketing strategy would be few for the USA, probably related to market performance beyond the control of the management, or exchange rate movements. For Uganda the difficulties are likely to be many, eg obtaining up to date information, currency movements, time delays between reporting and reviews and lack of current local knowledge.

73 KNOWLEDGE BASED SYSTEM

For knowledge based systems to be effective they need to carefully maintained to ensure that the knowledge base is **up to date and accurate**. In the developing world of electronic commerce, Amazon.com knows, from the information visitors bring to their web-site (without the visitor knowing or having consented to it being divulged), the other items any particular visitor will be interested in to complement the item initially chosen.

An on-line knowledge based system therefore enables a company to offer its visitors all the appropriate product offerings without the visitor having to take any action.

In the conventional world knowledge based systems based on **historic records** have been replaced by **EPOS** systems. These systems enable their operators to establish patterns of demand, methods of payment, contents of shopping baskets by value and volume of each item, and many other pieces of information.

This information allows for a more **dynamic approach** to marketing planning. Improvements in telecommunications allow M & S, for instance, to know what is happening in each of its stores around the world at any time, and provides the opportunity for management to alter any of the elements of the marketing mix to ensure optimum store performance.

For international planning knowledge based systems will assist in:-

Segmentation – through the continuous **definition and refinement** of segments within target markets and the creation of continually evolving **strategically equivalent segments**. Also, the understanding of the **expectations** of the consumers within the strategically equivalent segments will be enhanced through the continually developing knowledge base which will enable communications effort to be focused.

Marketing mix development - through the development of products and services that allow for the expectations of the target segments to be met more closely. Pricing policies can ensure **affordability** for the products and services by all members of the strategically equivalent segment, and **profitability** for the company. **Differential pricing** between markets to achieve a global position becomes easier with a knowledge-based system that allows **communications** to be developed. **Distribution channels** based on current knowledge rather than historic precedent will become the norm to ensure the effective delivery of the expectations of the target segment.

Implications for planning and control using knowledge based systems

(a) The continuous setting and re-setting of corporate and marketing **objectives** which reflect latest knowledge may have a detrimental effect on the motivation of both management and employees

(b) The creation of **standards** and **performance criteria** that have a short existence. The continual change in standards and their associated performance criteria may impact on motivation

(c) Creating **control systems** that can respond **effectively** to the performance data and information that is generated

(d) Creating **operating procedures** that take account of **differing commercial practices** and the degrees of **risk** that accompany trading on a global scale

Knowledge based systems will get smarter. It is the responsibility of all managers, and particularly marketing managers, to learn to use them effectively and profitably.

74 CONTROL SYSTEM

> **Examiner's comments**: This question was surprisingly unpopular considering that it was so straightforward. Those who did attempt it showed a general lack of understanding of what control is and how the factors affecting the effectiveness of control systems in an international situation should be taken into account.

There is a close correlation between effective control systems and successful organisations. The degree to which control systems are adhered to enables companies to distinguish themselves from the competition. Continuously analysing and identifying better methods of working and control leads to sustained competitive advantage.

Management commitment

The development and maintenance of effective control systems requires total commitment from management. This commitment needs to permeate all levels of the organisation. Active involvement from management in the design, development, implementation and evaluation of control systems will encourage widespread ownership of the procedures. Control needs to be positioned as a method of identifying opportunities as well as a means of ensuring performance.

Organisational structure

The **level of involvement of subsidiaries** in the strategic, operational and tactical management of the organisation will have an impact on the effectiveness of a control system. A centralised structure with little involvement of subsidiaries is unlikely to be as effective as a control system within a decentralised structure.

There are fads regarding preference for centralised or decentralised structures. At present the trend appears to be for centralised structures to extract as much **cost saving** as possible. If other objectives, such as profit or market share, are not achieved with centralised structures then costs of duplication may be perceived as of lesser importance than the achievement of market share and profit.

Financial controls

These are present in any organisation and invariably start with the requirements of the **annual budget,** whose estimated numbers for sales, cost of sales, gross profit, level of overheads and net profit form the control parameters for the coming year. Comparisons of actual performance against budget are familiar features of commercial life.

It is increasingly being recognised that there must be other more effective and more responsive performance measures in the largely computerised world of work. As the world changes so quickly should control systems be developed that operate in real time?

Information technology should enable companies to set much **shorter term** performance indicators that are more responsive to market movements than annual budgets. Performance criteria that are set using current data are more likely to be accepted and responded to.

Answer bank

Market research and marketing management information systems (MkMIS)

The maintenance of an effective MkMIS is crucial to the control system of any business. All the performance criteria in a control system should be related to the information stored in the MkMIS. No **environmental change** that has an impact on the business should escape recognition in the MkMIS, and, correspondingly no **performance criteria** should be set without reference to the MkMIS.

It is recognised that the above is an ideal and such detailed information is not available in many parts of the world. However, the **trading records** of the company can act as sound proxy measures and avoid performance criteria being set which are impossible to deliver.

Conclusion

Effective control systems must be based on realistic and timely performance criteria. All personnel must feel that they have contributed to and have ownership of these. Organisations should be in a position to use the real time data that they have in their IT systems.

75 KING CARPETS

> **Examiner's comments.** This case was generally answered well. There was a tendency to discuss the subject in general terms. Some answered as if King Carpets was a UK company and overlooked the cultural differences between Europe and the USA. Part (b) was not handled as well, perhaps reflecting poor time management.

(a) **Research programme for Europe**

Introduction

This programme of marketing research has been prepared to underpin the launch of King Carpets in Europe. It has been prepared on the basis of two assumptions.

1. The management of King Carpets have already conducted a **global market scan** and have selected the countries of the European Union as offering the best potential markets for their trading style, namely franchises, and range of floor coverings.

2. That King Carpets have the **financial resources** to undertake a full analysis of the potential in the markets of the European Union using secondary and primary research.

Objectives

1. To scan the markets of the European Union to identify and analyse the opportunities for King Carpets

2. To carry out detailed studies in order to:

    (a) provide an input to the development of appropriate **market entry strategies**

    (b) test the **feasibility** of the market and marketing mix options

3. To build a **marketing information** system to monitor trends in the European market for floor coverings by country

Secondary research programme - the scanning process

Using secondary research information and sources (such as Mintel, Keynote and EIU publications in the UK, and their equivalents in each of the countries of the EU), each of the fifteen member countries of the European Union will be scanned to determine the following.

1   The **accessibility** of each of the markets in terms of the setting up of franchises and the importation of floor coverings should these not be sourced from within the EU.

2   The potential **profitability** of each of the markets within the EU having regard for the trading style of King Carpets, namely, **franchising**. Profitability to the franchisee will be affected by the frequency with which European households (irrespective of whether owned or rented, family or single person) purchase floor coverings. Again sources such as Mintel, Keynote etc (or their European equivalents) will provide indications of the most likely purchasing patterns. Profitability to King Carpets beyond the start up payment of £15,000 will be dependent on the anticipated profitability of the franchises and the level of royalty payments.

3   A first order approximation of **market size** will be dependent on population size and number of households, which will be obtained from national statistics. National statistics on marriages will give an indication of new household formations and a first order approximation of the level of new demand for floor coverings. More refined estimates of market size will be obtained from production, export and import statistics for floor coverings for each of the countries, together with estimates for the levels of retail sales from publications such as Mintel, Keynote and their European equivalents.

4   The floor covering **buying behaviour** in each of the markets will need to be established. Again, Mintel and their equivalents can give some indications. For instance, in the UK most floor coverings are sold to customers who visit large, specialist, stores located on 'out of town' retail parks (similar to the USA practice which created the King Carpets approach) and select their floor coverings from a vast range of stock held by the retailer, who is usually a branch of a national or regional chain. Some detailed primary research would need to be undertaken to determine how UK buying behaviour could be changed to favour the King Carpets style of selling and whether UK customers would accept purchasing floor coverings in their homes.

5   A first order approximation of the most likely buyer behaviour can be established from combining the **demographic** and **economic data** from the national statistics, together with data from **household expenditure surveys** which will show how the various populations that comprise the markets of the EU spend their incomes, with particular reference to household durables such as floor coverings.

All this information on accessibility, profitability and market size will need to be assessed and prioritised to present the management of King Carpets with a decision making framework. The Harrell and Keifer matrix which assesses **country attractiveness** (market size, accessibility and profitability, from above) and **company compatibility** (use of franchises, rapid market entry, direct selling in customers homes) is an appropriate framework from which to prioritise the fifteen countries. A **segmentation analysis** will need to be performed to highlight the differences and preferences between the colder countries of Northern Europe and the warmer countries of Southern Europe. Further segmentation can be undertaken by style of floor covering, carpet, wood effect, or tile, types of patterns, and for carpets whether fitted or a standard shape.

Answer bank

Primary research programme - customer segmentation

The secondary research outlined above should result in a priority listing of the countries of the European Union. For the prime markets, which may be only two or three, some detailed primary research needs to be conducted to establish the customer segments to **target** together with their location.

The primary research must attempt to determine what **motivates** buyers to purchase floor coverings, how buyers behave towards the present method of selling floor coverings and what is their likely response to the King Carpets offerings. The use of **focus groups** in selected key cities is the proposed research methodology, as it offers the chance to capture the maximum amount of information in the minimum time.

This primary data relating to who the potential customer might be and how they buy can be used to create pan-European segments of similar customers. This can be cross referred to pan-European **marketing databases** such as ACORN and EuroMOSAIC to test applicability and utility of the information. A more extensive primary research survey can be considered after the launch to assess both the effectiveness of the launch, and the requirements of customers.

Marketing information system

For the management of King Carpets to benefit from this programme of research, the results will be presented in the form of a **marketing information system** that can be used as a basis for operating a continuous scanning programme of the markets of the European Union and for monitoring their achievements for **control** purposes. The **12 Cs approach** shown below is a suitable framework for a marketing information system.

FACTOR	INFORMATION
Country	The basic SLEPT data and any refinements to that data from other secondary sources
Choices	Competitor data
Concentration	Changes in the structure of the markets
Culture/Behaviour	Changes in the influences on buying behaviour
Consumption	Changes in the patterns of demand
Capacity to Pay	Changes that will have an impact on pricing decisions (eg changes in the rate of VAT)
Currency	Changes in exchange rates including the potential impact of the Single Currency - the EURO
Channels	Changes in the distribution channels
Commitment	Changes in the conditions which initially allowed entry into the markets of the EU. (eg changes in regulations regarding the sourcing of floor coverings.)
Communications	Changes to the media infrastructure and any potential impact on promotional activity
Contractual Obligations	Changes affecting the operation of franchises and/or the use of direct selling techniques.
Caveats	Any general changes that may have an impact on continuing to do business in the countries of the EU

Answer bank

Timescales and budgets

It is recognised that you wish to launch in all countries of the EU in mid 1997. We recommend that you defer that decision until the end of August to allow the programme of research to be completed. Completion of the above programme should be in mid August, assuming approval to proceed is received within the next 10 days.

The estimated cost of the programme, assuming that a maximum of three countries are selected for primary research, is £30,000.

(b) **Strategic planning and control issues**

Assuming that three countries are the initial target then **marketing objectives** need to be set for each of these countries and for the three countries as a group. Some suggested objectives are these.

1. To have 10 franchises in operation in each of the three countries by the end of 1997

2. Each franchise to have achieved positive contact with customer rates of 15 per employee per day by the end of 1997

3. Each franchise to have achieved visit to customer rates of 3 per employee per day by the end of 1997

4. Each franchise to have achieved orders placed rates of 1 per employee per day by the end of 1997

Whilst it is anticipated that the research will identify some **pan-European segments** of customers and their requirements, the marketing strategy must recognise and take account of potential differences between the colder north of Europe and the milder/warmer south and the impact these differences will have on the product strategy. (NB. King Carpets will have encountered and overcome similar climate differences in the USA). Hence, the objectives for the franchises are given in terms of **contact and response** from customers, rather than the more conventional basis of sales by product group. Also, by setting the objectives as given above the **control** issues are included since each **objective** contains a **performance criteria**.

The overall strategy needs to be one of establishing a **profitable presence** in Europe within a **timescale** acceptable to the management of King Carpets. Providing that the research confirms that an operating territory of 15,000 households will profitably support a franchise, the strategy can evolve since each franchisee will produce a cash sum of £15,000 to King Carpets. If the strategy is for the European operation to be self funding from the reinvestment of the £15,000 per franchise into specific marketing initiatives to stimulate **growth**, then results obtained by King Carpets will be fairly modest, given the level of **competition**. However, if the management of King Carpets are prepared to risk, $250,000 on developing the **selected target markets** then a much bigger challenge to the existing competition can be contemplated.

Product issues

A key element of the product strategy must be one of not restricting the franchisees in the **range** of floor coverings they offer to customers. As the implicit King Carpets product strategy is one of selling floor covering from samples and computer images direct from manufacturers, then the complete range of 1500 product lines used in the USA could be made available to customers in Europe. This range can be added to or subtracted from to take account of European preferences for floor coverings identified in the research phase. From a UK perspective, floor covering retailers tend to specialise in one type of floor covering eg carpets or ceramic tiles. The King Carpets approach of offering the complete range would be a significant **unique selling proposition** in the UK. The product strategy must take account any EU **import regulations** relating to floor coverings.

Pricing issues

In view of the established nature of the floor coverings market in each of the countries of the EU, a **penetration strategy** will be required. This strategy will be in line with King Carpets domestic strategy of offering customers lower prices than the conventional floor coverings retailers. Providing the European franchisees can select European suppliers of floor coverings (possibly helped in negotiations by suitably experienced King Carpets personnel), then the same low cost approach will apply in Europe.

Promotional issues

A high level of **promotion** will be required to effect the penetration strategy, thus the franchisees will need some **support** from King Carpets to **fund a suitable campaign**. The core of the campaign will need to be the King Carpets approach to selling floor coverings and the establishment of the King Carpets **brand** and its key elements of convenience, value and customer service. These should translate without significant alteration into the major markets and languages of Europe. The **launch promotion** will require funding from King Carpets to communicate the approach.

If the King Carpets concept is demonstrated by the research to be suitable for Europe then as mentioned above an intensive campaign to **recruit franchisees and create awareness** of the King Carpets presence in Europe is justified. It is possible that some floor covering manufacturers and suppliers may wish to use some of their promotional budget to support the new way of selling floor coverings, and reinforce their brand through assisting in the establishment of the King Carpets brand. Franchisees should be allowed to top up any corporate, or supplier, funded promotion in order to exploit any local advantages that may be forthcoming.

Distribution issues

The franchise is the method of distribution as seen by the final customer. However, the **nature of the agreements** with manufacturers will have an impact on the total distribution system. For instance, will the manufacturers impose **minimum order quantities** on the franchisees and, if so, how will the franchisee sell on the excess floor covering? If the existing European method of selling and distributing carpets is the 10 metre roll, then will customers have to buy this minimum quantity even though they need only a fraction of a roll? These issues will need careful thinking through, and some profound decisions taken at the **negotiations** with manufacturers and suppliers to commence supply contracts.

People issues

The King Carpets method of approaching customers will need to find empathy with potential European franchisees, and the management of King Carpets will need to satisfy themselves that their standards of delivery are not going to be compromised by the selection of an inappropriate franchisee.

(1) The potential franchisee will need to be **motivated** by the King Carpets approach and also by the opportunity offered to be his/her own boss. Clearly the ability to pay £15,000 is a key element of the selection process.

(2) Some empathy with **interior design** will be necessary in potential franchisees since invariably they will be assisting customers to make fairly extensive changes to their living areas.

(3) **Computer literacy** would be an advantage as the delivery of the unique selling proposition of King Carpets is dependent on the computer image of the room with the existing furniture and artefacts set against new(replacement) floor coverings.

Process issues

The research should demonstrate that the King Carpets process of selling floor coverings in customer homes will be acceptable to European customers. However, the **culture** of each of the regions of Europe must not be ignored. For instance, the management of King Carpets cannot assume that if the process is acceptable to customers in the South East of England, then the process will be acceptable in North Wales. The management of King Carpets should be sufficiently flexible in their market entry decisions to allow regional and cultural differences to be accommodated and catered for by the local franchisee.

Physical evidence

Again the differing cultures will have an impact on the physical evidence of the presence of King Carpets in each of the markets. Most Europeans are quite comfortable with pan-European brands and associated imagery, irrespective of country of origin. Similarly, Europeans are comfortable with sales staff in uniforms who present the same corporate image. However, differing regions and their cultures do not respond uniformly to 'scripted' sales pitches. The management of King Carpets should be prepared to allow their franchisees to develop their own sales pitches to suit their local needs.

Overall, it is in the best interests of King Carpets to set **objectives** for each of the target areas of Europe which include **performance criteria** such that there can be no ambiguity between the expectations of the corporate centre, European centre, and the franchisees. The management of King Carpets need to decide as a matter of some urgency whether they are going to create a European headquarters and staff it with Europeans. The ability to speak Spanish is not going to guarantee success in Europe.

A more acceptable approach, both strategically and operationally, would be to appoint **country** or **regional managers** who have an intimate knowledge of the floor coverings market in their areas and have them report to a VP Europe, who could be based anywhere in the selected target markets.

Providing the research is completed by mid August and the results are positive then King Carpets could have a presence in selected areas of the EU by the end of 1997. To have a presence in all countries by the end of 1997 is not practical. A more realistic objective would be to have a presence in each of the countries by the end of 1998.

The management of Kings Carpets should be prepared to sanction a **budget** of $500,000 to cover promotion costs, the costs of establishing a European headquarters and negotiating supply contracts with manufacturers capable of supplying both the European market as a whole and the individual countries and regions.

76 MCDONALD'S AND GLOBALISATION

> **Examiner's comments.** Far too many candidates wrote in general terms, with answers that could be applied to any product or company. This ignored the specific circumstances of the question. There was a lack of balance between answers to parts (a) and (b). Some candidates thought that part (b) was less important than (a), even though it carried 50% more marks. Greater emphasis is needed on structuring and focusing answers.

Answer bank

(a) **REPORT**

To: Global Competition Team
From: Jollibee Task Force 1997
Task Force Leader: Joe Smythe
Date: December 1997

(i) **Reflections on the task and the background**

The competition team may be well aware that I was delighted to be chosen to head up this particular task force, seeking to combat the existing, the imminent and the longer term potential **threat** to McDonald's position as global leader in the fast food market. Having worked for two years as a regional manager in the Philippines, when we were constrained by law from owning our retail chain there, and having been a training manager at the McDonald's Burger University for a time, helping to train our Filipino franchisees, I perceived the threat from Jollibee's to our position perhaps a little sooner than others at head office.

I say this to point up the fact that McDonald's had, perhaps, become a little **complacent** with its dominant position in the world and was beginning to suffer the fate of many major world corporations, before us, of rigidity and **lack of responsiveness** to **dynamic competition**. Kodak suffered at the hands of Fuji Film, while Chrysler and other US automotive multinationals suffered at the hands of Japanese and European competitors. IBM suffered at the hands of Bill Gates and the Microsoft empire. Yet the one thing we share with these earlier victims of **competitive innovation** is that we have a **huge brand equity** in the McDonald's name and our global product offering.

The golden arches are the biggest in the world and we are the best in the world - but we still have to keep the competition at bay in a rapidly evolving market place. McDonald's is the world **benchmark** in fast foods and we were instrumental in creating the world market by exporting our successful US formula in the first place. We are a **world brand in consumer recognition** terms.

My report that follows is directed at a **key analysis of the market**, not only in the Philippines, but in those country markets which may be threatened by the successful package developed by Jollibee's in their home market and which is being rolled out internationally. Essentially we must discover where we are good, where the competition may be better and try to analyse what the customers want from a revitalised McDonald's, in these threatened markets.

This will be followed with an outline plan to respond to the threat as we see it developing. Indeed, this may be the precursor for a general strategy in other markets, where we are suffering from strong local competition.

(ii) **The Philippines home market**

The Jollibee **threat** has come from a particular set of **circumstances** and market conditions in the Philippines and we must start our market analysis there.

We already know a lot about this key competitor from franchisee reports, from staff members who have worked for both organisations, from previous market studies when establishing new franchise outlets and from the Filipino press. This existing **dataset** needs to be collated with some urgency and my team will sift the information to gain whatever new insights we can. We also know a great deal of our own performance in this market, which needs to be reassessed in the light of the competitor's successes. What could we have done differently, better, more quickly to **minimise the threat**?

Answer bank

From this base of knowledge and other secondary information, we need to conduct a **full marketing audit**, both qualitative and quantitative in nature. What are our key **strengths** and **weaknesses**? What, exactly, are the market **opportunities** and **threats**? What is the Filipino market, both in terms of its differences and its similarities with other markets where we operate? In brief, we need to find accurate and clear answers to the following key questions.

(1) **Who are our customers?**

(2) **What do they buy?**

(3) **Why do they buy?**

(4) **What do they expect from the service marketing mix?**

   (a) **Product offering**: in terms of taste, flavourings and spices, portion size, options, complementary products, side dishes, packaging, party options for children, and so on...

   (b) **Price** pricing options, portion/price relationships, overall meal pricing, price relative to competition - given that we operate a premium price strategy in most, if not all of our markets, are there circumstances here which make this dangerous in terms of our market share?

   (c) **Place**. How important is convenience of access, bearing in mind that Jollibees appear to have got us outflanked in their home market, with more restaurants than we have and in more and better sites?

   (d) **Physical evidence** of our establishments and those of our competitors. What level of seating comfort, decor, music, temperature and general surroundings are customers looking for?

   (e) **People**. Our world-wide success has been built upon good, speedy, friendly service. Are we successfully fulfilling those expectations in the Filipino market and, if not, why not?

   (f) **Processes** in place. Do we handle peak times effectively with fast service, how do we handle complaints, do we always have quick change given from the tills? Is our management of servers and staff generally good, effective and discrete?

   (g) **Promotion delivery** - is it good, clear communication, friendly and humorous? What do customers feel about our in-store communications, are they informative and do they encourage enhanced buying from the customers?

We need to know all of the things discussed above, with respect to our **competitors** too, as well as further details of our own performance in the appropriate markets. We need to end up with a clear understanding of people's **perceptions** of our core values - how do they compare with the competition? And are our customers fully aware of the nature of our **brand equity** and that of our competitors? What are the critical differences?

(iii) **Research instruments**

We must be absolutely clear that this is not merely an interesting piece of ad hoc local research - it is a **fundamental market investigation** with potentially **global implications** for the future **strategic management** of our company. We must, therefore, approach the search for this information using all appropriate techniques to provide the fullest picture possible and in as many dimensions as possible, giving us the widest perspective on the real reasons for our competitor's success. We must omit nothing of significance, nor make assumptions.

We must therefore look at all aspects of the **distribution channel,** leading to our restaurants, using questionnaires and interviews, as well as researching the consumers directly. We must look at those people who are our customers and people who patronise the competition, as well as people who switch between the two.

We must look at **non-users** as well as users of fast foods. We must use interviews, telephone and personal, as well as observation techniques in and near restaurants. We should gain insights using **focus groups.** We should conduct taste tests with competitive offerings. We must be prepared to spend money on this research because it may have wide implications.

(iv) **Other issues and their impact upon the market**

As well as carrying out important **marketing research** as described above, our analysis must take into account a whole number of other factors and their impact upon the history of this market. We must assess the **political background,** how it is changing, its speed of change and similarities/differences with the political factors in other markets in which we operate around the world.

In particular, it seems that a significant component of the threat from Jollibee centres around the **availability and use** of retail properties and the difficulties we encountered because we could not own our sites outright. We must assess the way the **political and legal environment** is developing in the Philippines and other of our global markets.

As already mentioned the **human resources** of McDonald's have always been of central importance. Our market analysis should revisit this issue in the light of the competitive pressures we face and reassess where we stand in terms of **service** and the **management of the human resource** to continue providing our first-rate service.

(b) **Outline marketing plan, the next three years**

McDonald's: Company Response to Jollibee's

December 1997

Circulation: Board Members and Global Marketing Division, senior management team.

Report Author: Joe Smythe: Jollibee's Task Force Leader.

Introductory comment: Since this first draft of the outline marketing plan for responding to the Jollibee's threat in the Philippines and in other countries where such a threat exists is being presented before all the marketing research information has been gathered, certain assumptions have been made. Where appropriate these assumptions will be marked in the document text with a capital 'A' in square brackets.

1 **Background: corporate goals and strategy**

The company must spend some time reassessing its corporate strategy in the light of a rapidly developing global market, with competitors who are learning very quickly from our **key success factors** of service and quality and pursuing challenging positions with key success factors of their own.

Having developed the global market with the successful translation and roll-out of an American, **ethnocentric strategy** it may be time to consider tweaking the

Answer bank

company's market offering to suit more closely the local tastes, whilst at the same time retaining the most successful of our portfolio of strengths.

It is already apparent that we had lost the **flexibility** to respond quickly in the market place to new threats of competition.

1.1 Corporate objectives

Since McDonald's has been outflanked in the Philippines and we are under threat in other international markets as a result of Jollibee's activity (and that of other competitors) the key corporate objective is to **retain and re-establish our position** in the world fast food market. The overall goal must be to re-establish market dominance in those markets where the threat is greatest, and to begin to recover our leading market position in the Filipino market - recognising that this may take some time against a competitor who has already shown excellent marketing skills.

Since we have greater resources globally than Jollibee's we should not be unwilling to use them to stem this threat. See below for more detailed marketing objectives.

1.2 Corporate Strategy

Our corporate strategy is to re-assert our global position. In terms of **brand positioning** our customers must be informed from all our communications and from our product and service performance that we are the best and the benchmark against which other should be judged.

All of the company's controllable factors (the marketing mix and our organisational skills) must be directed towards delivering this value to the customer and I will deal with this in more detail below. We must use our global **brand equity** to its fullest extent, but we must take more note of differing local tastes and experiences. Consumers world-wide are becoming increasingly discriminating and we must recognise and provide different tastes for different palates.

2 Marketing goals

Dealing with the Filipino market, our long term goal must be to **re-assert market leadership**, through both market development and market **penetration**. This will take time, and we believe that the best we can achieve in a three year timescale is to regain parity with Jollibee's, providing a strong and stable base for future market expansion.

The marketing effort we are going to have to expend in order to achieve this is likely to expand the market at a rapid rate. Therefore, although Jollibee's and ourselves control 62% of the market at the moment, our rapid expansion (see below) will probably bring us jointly to 68 - 70% of this larger market. Thus our minimum market share in three years' time should be 35% of the Filipino market.

2.1 Marketing objectives

Making the assumption [A] that $20 million of Jollibee's turnover comes from outside the Filipino market, this gives an approximate market size of just under $330 million for the current year's total market. (Jollibee's 46% share = $150 million.) McDonald's therefore have sales of approximately $53 million in the current year. Our objectives for the next three years will be as follows:

Year one: 20% = $63 million
Year two: 25% = $100 million
Year three: 35% = $150 million

This represents **rapid market share growth** and it will entail considerable marketing expenditure. These figures will need to be kept under continual review, especially in the light of indications that there may be recessionary influences in the Japanese and other Pacific Rim markets, which may slow down the Filipino economy. In order to retain good control of the corporate and marketing effort, good **monitoring procedures** will need to be put in place and both marketing and sales **budgets** may be subject to modification. We may need to modify the total sales targets - but we should endeavour still to achieve the market share targets even if market growth slows down.

2.2 Marketing strategy

The overall strategy is to reassert the global brand equity in our key markets. Rather than go through each of the seven P's in this outline plan, for each year of the plan we will highlight one or two as the most significant elements and include more details in the final marketing plan, when all the market research data assembled.

Year 1

We must work quickly to consolidate our position by addressing the **product** offering, the **people**, the **physical evidence** of our stores and the **processes** used in our outlets.

Training will be key to the review and improvement necessary to make sure that the stores are as inviting as possible. The evidence suggests [A] that Jollibee's are getting more customer visits per store since they have three times the market share from twice as many stores. Since they have opened several stores recently they will be newly decorated, perhaps in better locations, bigger and better staffed.

Urgent action is needed here to make the most of our current resources. A large proportion of the outlets are still franchises and we must manage the franchisees with care.

As for the **product** element, we must target areas for product development tests to assess the viability of introducing new lines along the 'spicy' success of our key competitors. Where such new products demonstrate success we must be ready to roll them out very quickly.

In terms of **communications** we must use considerable promotional effort to re-establish the brand's global feel and market leadership. With careful planning we can tie this in to new store openings in the second half of this first year, which will be the start of our rapid growth phase.

Not only will we need to use a significant **advertising budget,** but we can use new openings to get free publicity in the Filipino media. One of the benefits of such an aggressive approach is that it may divert Jollibee's effort from expansionist goals, if they were to feel threatened. This will do no harm to our performance in other markets where Jollibee's are looking for growth themselves. We must not rely on this, however, to do any more than blunt their efforts.

Money must be spent to bring all of our stores up to the highest level of comfort and we must work with our franchise partners to discover if some modest decorative changes are needed to attract local customers. In doing this we must be careful not to dissipate existing branding strengths.

Continuous tracking and monitoring is vital during these important activity stages, throughout the three years covered by this planning cycle.

Place. This year will be important in identifying new store locations and putting through property purchases and leases.

Year 2

In promotional terms, it is vital we continue to restate our global brand equity and highlight the new store openings, which should be spread to maximise publicity.

Product. The tests conducted in year one will have led us to a renewal of our **product portfolio** and we will be in a position to go for a relaunch in the Filipino market, matching perceived local tastes but also delivering our core values as a company.

In terms of price we need to emphasise the value for money which is being delivered by the company, making it very clear why we are the premium priced company in the market place. We must not succumb to the danger of buying market share for a lower price.

Control. Everything should be kept under evaluation and we must have the right people in place to ensure proper and effective control of the whole marketing effort.

Year 3

Finalise the positioning of McDonald's as the global company in the Filipino fast food market, taking what Ohmae calls the 'insider' position. New store openings will continue throughout the year, perhaps slowing down as the year comes to a close in order to allow some time for **consolidation** of our leadership position.

Take the lessons learnt in the Filipino situation and begin to apply the principles to all of those other markets where McDonald's appears to be under threat from a flexible and well managed local competitor.

Product **quality** and **delivery** should be continually re-evaluated throughout all of our markets. Efforts should have been made to enclose and contain the potential threat from Jollibee controlled competitors in those markets where we have been coming under any kind of threat.

77 HARLEY DAVIDSON

> **Tutorial note.** This question gives you the opportunity to display your knowledge of local economic conditions. Question 1(a) required candidates to demonstrate an understanding of strategic thinking and not the detail necessary to create a strategic plan. Remember that your answer must refer specifically to the circumstances of the question. Merely reproducing a template answer with little reference to Harley Davidson or the selected area would gain few marks.
>
> **Examiner's comments.** Part (a) was often poorly answered, with candidates ignoring the instruction to write about strategic issues. Some focused instead on planning. Market entry strategy in part (b) was misinterpreted by some candidates as an invitation to write about market entry methods. Some of the recommendations were unrealistic and unsupported by any kind of justification. Many suggested that Harley Davidson should merge with a European motorcycle manufacturer without any supporting evidence.

Answer bank

(a) **Major strategic issues**

Market selection

The markets to be selected need to have a population with the following characteristics.

(i) Already supports a motor cycling segment of suitable size

(ii) Has a roads infrastructure that will allow the 'super heavyweight' motor cycles to be ridden in the manner for which they were designed

(iii) A wealthy segment that shares the American dream of long straight roads and wide open spaces

The markets represented by the countries of the European Union, South East Asia and Australia would satisfy some or all of these requirements.

Harley Davidson needs to consider both the **physical distances** involved in developing internationally and the **psychological distances**. For instance, Australians are probably more psychologically close to the Americans in terms of demand for superheavyweight motorcycles, but are at a great physical distance from the US. Physical distance will have an impact on **costs** and **profit**.

The numerous trade-offs in market selection can be analysed and evaluated using an appropriate **market attractiveness/company competence matrix** such as the Harrell and Kieffer matrix.

Market entry

The market entry method will depend on both the **financial resources** Harley Davidson can give to the expansion programme and the requirements of specific markets.

If financial resources are low, and a low level of control over market development is acceptable, then Harley Davidson could choose to expand internationally by using US based **export management** companies - an indirect method.

If a higher level of control over market development is required then Harley Davidson could choose a **direct method** of market entry through either the appointment of **agents** (lower cost) or **distributors** (higher cost). Custom and practice in the motor cycle market indicates that market entry and development strategies are most frequently based on using distributors.

If financial resources allow, or market entry conditions demand, then Harley Davidson may have to consider **overseas production** (direct inward investment). This is a high cost and high risk entry and development strategy which offers the greatest level of control and potentially the highest returns.

If market entry is dependent upon some of the value of the product being added locally, and Harley Davidson does not have the financial resources for direct inward investment, then a **strategic alliance** with an existing local manufacturer (who does not compete in the super heavyweight segment) could be a profitable entry and development strategy.

Internal resources

The market selection and entry and development strategies will be highly dependent on the internal resources of Harley Davidson. Clearly, the current 'very limited overseas **marketing budget**' will need increasing to support an increase in export sales from 30% of turnover to 50% of turnover within 3 years.

If the expansion strategy is to be determined by the internal financial resources available then in this case the low cost strategic options will need to be considered. Should external financial resources be made available from other sources (eg increased **borrowings** or the issue of more **share capital**) then a wider range of strategic options becomes available. This is a key decision for the management of Harley Davidson.

The suitability of the existing **staff** to support an overseas expansion programme needs to be assessed in the light of the chosen strategy. Key management decisions need to be made with regard to the balance of **skills** of the existing staff and the skills required to deliver the expansion programme. Re-training existing staff may be an option. The recruitment of experienced staff may be a more expedient approach.

The **physical resources** of Harley Davidson will need careful evaluation to establish their suitability to supply the products required by the expansion programme. Key questions for management would include **plant capacity** in terms of machines and labour.

(b) **Overseas development in Europe**

Introduction

The markets represented by the countries of the European Union have been selected as the **target geographic area** for the overseas expansion programme of Harley Davidson. Specific target markets for the initial 3 year expansion programme are Germany and the UK. Successful performance in these markets will lead to a **market spreading strategy** being applied to the other countries of the EU. The switch from the initial market concentration approach to a market spreading approach can occur at any time during the 3 year period subject to the success of the programme.

Market entry - strategy options

Harley Davidson is considering a long term commitment to overseas expansion and should, therefore, review those **entry strategies that will deliver the corporate objective** of increasing export sales from 30% of turnover to 50% within 3 years.

A **market extension strategy** with a focus on selling products developed for the domestic market with no adaptation to take account of the target market could be used effectively providing there is sufficient customer empathy. This strategy would be totally dependent on overseas customers wanting to buy the US product and its associated imagery. A market extension strategy may be more appropriate to Germany with its large number of US military bases (and consequential significant numbers of US nationals) and unrestricted speed limits on some autobahns. Whilst this strategy could deliver the corporate objectives it is felt that the **underpinning assumptions** present a significant **risk** to success, in spite of the relatively low cost to implement such a strategy.

A **multidomestic strategy** would be an appropriate entry strategy as the company would need to consider each country on its merits and avoid looking for interdependencies. The British motivation to buy a premium US motorcycle may be more to do with perceived product excellence. This strategy is considered to be less risky although more investment will be required to provide the appropriate imagery for each market.

A **market spreading** or **regional expansion strategy** throughout the countries of the EU is encouraged, following the successful establishment of a multidomestic strategy in Germany and the UK.

To effect a multidomestic strategy it is necessary to adopt a direct approach to market entry, as this is the most appropriate and adaptable in the future. Some **direct inward**

investment will be required to establish a country office and workshop in each target market. The other market entry methods of indirect exporting, overseas production (intensive direct inward investment) and strategic alliances are not given any further consideration.

Market entry choice

The chosen market entry strategy is to develop a network of **independent distributors** which will be appointed, developed and controlled through a Harley Davidson country office and workshop in both the UK and Germany. Each distributor will be contracted to stock one of each of the basic models and the complete range of options available to customise the motorcycle. All motorcycle final build and customisation will be undertaken at the country workshop with final cosmetics being applied by the distributor along with the after sales service package. This allows the distributor to develop a relationship beyond the sale of the motorcycle.

Marketing objectives

The current **level of awareness** of the Harley Davidson product and brand by the population of each target country needs to be established and **marketing communications objectives** set which build on this level, particularly amongst the target segment. An appropriate objective would be to double the level of awareness over the 3 year programme.

Sales objectives will have to be based on an analysis of the motorcycle market in both Germany and the UK which identifies the size of the super heavyweight segment. As there is **local competition** in Europe from BMW in Germany and Norton in the UK, both of whom are selling dreams and images as well as motorcycles, sales objectives to achieve a 20% share of segment by the end of year 3 would appear to be appropriate.

Distributors will be selected and appointed in each of the major contributions first and, subject to successful **sales penetration** in these areas, other distributors will be appointed in the next level of population density. Selection of the distributor will be based on empathy with the Harley Davidson product and the **strategic fit** of super heavyweight motorcycles with the existing business. Distributors of BMW and Norton motorcycles would not be excluded from the selection process but care would be exercised in their appointment.

Management issues

Organisation

The organisation structure for this expansion programme can be relatively small whilst being highly effective. In the US, a senior manager needs to be given full **responsibility for the expansion programme**, including the appointment of a US national to head up each of the UK and German sales offices. The US senior manager will need the support of an experienced **export administrator** to cover the day to detail between the US, the UK and Germany.

In the UK and Germany, the **sales office manager** needs supporting by a local workshop manager, totally familiar with the local requirements for motorcycles, and 2 or 3 mechanics, depending on the level of demand.

Budgets

It is estimated that the development of the European market will require a **marketing budget** of $500,000 (around £340,000) per year. This will cover the costs of creating and maintaining offices in the UK and Germany. An initial sales budget needs to be set of $1,000,000 for each market, equivalent to selling 50 - 70 motorcycles at $15,000 to

Answer bank

$20,000 each. This initial sales budget can be amended as appropriate when the size of the super heavyweight motorcycle **segment** is known.

Timescales

It is anticipated that the research should be completed by the end of September 20XX, allowing for a launch of Harley Davidson around Christmas time 20XX to coincide, and compete, with the promotional pushes for summer holidays. The UK and German sales offices should be operational before the launch, say early December 20XX.

People requirements

The key operational staff outlined above will need administrative support, initially provided by one suitably experienced person. Depending on the final sales budgets set and the number of distributors appointed the type and number of support staff will need to be reviewed.

Controlling the expansion programme

Initially, **weekly visit reports** will be required to monitor the distributor appointment programme. When the distributors are appointed, monthly **sales reports** will be required comparing actual sales against budgeted sales. Quarterly **financial accounts** will control each of the country operations.

78 SRI LANKAN TEA

(a)

> **Examiner's comments**: The mini case was one which most candidates should have been able to answer with considerable ease. The case was designed to enable them to display their knowledge of the basics of an international plan, ie an outline market entry plan and the operational issues associated with it.
>
> Part (a) was generally poorly answered. In many cases the answer provided did not relate to the question and could have been referring to any marketing plan. Many candidates failed to identify the branding issues or carry out any environmental or buyer behaviour analysis. Strategic thought was constantly missing and 'analysis' and 'strategy' were clearly mixed up.

UK Market Entry Plan for the Sri Lankan Tea Consortium

Introduction

It is assumed that this initiative will not compete directly with the existing bulk tea business of Sri Lanka. It will instead attempt to **expand the market** through developing the premium tea segment with a **product offering** that has many distinguishing features. Correspondence with, or ideally a visit to, Jacobs Creek in Australia would be invaluable in enabling the Tea Consortium to establish the requirements for **brand development** in the crowded UK market.

Objectives

(a) Establish a high level of **awareness** (75%) of Sri Lanka as a producer of high quality tea with the UK adult population within 1 year

(b) Develop a tea processing and packaging **plant** in Sri Lanka capable of producing tea in the pack sizes and formats required by UK consumers. To be operational within 6 months

(c) Achieve a 30% **share** of the UK premium tea market by the end of the 3 year period.

Secondary research

With reference to the UK Target Group Indicators (TGI), produced by BMRB, UK tea consumption patterns can be established by:

- Age
- Geographic area
- Socio-economic group
- Pack format (loose leaf or tea bag) preference
- Brand share(Typhoo, PG Tips etc)
- Outlet (supermarket or convenience store)
- Extent of usage
- Country of origin of the tea (possibly)

Primary research

The consortium needs to establish the **attitudes** of UK consumers to tea drinking in general and Sri Lankan tea in particular. The research also needs to determine the understanding and **perceptions** of UK tea consumers towards **premium brands** of tea. Tasting panels and **focus groups** can be used to examine these **qualitative** aspects of tea consumption, together with the most appropriate **pack formats** for premium tea, **price levels** consumers are most likely to pay, and likely **place** of purchase.

Market entry

Given the dominance of supermarkets in UK food retailing (around 80 % of all grocery spend is with the top 10 supermarkets) the Tea Consortium must have a presence in these outlets. A Tea Consortium **sales office** in the UK is considered to be vital to establish and develop **relationships** with the buying teams of the supermarkets. This will involve minimal cost, preserving most of the Sri Lankan government support to invest in processing and packaging facilities in Sri Lanka, and marketing communications in the UK.

If processing and packing in Sri Lanka and the shipping time between Sri Lanka and the UK can be synchronised with the demand from the supermarkets, then in principle the packed tea could be shipped direct to the **regional distribution** centres of the supermarkets. This would ensure optimum freshness on the shelves, commensurate with the premium image to be developed and the premium price to be charged. **Synchronisation of delivery with demand**, including taking account of shipping time, would give the consortium a significant **competitive advantage**. It would also avoid the Tea Consortium incurring storage costs in the UK and allow it to exploit the lower operating costs in Sri Lanka whilst using the latest tea processing and packing **technology**.

Marketing mix

The Sri Lankan tea will be positioned as a **premium product** through the use of a **suitable advertising and promotional campaign**. Images of Sri Lanka will be used to demonstrate the heritage of tea production and processing on the island and the care with which the tea is grown, harvested and processed. A similar theme to the Kenco coffee advertising will be used. This has succeeded in creating Kenco as a premium brand, with a price premium over the market leader Nescafe and the supermarket own labels.

Distribution on the shelves of supermarkets is vital to the success of this initiative and the Tea Consortium must make themselves distinctive to their supermarket buyers. A **premium price** to consumers will enable the supermarkets to generate a higher **margin**. This will encourage the supermarkets to stock the tea, and the Tea

Consortium will be able to charge the supermarkets a competitive price due to all the **value adding activities** taking place in Sri Lanka with its considerably lower operating costs.

Controlling the initiative

Research needs to be undertaken as soon as possible to enable the **costs** and **timescales** of the market entry plan to be established. Ideally, this should be completed by early March 1999.

A **budget** needs to be set to cover the advertising and promotional expenditure in the UK. Expenditures against this budget will need careful **monitoring** to ensure the awareness and sales targets are achieved. It is highly likely that the presence of premium Sri Lanka tea on the supermarket shelves will be dependent on the level of promotional spend.

Timescales need to be set for targets to be met. These need to take account of the time required to **negotiate** access to the supermarket shelves and the start of the promotional campaign. It is highly likely that one year will be required to negotiate shelf space, hence indicating a launch of the premium product in late 1999/early 2000. Therefore the earlier the negotiations start with the supermarkets the better, so that the maximum time is available for making the investment in processing and packing equipment.

Conclusions

Although the UK is widely regarded as a nation of tea drinkers, this does not necessarily translate into a premium tea market. A lot of work will need to be done to verify the plan outlined above before committing to major capital investment in the project. It is recommended that an initial budget of £50,000 is set to **fully research** the UK market to establish the likelihood of success and that this research be completed by end March 1999.

(b)

> **Examiner's comments**: With few exceptions this was poorly answered. Answers were far too general and failed to display even a basic knowledge of the strategic and operational elements of an international marketing plan. Too many answers contained bullet points which did not relate to the question. Few candidates addressed the management issues thrown up by the plan suggested in 1(a).

Implementing the market entry plan

Introduction

It is assumed that research has been undertaken and that the project is to proceed to the next stage of setting up the UK sales office. Suitably experienced Sri Lankan nationals have been recruited to head up the UK sales office.

Operational Issues

In the UK a suitable **location** for a sales office needs to be found and arrangements made to start the **recruitment** process for the UK support/administration staff. One of the selection criteria would be the availability of regional or local authority **financial assistance**.

Suppliers of suitable processing and packing equipment need to be identified and **contracts negotiated** to supply the equipment to a location in Sri Lanka. The buildings will need to be suitable for holding inventory of packed product in its final form ready for transportation. Suppliers of all packing material will need to be identified and the supply chain created to feed this to the Sri Lankan plant. **Storage**

facilities will be required at the plant to ensure the packing materials do not deteriorate prior to use in the packing plant. All processes, including storage, will need to take account of UK food hygiene **regulations** that may be imposed by the UK supermarkets.

Human resource issues

The UK office needs to be established and staffed by a team of two Sri Lankan nationals supported by two or three UK nationals as administrators. The administrators will need to be experienced in dealing with the buying teams from UK supermarkets and the selling teams of UK advertising agencies. The Sri Lankan nationals will have been recruited on the basis of their experience of negotiating with powerful buyers. The candidates appointed will have been educated and worked in the UK at some point in their career. Refresher training in sales negotiations needs to be arranged in the UK.

Financial issues

As the target market is the UK then the Tea Consortium should experience no **political risk** and very little **exchange risk**. However, they need to be aware of the **credit periods** UK supermarkets impose on their suppliers of between sixty to eighty days. This will have an impact on the **working capital** requirements of the Tea Consortium. It is anticipated that the Sri Lankan government will contribute the **capital costs** of the buildings, plant and equipment in Sri Lanka.

Production issues

The Tea Consortium can become distinctive with the UK supermarket buying teams through the **synchronisation of supply with demand**. Hence, the plant management will have to ensure that the supply from the growers and the storage of the unprocessed, part processed, and packed tea is to a very high standard so that it is delivered to the UK supermarkets in perfect condition all the year round.

Controls

Financial objectives need to be set with respect to the usual measures of **return on assets**, return on capital employed, net **profit** and cash flow. **Marketing objectives** need to be set with respect to sales volume, market share, consumer awareness and product image.

Performance measurement

The UK sales office will need to send detailed quarterly **reports** to the Sri Lankan headquarters, which will complement headline weekly reports based on EDI data from the supermarkets. The provision of **weekly sales data** from the **EPOS systems** of the supermarkets via EDI needs to be negotiated along with the contract to supply. It is suggested that **meetings** between the UK sales office and the management at Sri Lankan headquarters take place every 6 months to review progress and to set objectives. As much use as is practical needs to be made of **information technology for communications**.

79 ZIMFLOWERS

(a)

> **Examiner's comments.** Responses to this question allowed candidates to demonstrate their knowledge of PEST and 12C's analysis, with the more able candidates selecting a particular area and a country or countries in that area. It was remarkable how few candidates bothered to nominate a country in either region, resulting in the PEST/12C's analyses being little more than a parade of abstract speculations. It was baffling when examining answers to this question why so few candidates used their home market as a benchmark to show how HPC should enter other markets in the target region. Also, the ability of candidates to present "…factors….to consider…" in a meaningful and professional management style was very poor.

Assumptions

If the existing growing capacity (glass or polythene houses) is fully utilised in providing the current level of exports, then the Horticultural Promotion Council must be fairly certain that the growers will **invest** in sufficient **capacity** to double the level of exports over a 6 - 7 year period.

The growers will almost certainly want to see any expansion in capacity and the consequent increase in exports generating better **returns** for them, through increased **prices** from both existing and new markets. Also, expansion of cool-store and chilled transport facilities could be needed to ensure the cut flowers reach the air freight terminal and the customer in prime condition.

Therefore, the Horticultural Promotion Council needs to consider the **internal factors** that will affect the flower growing industry in Zimbabwe in conjunction with the **external factors** and **business environment** of the target market area.

Internal factors

With some growers feeling that they are not getting the best possible prices from selling through the Dutch auction, there may be some resistance to increasing the level of exports, based on a belief that better prices may be obtainable from other markets for the same volume of output. This may be a more attractive option for the growers.

To persuade the flower growers to increase their capacity, HPC may need to consider lobbying the Zimbabwean **government** for some **investment assistance** to the growers, in advance of the increased flow of **foreign exchange receipts** that the growers will generate.

The HPC will need to consider that the most likely response from the government to this request will be for an assured increase in **hard currency** receipts. All exports would need to be priced in US$, or other hard currency. This would automatically focus the **market selection** process on Europe with its plethora of hard or freely convertible currencies, and focus the **market entry decision** away from reliance on the Dutch auction.

Government investment assistance to growers may need to be extended to the cool store operators and chilled transport operators, putting more pressure on HPC to earn foreign exchange.

> **Note to students.** This line of reasoning would not preclude a consideration of ASEAN countries, but as all the countries of ASEAN except Japan have soft currencies, pricing in US$ would need to be considered throughout the consideration of the factors.

The volume of air transport to and from Southern Africa is most likely to increase in the North/South direction rather than West/East. Thus, HPC may wish to consider

Answer bank

routing some of their planned increase in exports through the much larger facilities in South Africa (Johannesburg) whilst the Zimbabwean facilities are improved and increased.

> **Note to students**. Using Johannesburg as a hub may give HPC and the Zimbabwean growers access to cost effective transport to the countries in ASEAN (West/East) by using the airlines and airfreight companies that fly West/East out of South Africa.

External factors

The **business environment** in the countries of the selected region or trading bloc will need to be scanned to determine the significance of any of the following effects on the market demand for cut flowers.

- **Social** (flower use, flower buying and giving)
- **Legal** (restrictions on the importation of cut flowers)
- **Economic** (income levels, prices of cut flowers and capacity to pay)
- **Political** (country relationships with Zimbabwe, currently under strain due to land reform policies)
- **Technological** (cut flower substitutes)

As the individual growers are uncomfortable with the prices obtained from the Dutch auction, HPC needs to consider alternative, possibly more **direct market entry methods**, to improve the prices the growers receive and to encourage them to invest to meet the predicted increased demand.

At one extreme all exports of cut flowers could be **centralised** through HPC, with HPC creating **relationships** with flower distributors, or large flower retailing chains (such as the supermarkets in the UK) in each of the countries of Europe. This approach would ensure that all flowers leaving Zimbabwe and all foreign currency receipts into Zimbabwe from the sale of the flowers are channelled through one agency (HPC).

In this approach the growers would receive a standard, local currency, price agreed between the growers and HPC. HPC would take responsibility for, and incur all **costs** relating to, promotion, price setting and physical distribution with the export customers.

This **standardised approach** may allow for some differentiation through **branding** (eg long stem Zimbabwean roses differentiated from the short stem English rose).

Given the **command style of economy** operating in Zimbabwe (in common with many of the other countries in Africa), then the government could favour this approach to increasing exports and **foreign currency receipts**, and possibly offer investment incentives to growers to increase capacity.

At the other extreme HPC could encourage each grower to develop relationships with their selected customers in the target market. This may be more attractive to the growers as it gives them control of where they develop their business. However, given the **power of the buyers** (flower distributors and, particularly, supermarkets in the UK) in the European markets such a fragmented approach would give HPC very little influence in the export markets and could hinder market development.

The costs to the individual growers could increase, as each grower would be negotiating to sell and ship relatively small volumes in proportion to total demand and industry output. Also, **differentiation through branding** would be more difficult to establish with a fragmented approach.

A middle position could be HPC encouraging small groups of growers to **co-operate** to meet the needs of a particular target customer (e.g. a group of 12 growers satisfying the flower needs of Sainsbury's in the UK, or KaiserMarkt in Germany).

Promotion, price setting and physical distribution could be undertaken jointly between the co-operating group and HPC, and give some balance to the negotiations. This approach would allow for differentiation through branding, as the buyers would see HPC taking a leading role in establishing the relationship between grower and buyer.

Conclusion

HPC must balance the internal and external factors to ensure that HPC meets its implied objectives (doubling export volumes by the millennium) and the interests of the growers.

(b)

> **Examiner's comments.** Many candidates must have seen the words "generic ...... strategy" and thought that all that was required of them to answer this question was to provide the examiner with all they knew about Porter's generic strategies without, in most cases, applying them to HPC and/or the flower growers. As a result the responses did not include a marketing strategy, any objectives, any budgets and time-scales, and no opinions regarding implementing and controlling a cost leadership or differentiation strategy. Some candidates chose to attempt to use the Ansoff approach in a similar way - no marketing strategy other than penetration or development, no objectives and no budgets. A significant number of scripts demonstrated an encyclopaedic knowledge of market entry strategy, including much effort spent on overseas production! This specimen answer is based on a generic marketing strategy based on the McDonald approach.

Analysis

Europe has been chosen as the target geographic area, due to the majority of countries in Europe having stable and **freely convertible currencies**. The target market is France since it is assumed that the flower use, buying and giving **behaviour** will be similar to that in the UK and Germany, both established markets. Certainly, Germany and France with their strong Catholic **cultures** will share the same religious festivals that are significant flower using occasions.

Coincidental with the **development** of the French market, the UK and German markets will be subjected to further **penetration**. All of the major retail chains in Europe that sell cut flowers and have pan-European expansion plans such as Tesco in the UK and Aldi in Germany will be targeted as the lynchpin of the marketing strategy. This should ensure that the implied HPC objective of doubling exports over a 6 - 7 year period is achieved.

Marketing strategy

The generic marketing strategy is one of **market development of a target country**, France, complemented with **market penetration of existing markets**, UK and Germany.

The generic strategy of development and penetration will enable a supplementary **market spreading strategy** to be effected through the development of relationships with key pan-European retailers.

Objectives

For a generic strategy to be implemented a combination of marketing and financial **objectives** need to be set. In the context of the overall objective of doubling exports (ie exporting an additional 4000 tonnes per year) the following marketing objectives are recommended.

Answer bank

(i) The French market to be importing 1000 tonnes of cut flowers per year by 1999, valued at F.Fr x million. (Assuming a minimum amount currently via buyers at the Dutch auction)

(ii) The UK and German markets to be importing at least 2500 tonnes of cut flowers each per year by 1999, valued at £a million and DMb million respectively. (Assuming that currently UK and German buyers are importing 1500 tonnes per year each, excluding the major supermarkets)

(iii) The pan-European retailers (Tesco, Aldi etc) to be importing at least 2000 tonnes of cut flowers collectively per year by 1999, valued at US$c million. (It is assumed that this group of buyers will distribute the cut flowers throughout Europe from their own strategically placed regional distribution centres supplied by HPC)

(iv) To have no more than 1000 tonnes of cut flowers sold at the Dutch auction in 1999, valued at d million Guilders. (Assuming that at least 1000 tonnes are currently sold via the Dutch auction and are transhipped to a myriad of unknown destinations)

Marketing mix considerations

It is recommended that the **product strategy** concentrate on roses, since this is causing other flower exporters to view the Zimbabwean rose as a major competitive challenge. Other cut flowers can complement the rose to present the buyers with a balanced portfolio of flowers from which to choose, but the rose gives the **portfolio** of cut flowers from Zimbabwe its **distinctiveness**.

The rose can be used to start the market development programme in France. Market penetration in the UK and Germany can be based on the rose. Negotiations with the buying teams of the pan-European retailers can start with the distinctive features of the Zimbabwean rose.

The current evidence suggests that the rose should command a **premium** price - it is sufficiently distinctive and is viewed as a challenge. Thus, the product/price mix needs to position roses from Zimbabwe and the complementary ranges of other flowers as premium products. If the majority of flowers purchased by consumers are for special occasions such as birthdays or anniversaries, then demand is unlikely to be **price sensitive**. Therefore, with a distinctive portfolio of cut flowers a premium position should be achievable.

This positioning needs to be created in France, the market under development. In the UK and Germany a compound annual growth in volume sales of 10% should be achievable with a premium positioned range of flowers. The pan-European retailers will need to be convinced that they will benefit from the better **margins** that can be obtained from premium flowers purchased on impulse. It is unlikely that a premium position can be established at an auction.

Achieving a premium position from the outset in the development of the French market and penetrating the existing markets of the UK and Germany will require a promotion mix based on **personal selling** direct to **key buyers** and building lasting relationships with them.

The buyers will need convincing that buying direct from the growers via the HPC will result in cut flowers reaching them in perfect condition to command premium prices. Whilst the buyers may be paying more for their flowers direct from Zimbabwe than from traditional channels, the **price premium** they can obtain from the consumer will ensure they make a better **margin** with Zimflowers. A **communications** strategy based on personal contact will be essential to deliver these messages.

On-time deliveries of perfect flowers in the quantities ordered will be the key to building long term relationships with key buyers and ensuring that the premium position is achieved and maintained. Using Johannesburg as a hub should result in more frequent fights to Europe, and with potentially more airlines using Johannesburg than Harare, the increased **competition** between the airlines may result in lower **airfreight charges**.

Budgets and timescales

HPC needs to set itself a budget for each of the years to the millennium that identifies the pattern of **costs** to be incurred, and how these patterns will change as the market development and penetration strategies start to take effect. It is estimated that an initial budget should be set of US$250,000 per year to cover general market visits, promotion costs (point of sale material), and selling costs.

Whilst the objectives given above are for the **long term**, control of the 7 year programme will depend on careful **monitoring** of the **objectives** and **budgets** set for each year. **Independent research** of cut flower demand and consumption in each of the market segments will be a major element of the control system.

Conclusion

HPC needs to consider a market development and market penetration strategy running concurrently in different markets, with a **marketing mix** clearly focused on creating a premium position for cut flowers from Zimbabwe. Tight **budgetary control** will have to be exercised over the expansion programme given its 6 – 7 year life.

80 LEVI STRAUSS

> **Examiner's comments.** The minicase was one which should have been familiar to all candidates. The questions were aimed at testing the ability to design an international plan with a strategic focus. Such questions are regular and standard on this paper. Many candidates found this difficult and answers were often only of average standard.
>
> In part (a) many candidates were unable to show how an MkIS could have helped Levi Strauss to identify the environmental changes that were giving it such problems. General answers on MkIS, that did not relate specifically to Levi Strauss, were also in evidence.

(a) **Marketing information**

Introduction

The environmental variables impacting upon Levi's should have been recorded and classified according to the **SLEPT framework**, although not all of these variables would have accounted for the problems facing the company. To be effective the results of any scanning process, irrespective of the framework used (e.g. SLEPT, 12 C's, etc.) need to be stored and maintained in a **marketing information system**. The MIS must be responsive to changes in the environment and also be effective in reporting the potential consequences of the changes to management.

Environmental variables

The major change in the environment that appears to have been missed by the management of Levi's was the **change in consumer taste** for both jeans and the Levi's brand. This is a social phenomenon, usually characterised by fairly gradual changes over a long period, which needs a sensitive Marketing Information System to monitor and report to management. Irrespective of the sensitivity of the MIS, management need to recognise the value of interrogating the MIS to inform their actions at both the strategic and operational level.

Changes in the **economics** of manufacturing and marketing jeans have had a significant impact on the fortunes of Levi's. When market share falls even after considerable promotional expenditure has been incurred, action needs to be taken to identify the causes. A responsive MIS would have informed management that competitors were gaining market share at the expense of Levi's. Appropriate management action could have been taken.

The **new entrants** to the jeans market were creating **fragmentation** and increasing the level competition in the jeans market. Fragmentation is a combination of social and economic phenomena and occurs over an extended time period. Again a sensitive MIS would have alerted the management of Levi's to the new entrants and the impact they were having on the marketplace.

New entrants, irrespective of whether they were the fashion houses and brands moving into the jeans market, or organisations exploiting **production technology** in low cost labour areas of the world, were contributing to both the fragmentation and change in consumer taste. This was being achieved through the same generic product being offered with either a more fashionable label or at a much lower **price**, and, in some instances made to measure using **Internet communications** between consumer and supplier.

Marketing information systems

For marketing information systems to be effective they must be current and must be believed in, particularly by the senior decision-makers in organisations. An effective MIS is expensive to create and maintain and hence must be capable of showing a return on the investment.

Levi's should have created a marketing information system with some clear **objectives** relating to the data to be collected and maintained, and its analysis and reporting. The objectives for the MIS should have been set based on the information required by the decision-makers. The **analysis and evaluation** of such data would provide quality information to meet the precise needs of the decision makers. A sensitive MIS, incorporating **knowledge management** principles, would indicate to decision-makers possible future outcomes for differing interpretations of the information.

Change in strategy

The information from the MIS should have been informing management of the changes occurring in the marketplace. The first changes to appear would have been the **new entrants**. The MIS should have been recording data relating to, at least, country of origin of products, materials, styles, retail prices, type and estimated expenditure on promotion for all the competing offerings.

This information would have enabled Levi's to make decisions relating to their **target market**, for instance, were the new entrants creating **new niches** (i.e. expanding the market) or attacking Levi's segments (i.e. **fragmenting** the market). Knowledge of the effects of the new entrants could have been used to direct Levi's efforts in changing its target market (e.g. from the youth market, to, possibly, thirtysomethings). This knowledge would have assisted Levi's in adjusting or altering its **strategic focus** (e.g. from a mass producer of premium jeans to a differentiator or customiser of premium jeans).

The MIS would have informed changes to the **marketing mix**, particularly the **promotion** and **distribution** elements. If new entrants were gaining market share from Levi's with very little promotional expenditure, then clearly Levi's needed to change its approach to promotion to ensure that the majority of the benefits arising from the expenditure accrue to Levi's. Similarly, Levi's approach to distribution needs to be critically reviewed to ensure that Levi's gain maximum exposure in the high street and shopping malls, and gain competitive advantage from their investment in specialist Levi's stores.

Answer bank

Conclusion

To be effective the MIS must inform the whole of the **planning**, **implementation** and **control** cycle. Additionally, everyone in the organisation with responsibility for contributing to the cycle must have access to, and believe in and act on, the information contained in the MIS. Believing in and acting on **perceptions** has had disastrous consequences for Levi's.

(b)

> **Examiner's comments.** This should have been a straightforward exercise in strategic planning, but the following problems were in evidence
>
> ○ Repetition of case study material
> ○ Overelaborate SWOT analysis
> ○ Generalities rather than specifics
> ○ Use of bullet points rather than detail
> ○ No statement of assumptions
> ○ No timescales or budgets
> ○ Unrealistic and unattainable objectives
> ○ Inadequate focus on control methods
> ○ Emphasis on operations rather than strategy

Strategic International Marketing Plan 1999 - 2002

Objectives

1. To restore the turnover to $6 billion by the end of Financial Year 2002
2. To generate a net profit of at least $0.5 billion by the end of Financial Year 2002

Assumptions

1. Financial years and calendar years coincide
2. It is now December 1998
3. That Levi's have the senior management commitment and the financial resources necessary to invest in and implement the plan
4. That the Levi Stores concept is retained as the vehicle for getting as close to the consumer as possible

Analysis

A detailed analysis of the global market for jeans needs to be completed urgently. This plan is based on the global analysis being completed and presented to senior management by the end of Quarter 1 1999. This analysis must include a critical review of the effectiveness of the Levi Stores concept in order to verify assumption 4 above.

The analysis will identify the major **geographic** jeans markets of the world and then proceed to **segment** each market to a common format, such as **12 C's**, in order to establish a **priority** list of countries to target to achieve the objectives. A Harrell and Kieffer, or similar **market attractiveness/company compatibility matrix** will be used to classify the countries and compile the target list.

If time permits, an analysis using a **SLEPT** format could be undertaken to provide a higher level validation of the 12 C's results.

Answer bank

Planning

From the analysis **annual objectives** will need to be set to demonstrate that the overall 2002 objective can be achieved. Typically the annual objectives may appear as:-

End 1999:- Turnover $3.5 billion   Net Profit $0.25 billion

End 2000:- Turnover $4.5 billion   Net Profit $0.30 billion

End 2001:- Turnover $5.0 billion   Net Profit $0.40 billion

End 2002:- Turnover $6.0 billion   Net Profit $0.50 billion

A **strategic focus** needs to be set that concentrates on positioning the Levi Stores to generate the maximum value from each sale for Levi's and provides a significant point of **differentiation** for the consumer. Investment in state of the art EPOS systems and associated communications systems will provide the management of Levi's and their planning teams with information on levels of consumer activity in each store. Thus, the strategic focus becomes one of **managing information** about consumers and their buying behaviour as they make purchases.

The **target markets** are expected to include the countries of Europe, the countries of the Pacific Rim, and the major emerging markets such as Russia and China, as well as the domestic market including Mexico and Canada.

A **marketing mix** needs to be developed which places as much emphasis on the Service P's of People, Processes and Physical Evidence as it does on the traditional 4P's. In effect, Levi's should be planning to create through their stores a service that is differentiated to meet the needs of the consumers whilst extracting economies of scale out of the other elements of the marketing mix. Thus, the product, its promotion, and distribution through the Levi Stores may be standardised, but the price, and the Service P's are adapted to a particular location or country.

Restoring lost sales does not happen without considerable investment. The senior management of Levi's needs to be investing a minimum 10% of projected turnover each year in marketing activities, particularly promotion activities, to realise the objective of doubling sales. A total **marketing budget** may be:-

Year	Target Sales $ bn	Marketing Budget $ bn	% of Sales
1999	3.5	0.5	14
2000	4.5	0.5	11
2001	5.0	0.5	10
2002	6.0	0.6	10

The marketing budget will need to be appropriately **allocated** between the geographic markets. The **promotional mix** in each market, particularly point of sale promotion, and developing suitable e-commerce activities will also require consideration when allocating resources.

Implementation and control

The **organisation structure** of Levi's will need to be reviewed to ensure that it is effective for managing a manufacturing and retailing company on a global scale. A restructuring needs to be commenced after the analysis has been completed and the revised structure needs to be operational by the end of Quarter 3 1999.

Investment in the EPOS system and its associated communication system is an essential first step in delivering the proposed **forward-integrated strategy**. The stores in the primary target markets must be the first to receive the EPOS investment. Investment in the secondary target markets can be phased in over the duration of the plan.

All stores in the primary target markets need to be in operation by the end of 1999. This will allow Levi's to make decisions regarding the effectiveness of promotional expenditure on sales by both value and volumes. Close monitoring of sales and cost of sales is an essential activity in attempting to restore business.

The EPOS system will be the primary **control process** for Levi's since it will track **sales by product,** and inform management of optimum stock levels in stores to keep **inventory** costs to a minimum and **customer service** levels to a maximum.

The marketing communications programme needs to be commenced in the primary target markets during the second quarter of 1999. This programme needs particular emphasis on getting customers into the Levi Stores so that they can benefit from any incentives Levi's may wish to include in its marketing budget.

Conclusion

The management of Levi's have a mountain to climb to restore their lost business. It is unlikely that traditional approaches will be able to deliver the level of recovery required.

The management of Levi's has two choices, namely, use traditional approaches to market recovery which may result in them standing still, or invest in and use state of the art information systems in an attempt to gain competitive advantage through having superior knowledge of the behaviour of jeans consumers.

Test your knowledge

Test your knowledge: questions

1 Which of the following is the most 'customer orientated' method of quoting a price in an export market?

   A   Ex works
   B   FOB
   C   CIF
   D   DDP

2 Which method of payment is the most secure from the supplier's perspective?

   A   Open account
   B   Bill of exchange
   C   Documentary credit

3 'An ethnocentric organisation adapts its products to meet its overseas customers' needs.'

   TRUE OR FALSE?

4 What is AIDA?

5 Briefly describe three types of invoice used in international trade.

6 Identify the competitive forces in the environment of any firm.

7 Describe economies of scale.

8 Identify the elements of the Ansoff matrix.

9 What is the WTO?

10 Describe export-led growth.

11 What are the key aspects of a geocentric approach?

12 Identify the key INCOTERMS.

13 What are the key features of a joint venture?

14 Which currency would minimise the risk to the supplier in an international sales contract?

   A   A third, stable currency
   B   The supplier's currency
   C   The customer's currency

15 Identify the most frequently encountered non-tariff barriers.

16 Describe an 'own brand'.

17 What is undifferentiated marketing in an international marketing context?

18 What are consignment stocks?

19 What is secondary data?

20 Distinguish between products and services.

21 What is a quota, and what is it used for?

22 Describe the features of the product life cycle concept and how it can be applied to international markets.

23 What is the difference between GDP and GNP?

Test your knowledge: questions

24 What is import substitution?

25 What determines exchange rates?

26 What have been the major achievements of GATT?

27 What are the three main forms of regional trading groups, and how do they differ?

28 Identify the problems of using secondary data in international marketing.

29 What are the three main modes of entry into international markets?

30 Identify the advantages of a polycentric approach to international marketing.

31 What are the steps taken by a firm when it moves from a domestic business to an international business?

32 What are the four recognised branding strategies?

33 Identify the quadrants in the BCG growth share matrix.

34 What are the stages in the product development process?

35 What are the elements of the marketing communications mix?

36 What are the key differences between advertising and sales promotion?

37 Identify the elements of the total distribution cost approach.

38 What are the five characteristics of a product which are important in pricing?

Test your knowledge: answers

1   DDP (Delivered Duty Paid).

2   C. (Documentary or Letter of Credit, irrevocable and confirmed by a bank in the suppliers country).

3   False. Ethnocentric organisations operate with a standardised approach to international markets.

4   An acronym for the elements of a marketing communications strategy. A for generating Awareness of the organisation or product; I for creating an Interest in the potential buyer; D for arousing Desire to purchase; and A for Action in the form of a purchase decision.

5   Any three of the following.

    (a) Proforma invoice which can: act as a quotation; enable a foreign buyer to apply for import licences and/or foreign exchange; or ensure a cash with order transaction

    (b) Commercial invoice (a demand for payment).

    (c) Consular invoice (which is issued and approved by the consulate of the buyers country in the suppliers country and is used to control imports).

    (d) Certified invoice which indicates that the goods supplied have been subjected to some form of inspection before shipment.

6   The competitive forces used in the Porter model of industry analysis are: the power of the buyers, the power of the suppliers, the threat of new entrants, the threat of substitutes and the competitive rivalry amongst the existing organisations active in an industry or market.

7   Reduction in the average cost of producing a product in the long run as the volume of output (production) increases.

8   Market penetration. Market development. Product development. Diversification.

9   The World Trade Organisation: an organisation of some 150+ countries with the aim of increasing the level of international trade.

10 Approach adopted to generate economic growth through exporting; sometimes achieved in conjunction with creating protected home markets through tariff and non-tariff barriers.

11 An organisation which adopts a geocentric approach will standardise its marketing approach where appropriate, and adapt its marketing approach where necessary.

12 Ex Works, FAS (Free Along Side), FOB (Free on Board, named port of departure), CIF (Cost Insurance and Freight, named port of destination), DDP (Delivered Duty Paid, named town).

13 A joint venture involves two organisations forming a third company in which the shareholdings and risks are shared. Joint ventures are popular with governments in the developing countries as they enable necessary technology transfer and transfer of essential management skills (including marketing skills) from the developed country to the host country to utilise local resources. From a developed country's perspective a joint venture can enable an organisation to enter an otherwise difficult market.

14 B. The supplier's currency: in this case the buyer is taking all the risks relating to exchange rate movements.

15 Technical barriers. Restricted port of entry barriers. Quotas (restricted import volumes). Restricted use of hard currency (payment difficulties), packaging and labelling requirements.

16 A brand created and supported by a retailer, or a generic term covering goods sold under the retailer's name.

17 Undifferentiated marketing in an international context would be the standardised or ethnocentric approach. An organisation using undifferentiated marketing does not segment the market and hopes as many customers and/or consumers as possible will buy the products. There is no adaptation of the marketing mix.

Test your knowledge: answers

18 Consignment stocks are stocks held by an overseas distributor, but owned by the supplier. The overseas distributor pays for the stock when it is sold on.

19 Data that is collected by third parties (research agencies, government departments etc) for general use. Secondary data is usually not specific for its users' requirements since it will have been collected under unknown conditions. Such data can be highly aggregated and is invariably historic. However, it is usually inexpensive and can assist in specifying the requirements for primary data.

20 Products are tangible items that can be stored, shipped etc, or can be consumed or used away from their point of production. Services are intangible, production (supply) and consumption is usually simultaneous: services cannot be stored.

21 A quota is a non-tariff barrier which restricts the quantity of goods that can be imported into a market. In rare cases a quota may apply to exports. It is a protectionist measure.

22 The main features of the product life cycle are introductory phase (the period after the product launch), the growth phase (the period of growth in demand for the product and a period when competition is attracted), the mature phase (the period of fairly stable demand, competition is usually limited) and the decline phase (the period when demand starts to fall). The international trade product life cycle has the same phases but products can be at different stages of their product life cycle in each market. Trading a product internationally can significantly extend its life cycle.

23 GDP is gross domestic product and is the value of the goods and services produced by an economy in a given time period. GNP is gross national product and is GDP plus income from investments abroad less income paid on foreign investments in the home economy.

24 Import substitution is an approach adopted to create local production facilities thus avoiding the need for imports.

25 Exchange rates are determined by the level of supply and demand for a currency based on the level of international trade.

26 GATT has achieved a significant lowering of tariffs between its member countries. This has led to an expansion in international trade.

27 A free trade area is a regional grouping whose numbers agree to lower barriers to trade amongst themselves. There is very little other form of economic cooperation.

A customs union is a regional grouping where members agree to lower barriers to trade amongst themselves and adopt a common policy on tariff and non-tariff barriers to external countries. The internal barriers amongst the members will be harmonised in the longer term.

An economic union is a regional grouping in which members surrender all decisions relating to internal trade to the union itself. The union will adopt a common policy on tariff and non-tariff barriers to external countries. The members of the union become a single entity.

28 The major problem of secondary data is that it was not originally created for your purposes, therefore problems of interpretation, accuracy and timeliness arise.

29 Indirect exports, direct exports, wholly owned overseas facilities.

30 A polycentric approach is totally customer-focused with the whole of the marketing mix and management control systems adapted to meet the customer's needs.

Test your knowledge: answers

31 *Present activity: domestic marketing*

   Step 1 Experimental involvement usually prompted by an unsolicited order from an overseas customer

   Step 2 Active involvement in which resources are made available to obtain overseas customers

   Step 3 Committed involvement in which the organisation makes a long term commitment to overseas markets usually through direct inward investment in the market.

32 Corporate umbrella brand (eg Heinz, Kellogs, Cadbury's).
    Family umbrella brand (eg own label brands, such as Tesco, used for a wide range of products).
    Range branding (eg Blaupunkt for its range of car entertainment systems).
    Individual brand names (eg Daz used to identify an individual product).

33 Cash Cow. Star. Question Mark. Dog.

34 Idea generation, initial screening, business analysis/appraisal, product development, market testing, commercialisation and launch.

35 Advertising. Sales promotion. Personal selling. Publicity/public relations.

36 Advertising is largely untargeted and impersonal with long term effects. Sales promotion is highly targeted and personal with short term effects.

37 $D = T + W + I + O + P + S$

   Where D = total distribution cost
   T = total transport costs
   W = warehouse cost
   I = inventory cost
   O = order processing and documentation cost
   P = packaging cost
   S = total cost of lost sales for not meeting in performance standards set

38 Frequency of purchase. Degree of necessity. Degree of comparability. Degree of fashion or status. Unit price.

Diploma in Marketing

Test Paper: June 2000

9.52 International Marketing Strategy

3 Hours Duration

> This examination is in two sections.
>
> **Part A** is compulsory and worth 40% of total marks.
>
> **Part B** has six questions, select three. Each answer will be worth 20% of the total marks.
>
> **DO NOT** repeat the question in your answer but show clearly the number of the question attempted.

DO NOT OPEN THIS PAPER UNTIL YOU ARE READY TO START UNDER EXAMINATION CONDITIONS

Test paper: June 2000 questions

PART A

The Mini Case

Knowledge Interact Ltd

Knowledge Interact Ltd, a consultancy specialising in advising organisations how best to make use of their intellectual assets, is a strategic business unit of a large UK based global Information Technology (IT) corporation. Formed in 1996, it had grown rapidly into a £15 million operation. The Board was considering the company's next strategic growth direction.

Knowledge Interact Ltd was one of many organisations which saw early on the power of intellectual capital as contributing more to growth and competitive advantage than the contributions of finance and physical assets have ever done over corresponding periods in the past. The emphasis on raw materials, finance and manpower until the late 1980s saw many companies missing the vast opportunities presented by an organisation's people, process and structures. The Swedish global insurance agency, Skandia, is a classic example. It markets best practice leaflets, manuals and software on internal and external computer networks. Once Skandia had developed an Intranet, intellectual capital was available in hundreds of places simultaneously, giving it a huge potential to lever its earnings and growth. This was witnessed by the fact that Skandia's turnover leapt from £300 million in insurance premiums to £4 billion in less than 10 years.

Knowledge Interact Ltd had gone into the business of advising organisations how to unlock their intellectual capital. It sold its services over the World Wide Web, and provided consultants to clients who responded. It was a natural progression for Knowledge Interact Ltd to start providing more services on the web including online global brand strategy development services and global e-business research sites amongst many other potential activities. It would still need consultants to engage with companies to deliver its core service - that of 'intellectual engineering'.

To aid the decision where to grow next, the company undertook some market research. Basically it required to reach marketing organisations with access to web site facilities, and for Knowledge Interact Ltd itself, it needed a pool of consultants on hand to deliver in-company services. Research showed that North America had the largest number of Internet users in the world (57%), followed by Europe (21.75%) and Asia (17%). (*Source: Nua Internet Services, 1998*). In terms of online money spent, North America far outstripped anywhere else in the world ($4930 million in 1998) compared to the next highest, Europe ($298 million in 1998) of which Germany and the UK were by far the highest online spenders (*Source: Datamonitor and Yankee Group, 1998*). However, this data was insufficient for Knowledge Interact Ltd to make decisions as it was the companies that sold their products online it needed to know about, not the consumer purchases on the various web sites.

The Board of Knowledge Interact Ltd decided on two things. Firstly, it needed to locate its headquarters outside of the UK and nearer to the 'heart of the knowledge industry action'. Secondly, it needed much more research data to aid the decision where to locate and what services to develop online to aid marketers to sell their products and services in a global e-commerce marketplace.

Test paper: June 2000 questions

Question 1

(a) As a consultant contracted to Knowledge Interact Ltd, write a report to the Board indicating clearly the types of market information which it would require to collect to aid the decision:

   (i) On where to locate its new headquarters.

   (ii) The type of online services it would offer to potential web site marketers. (20 marks)

(b) Assume any country of your choice for Knowledge Interact Ltd's new headquarters location. Based on the information suggested in your answer to Question 1(a), write an International Marketing Plan for Knowledge Interact Ltd for the first 3 years of its operation in this new location. (20 Marks)

(40 marks)

PART B - Answer THREE Questions Only

Question 2

Recent mega mergers in the car industry are typical of the late 1990's 'merger mania' trend. What is the rationale behind such mergers and how will it lead to global competitive advantage? **(20 marks)**

Question 3

A UK based tourism company is wishing to break into long haul holidays in either India, Malaysia, Zimbabwe or South America. Identify the marketing intelligence required to aid the company's decision on one destination only. **(20 marks)**

Question 4

Manchester United Football Club (MUFC) is one of the world's best known brands. Explain why, with its apparent 'standardised' product/market strategy, MUFC has been able to establish this position.

(20 marks)

Question 5

It has been suggested that the best way for developed countries to market into developing countries is via another developing country. Using examples, explain the reasoning behind this proposition and its implications on the organisation and resources of a developed country based multinational.

(20 marks)

Question 6

Answer only **one** of the following.

EITHER

(a) Traditional methods of planning and control in international marketing are becoming increasingly questioned due to the effects of the rapidly turbulent environment. Outline the

Test paper: June 2000 questions

more recent developments in planning and control and show how they are more suitable to today's marketing environment. **(20 marks)**

OR

(b) The increasingly turbulent environment makes international planning and control activity difficult to operationalise. How can planners attempt to cope with this problem? **(20 marks)**

Question 7

Answer only **one** of the following.

EITHER

(a) Identifying specific examples, show how recent developments in marketing software can help international marketers target their marketing strategies more precisely. **(20 marks)**

OR

(b) Citing specific examples, show how marketing databases can help international marketers target their marketing strategies more precisely. **(20 marks)**

Suggested answers

**DO NOT TURN THIS PAGE UNTIL YOU
HAVE COMPLETED THE TEST PAPER**

1 (a)

Report to the Board

Subject: International Marketing Information

Prepared by: Chaucer Consultants

Date: June 2000

Introduction

This report outlines the types of **market information** which you, the board of Knowledge Interact, need to collect, analyse and evaluate to inform your decisions regarding the location of your new headquarters. As your consultants we would be delighted to be allowed to bid for undertaking the necessary research.

The process for specifying the information required

With so much data and information available, the **objectives** for the information collection will be closely focused on that information that will assist a location decision and the service portfolio to offer clients.

Accordingly, the majority of the information relating to location will come from **secondary sources** due to its immediate availability and low cost. This secondary information will be screened in order to select a shortlist of candidate locations from which **primary** information can be obtained which will allow a final choice of headquarters location to be made.

The information will be collected under the broad headings of **environmental**, **market** and **competitive** factors and will be analysed using a suitable form of location attractiveness/company compatibility matrix.

Location information - secondary sources

Initially broad geographic areas of the world will be selected, i.e. Pacific Rim, West Coast USA, East Coast USA, Western Europe, Australasia, from which to gather information and classify it for analysis.

Environmental information

This will include in the following.

(i) National government or regional government incentives for attracting business to the particular region or location

(ii) Specific incentives to attract high-tech, knowledge based, companies

(iii) Levels of education in general and particularly in the management strata from which the consultants will be recruited

(iv) Levels of use of English

(v) Acceptance of management consultants within the local and regional business community

(vi) The level of rent, rates and local taxes

Market information

This information will focus on establishing the dynamics of the market place, particularly with respect to growth in the use of intellectual assets.

(i) The creation and availability of brands in the local economy estimated from assessing the concentration of advertising for particular products and/or services

(ii) The use of web-sites and e-commerce for the promotion of both products and services

(iii) The number of consulting firms specialising in the general area of e-commerce assessed from web-sites or Yellow Pages

(iv) The number of specialist logistics companies

(v) Significant changes in employment patterns between the manufacturing sector and the service sector

Competitive information

These will include identifying the following.

(i) The number of major companies with either corporate headquarters or regional headquarters in the various locations which could be attracted to the concept of exploiting their intellectual assets - this will give an approximation of the size of the potential customer base

(ii) Salary rates and scales for the types of people likely to be attracted to, and be suitable for, the highly specialised consulting posts to be offered by KI

(iii) Political, economic and financial stability of the local and regional infrastructure

(iv) Estimates of the costs of operating in locations within the selected regions, which will have an impact on the level of fees charged and the profitability of the location

Location Information - primary sources and the type of on-line services that KI should offer.

The primary information will be collected using **interviews** with the local regional development authorities, and the major companies operating out of the selected locations in order to verify the information obtained from the secondary research phase.

As well as verifying the location information the primary research will need to focus on obtaining information that will help to establish the type of services the potential clients in the locations require. This primary research can either be undertaken by suitably experienced KI personnel or contracted out to a local research agency.

Typically, the information required will be as follows.

(i) The types of consulting services the potential clients are likely to require and whether they will be prepared to pay for such a service. Also it will be vital to establish whether the service will be expected to be provided on-line and remotely or will require personal contact.

(ii) Should the services be required to be provided through personal contact then the distribution density and location of potential clients becomes important. This will be key information if personal contact is required as it will have a major impact on the overall charge to the client.

(iii) The size and type of potential client businesses. This can be used as a first approximation of the level of fees that can be charged.

(iv) The level of fees the potential clients may be prepared to pay for the services, together with estimates of the level of fees for consulting services in the region.

(v) The type and nature of competitive or substitute offerings available in the location. This would include other consulting firms as well as education providers in the region, and the willingness of potential clients to develop their own in-house skills.

Test paper: June 2000 suggested answers

(vi) An assessment of business practice with respect to the use of consultancies and whether there is evidence of long term relationships between consulting firm and client or whether consulting services are purchased on an as needed basis

(b) Marketing plan for Los Angeles for 2001/2003

Introduction

Los Angeles has been targeted as the location of the KI's headquarters due to its central position in California and the dominant role in Internet technology played by companies located on the West Coast of the USA. US companies are known to use consulting firms on a long-term basis, unlike companies in the UK. Also, the West Coast of the USA is almost equidistant to the growing technology markets of Europe and South East Asia.

Company objectives

- To triple turnover within three years to £50 million pounds
- To achieve a net profit of at least £5 million per year

Assumptions

KI has the necessary financial resources to invest in a programme of market development.

The marketing plan

Marketing objectives. By the end of year 1 to have achieved a base of 50 clients, which by the end of the planning period in 2003 should have increased to 250.

Target markets. The specific target markets will be the companies developing state of the art technology products and services, who are looking for ways to get their products and services to the widest possible marketplace in the shortest possible time. It is estimated that for KI to generate between £30 and £40 million of sales from California and neighbouring States an investment in marketing of around £3 million pounds will be needed for each year of the three-year period.

The bulk of this investment will be in the **promotional mix**, potentially **personal selling** costs. Hence the target clients must be capable of spending around £160,000 each, per year, on consulting services. Thus there is a need to develop long term relationships with the clients through appropriate use of the service elements of the marketing mix.

Marketing mix. This will concentrate primarily on the promotional aspects and the **service** elements of the marketing mix, such that the promotion creates a high level of **awareness** of KI's presence in the market place and the customers it is attempting to target, together with establishing the service KI is offering.

Product. This will be a range of consulting services that will allow clients to exploit their intellectual assets. This may range from modifying the existing databases of clients through to developing new internal processes for clients, such as period end reporting processes based on web technology.

Price. KI should aim to achieve a **premium price** wherever practical after taking into account local competition. If a premium price cannot be obtained then the marketing objectives may need to be re-visited since as set they are based on clients willing to spend £160,000 per year on consulting services.

Place and the **service elements.** Since the product is a consulting service it is essential that the appropriate calibre of people are recruited who can be developed to deliver the KI solutions. Unless the product/service can be delivered remotely over the Internet then the

Test paper: June 2000 suggested answers

place will be the client's premises that will demand highly competent people to deliver the client's expectations.

The **process** will have to be distinctive, which in consulting terms means completing the assignment on time and to initial cost estimate. This ensures a good chance of repeat business. The **physical evidence** is linked closely with the people and the process, and needs to concentrate on developing clients for the long term.

Implementation and control

An organisation structure needs to be in place with a Country Manager supported by local staff. One of the key issues that needs to be decided is whether KI should employ all its own consultants, or sub-contract on an as needed basis from appropriate small consulting firms. This will have a major impact on the service elements of the marketing mix. If KI decide to use local consulting service providers the people element will need careful control, otherwise KI could be training and developing its own competitors.

The major **control measure** for the three-year programme will be the rate at which clients are acquired and retained. A primary control mechanism will need to be established based on the ratios between numbers of enquiries received, numbers of visits and quotations to potential clients, and number of clients obtained. Secondary control measures will be based on the level of repeat business by client and service type.

These control mechanisms can be in terms of numbers of **clients** or **monetary value**. The control mechanism will need to be sensitive to the sources of the enquiries such that the promotional effort can be targeted at the clients showing the greatest prospects for KI.

Conclusion

KI is entering a **highly competitive marketplace** and will need to be both distinctive and agile to ensure that the services it provides are always at the leading edge of client's needs. To be highly effective in this market KI will need to be **developing services** that their existing and potential clients do not yet know they require.

2

The rationale for **mergers** within any industry can be classified under two broad headings, namely, the **economic rationale** and the **marketing rationale**. The global car industry is no exception to the merger phenomenon. Mergers are always justified from the perspective of **improving competitive advantage** for both parties to the merger, regardless of how short lived the advantage may be.

The economic rationale

The principal rationale behind a merger is to gain **economies of scale** in terms of production (numbers of cars produced), the range of cars produced, and in research and development Competitive pressures from previous mergers also add to the argument and justify merging to avoid the fear of being left behind. Mergers can give access to **technologies** or **cash** (for R and D or market development) which may not otherwise be available.

Rationalisation of production lines and product lines are both a rationale for a merger and a consequence of a merger. Mergers tend to demonstrate **risk averse behaviour** in which the management teams of both parties are staying close to their comfort zone of knowledge and practice.

Test paper: June 2000 suggested answers

The marketing rationale

Economies of scale also apply to marketing activities, particularly **promotional expenditure** and the **distribution costs** of vehicles. Market development costs may be minimised due to the marketing presence of the merged companies complementing one another. Product development costs may be minimised due to product lines complementing one another.

Market shares will increase for the merged company that can act as a **deterrent** to predators. Alex Trotman, a former Chairman of Ford, claimed that a merger between Ford and Fiat in the mid-1980s would have produced a combined company with a 25% share of the European car market which would be considerably stronger than Fiat and Ford's individual 12% market share.

Mergers allow for rationalisation of marketing effort and associated reduction in marketing expenditure.

Aspects of competitive advantage

Economies of scale in both production and marketing will lead to lower costs and hence more competitive **prices**. Economies of scale in R and D should lead to **better products** offering wider customer choice hence enhancing **market share**. Consumers tend to be reassured by the size of an organisation.

Products can be **standardised** in particular locations with the pre-sales, sales and after sales **service** being **adapted** to suit the requirements of particular locations. Thus the merged company may **think globally** in terms of where it chooses to produce its vehicles, but **acts locally** in terms of the presentation and service to its vehicle owners.

Mergers can also allow significant support for **niche products** that otherwise may not be available. For instance, the support the Jaguar brand receives as part of Ford is significantly greater than Jaguar could offer the brand as an independent or as a brand within a much smaller vehicle manufacturer's portfolio.

3

For each of the prospective countries and region the Tourism Company will need the following information and intelligence:-

(a) A rigorous assessment of its own **resources,** (financial, human, operations and market) and capabilities to ascertain whether it is practical to break into the long haul holiday market. Although this market may appear attractive from the outside, the company needs to be aware that unless the internal resources are available, and capable of supporting an entry into this highly competitive market (in which it may take a long time to become established) then the internal issues become the controlling factors for the decision

(b) **Country/region characteristics**

    (i) **Geography.** Particularly climate and its seasonality, any natural attraction such as Victoria Falls in Zimbabwe. The general infrastructure, particularly transport in the region, will be critical to the success of the area.

    (ii) **Language.** Use of English

    (iii) **Political factors.** The stability of the selected regions need rigorous assessment as tourists have demonstrated that they will shun any areas of instability and any long haul holidays if any conflict is around, irrespective of whether the destination is affected. Currently, mid-2000, Zimbabwe looks politically unstable with land reforms creating significant problems for the minority white population.

(iv) **Security.** As above, personal security goes hand in glove with political stability. Any anti-West feelings have a significant impact on tourist buying behaviour

(v) **Demography.** This will impact on the type of person likely to be employed in the tourist sector of the economy and their attitude towards tourists particularly those from the west/Northern Europe.

(vi) **Economic development.** The level of economic development will give an indication of how well the service sector has been developed. This is vital information for tourists, as hotel accommodation and restaurant populations are essential.

(vii) **Technology.** Particularly the technology relating to access to money and telecommunications

(viii) **Religion.** Any taboos or particular festivals which may impact on Western tourists

Most of this country information will be available from **web sites** promoting each of the countries for both inward investment and tourism, and should be of sufficient quality to make a choice of destination.

The information will need to be **screened** on a country by country basis, as illustrated in Table 1, in which each factor for each country/region will be given a score out of, say 10, and the country with the highest score becomes the selected destination.

Alternatively, for each country/region a much more detailed **country attractiveness/company capability** and position to compete screening process could be undertaken as shown in Table 2. Again, each factor for each country/region will be given a score and the country with the highest score becomes the selected destination.

	India	Malaysia	Zimbabwe	South America
Geography				
Language				
Political				
Security				
Economic Development				
Technology				
Religion				
TOTAL				

Table 1 Country Selection

EG. India	Company capability or position to compete		
	Weak	Average	Strong
Market Attractiveness			
Number of attractions			
Language			
Culture			
Stability			
Infrastructure			
Etc			
TOTAL			

Table 2 An alternative selection matrix by country

4

Football is a standardised game played to standardised rules on a global scale. Thus, any football supporter, irrespective of where they are in the world, is intimately aware of the game, the pleasure to be gained from watching the matches and the feeling of belongingness to the game that is obtained by acquiring the merchandise associated with football and its teams. Football supporters during the last ten years have been able to enjoy matches played live via satellite TV irrespective of location.

Football clubs all around the world have realised the power of the game and also the **business benefits** that can be derived from the desire to buy merchandise and products relating to the club. Thus standardised **marketing strategies** have been developed around the game of football. Many of the larger clubs (particularly clubs with global reputations such as Manchester United) make more money from merchandise sales (e.g. replica playing strip for casual wear) than they take at the gates. It is frequently claimed that fewer than 8% of the members of Manchester United's global supporters club have ever visited Old Trafford.

All the major football clubs of the world are exploiting the global **youth culture** that football and satellite broadcasting has helped to create. Young people all around the world enjoy wearing and promoting the merchandise of their favourite clubs.

Manchester United is one of the few clubs to have its own web-site incorporating TV, exploiting the latest **technology** to ensure it provides its supporters/customers with what they require. **Sponsorship** of football clubs by product and service providers gives the clubs another source of revenue and gives the sponsor 90 minutes of TV exposure every game, for the cost of the sponsorship rather than the cost of the air-time.

Aspects of consumer behaviour

The standardisation of sport scale enables supporters of particular sports to be organised into **segments** with identical attitudes, values and opinions, irrespective of all other cultural differences. Thus a Manchester United supporter in Hong Kong is likely to behave towards the game in the same way as a supporter in Halifax or Hamburg. Their life styles may be significantly different but their interest in football and the club will be the same, and therefore they will want the merchandise to demonstrate their allegiance to the club.

In general, supporters of any global sport demonstrate **segmentation by connection** rather than the traditional **segmentation by division**, and organisations can effectively exploit those factors that connect the supporter with the sport.

Brand loyalty

Football can be considered to be a brand of sport, and MUFC as a brand within the sport. The brand football is globally standardised as mentioned above - it is played to globally standardised rules, and MUFC has developed to become a standardised club brand within the football brand. Therefore, it is probable that a football supporter develops loyalty to the sport first, followed by loyalty to a particular club, e.g. Manchester United. High levels of customer loyalty and a standardised global brand are a powerful combination of forces, especially when linked through global broadcasting.

It is this loyalty to both the game and the club that is exploited through sponsorship, both by the club and the sponsoring organisation. The supporters of a particular club are often of a type that the sponsoring company would like to have as brand loyal to them. For instance, Sharp who sponsor Manchester United are probably anticipating that Manchester United supporters will be drawn to the Sharp portfolio of products.

5

Empirical evidence from regions of Africa seems to support the view that it is easier to enter a second African market from an existing African market than it is to enter the market from Europe, the United States or any other developed country. Similar phenomena can be observed in the patterns of trade between Singapore and Malaysia. For some organisations it is easier to enter Malaysia from Singapore, and vice versa, than it is to enter from Europe or the USA.

Reasons found to support the view include regional similarities of **culture,** for instance, Zambians are psychologically closer to Zimbabweans than they are to the English. Both countries are at similar **levels of development**, having similar **literacy** rates, **employment** rates and **personal incomes**, which will impact on product demand and response to promotion.

Both countries have a similar climate that will impact on **product characteristics** of presentation and distribution, and both were former colonies of the UK. Thus, trade between Zambia and Zimbabwe is likely to be easier to exploit than trade between the countries of Europe and either country individually (except in those instances when trade is tied to aid).

Other areas of Africa, particularly the neighbouring West African States of Nigeria, Ghana and the Ivory Coast, also share similar cultures and entry into one and using this as a staging post to enter the others is frequently exploited by European multi-nationals, e.g. Unilever.

In general, developing countries typically have very similar **infrastructures** including, usually, very similar **political systems** (these countries usually have a dominant ruling party) and **economic systems** (usually a form of **centrally planned economy**).

Many of these countries have been created from boundaries drawn by the European colonising powers of the last 500 years, and do not take into account the historical tribal and territory boundaries. Therefore, what Europeans see as cross-migration between countries is, in reality and practice, movement within the territories of the historic tribal communities - a single market. The customers in these cross border territories have common cultures, beliefs, opinions, and do not accept totally the precision used by the European cartographers to define country boundaries.

Test paper: June 2000 suggested answers

In terms of organisation, the developed country based multinational may have to set up a **decentralised locally ethnocentric organisational structure** that takes account of the tribal boundaries, territories and groupings as well as respecting the imposed political boundaries.

To be effective this locally ethnocentric organisation will require a fairly high level of **autonomy** so that it can exploit **local opportunities** in its terms rather than the terms imposed from a distant headquarters. The local headquarters will have to employ more **locals** than **expatriates** so that customers can relate to the people as well as the product.

The product and market development will be based more on the needs of the **regional groupings**, rather than from exploiting economies of scale dictated by global headquarters. Hence there will be less of a need for standardised products and services and more **adaptation**. Promotion adapted to suit the local culture will be more effective than the promotion used in the markets of the developed world.

The organisation that chooses to adapt in order to exploit the trading phenomena in the developing world will undoubtedly require more resources. The rewards will be greater from adapting operations to suit local conditions than the rewards produced from insisting on a standardised approach.

More investment in **training** will be required for the local staff to understand the product and service and how it can be adapted to suit local needs. The staff in the headquarters in the developed country will require more training in order to learn how to maximise profit from adapted operations.

Using and expanding resources in one developing country to gain entry into a neighbouring developing country may appear on the surface to conflict with economies of scale arguments practised by the organisations of the developed world. However, when the wider **cultural** and **customer behaviour** aspects of the developing region are considered this may be the most effective and profitable approach.

6 (a)

The rapidly changing business environment is influenced by the following factors.

(i) Changes in the **competitive offerings** (products and services) resulting from organisations wanting to differentiate their offerings to gain competitive advantage

(ii) **Competitive advantage** being achieved through exploiting changes in **technology** or through developing new technology to create both differentiated products and new products

(iii) Both of the above will result in changes in **consumer tastes** which will be exacerbated by the **shorter product life cycles** created by organisations exploiting differentiation and new technology

(iv) Greater **environmental awareness** amongst consumers creating pressure to change the old ways of doing things

(v) **Consumer reactions** to changes in governmental and economic solutions

(vi) **Rapid innovation**, particularly with respect to **communication technology** which is resulting in more awareness of what is going on in the world

Traditional **planning and control methodology** is based on the assumption of a stable or slowly changing environment. The introduction of the principles of **mass production** by Ford in the 1920's demonstrated that standardised products and reducing prices due to improving economies of scale could create a steadily growing and manageable demand pattern. This has led to planning processes which are very time consuming to execute and which run the risk that the environment could change.

Traditional planning activities have developed and produced the following.

(i) An obsession with attempting to collect all the data and information rather than the essential data. This results in **information overload** and adds to the time required to develop the plan due to the level of analysis required.

(ii) Too many activities and people involved in the process

(iii) Planning documents of such complexity that the resulting implementation of the plans are poor

(iv) Inadequate and inappropriate **feedback and control systems** built into the plans, which add to the problems of implementation

(v) A planning methodology that is out of date

New approaches to planning involve the following.

(i) The use of **computerised decision support systems** which perform much of the traditional manual analysis and can produce numerous "**what if**" scenarios for the planners to choose from

(ii) The development of **expert** or **knowledge systems** out of existing management information systems, which will produce the optimum plan from a given set of data and information

(iii) The development of planning processes based on recognising **incremental or emerging changes** in the business environment. Henry Mintzberg and James Quinn have created a methodology around working with **emerging strategies** and **logical incrementalism**.

The new approaches to planning concentrate on obtaining and processing the **relevant data** only, thus reducing the number of people required to undertake the process, and speeding up the planning process. The speed with which plans can be prepared, approved and implemented is an essential factor for success in a rapidly changing business environment.

6 (b)

Turbulent markets have been created by the following influences (as for the previous question).

(i) Changes in the **competitive offerings** (products and services) resulting from organisations wanting to differentiate their offerings to gain competitive advantage

(ii) **Competitive advantage** being achieved through exploiting changes in **technology** or through developing new technology to create both differentiated products and new products

(iii) Both of the above contributing to changes in **consumer tastes** that have resulted in **shorter product life cycles** from organisations exploiting differentiation and new technology

(iv) Greater **environmental awareness** amongst consumers creating pressure to change the old ways of doing things

(v) **Consumer reactions** to changes in governmental and economic solutions

(vi) **Rapid innovation,** particularly with respect to **communication technology** which is resulting in more awareness of what is going on in the world

Turbulent markets require very **rapid responses** in order for organisations to survive. Some of the methods planners are adopting to enable them to plan effectively in an increasingly uncertain environment are as follows.

(i) The use of computerised decision support systems which perform much of the traditional manual analysis and can produce numerous "what if" scenarios for the planners to choose from

(ii) The development of **expert** or **knowledge systems** out of existing management information systems, which will produce the optimum plan from a given set of data and information

(iii) The development of planning processes based on recognising **incremental** or **emerging changes** in the business environment. Henry Mintzberg and James Quinn have created a methodology around working with **emerging strategies** and **logical incrementalism**.

Some organisations (notably Saatchi's) have abandoned the annual budget and 3-year planning methodology in favour of working to 100-day plans. The rationale for this significant departure from tradition is that the senior management team can be fairly confident of what is likely to happen over the next 3 months, and can manage the business very effectively and profitably over this time horizon. In turbulent markets the prospects for being able to stabilise the environment are not good, so organisations need to develop strategies to enable them to cope with a rapidly changing environment, i.e. rapid response.

In general, the planning horizon will reflect the **risk profile** of the planners and decision-makers. Risk averse planners and decision-makers will have to learn to adapt to making and changing plans in rapid succession to allow them to minimise their risk and exposure. Risk neutral planners and decision makers are likely to use a combination of the traditional (3 - 5 year planning horizons) and the new (quarterly planning horizon) to establish which is the most effective and profitable. Risk taking planners are likely to stay with the traditional methods as they are more prepared to take risks over the long term.

7 (a)

The most significant developments in marketing software over the last ten years have been in **database** and **web based software**.

Databases, particularly those linked to **EPOS systems** through loyalty schemes allow marketers to understand and segment their customers with levels of precision not achieved in the past. EPOS systems were once considered to be stock control systems but the data such systems capture about consumer buying behaviour give them a value to marketers way beyond the designers original specifications.

Most retailers in the developed world with EPOS systems and loyalty card schemes combine the two sets of data into a common database to mail-shot customers with information regarding special offers and forthcoming new product launches. This is highly **targeted promotional activity** since the EPOS system will have tracked customer purchases over a period of time and will know that, for instance, a particular customer has a propensity for responding to special offers or for trying new products.

Marketing database software enables organisations to develop marketing plans that more closely meet the needs of customers. In particular, marketing objectives can be set which reflect the potential customer's individual characteristics, so that market segments of one could be considered for **target marketing**. **Segmentation software** based on postcodes, such as PINPOINT, can get down to market segments of a handful of households. The assumption underpinning this degree of detail is that very similar people will live in close proximity to one another. Similar assumptions underpin both ACORN and MOSAIC.

Web based software allows site owners to identify visitors to their sites and from the click trails enable profiles of these potential customers. Several organisations using web-based technology are offering customers **products produced to specification** and delivered to them very quickly. The National Cycle Company of Japan pioneered the concept of producing bicycles tailor made to suit individual specification, irrespective of where in the world the customer is located. Jeans manufacturers have followed suit and some motor companies, notably Daewoo, are allowing customers to specify their particular cars from a Daewoo controlled menu. **E-commerce** in its widest possible context is impacting significantly on the **product element** of the marketing mix.

Much is currently being written regarding the **pull effect** of marketing communication between consumers and web sites, compared with the **push effect** of conventional advertising and promotion. The software used to promote an organisation through a web site needs to be capable of connecting with as many people as possible through the use of images, language and site navigation to ensure the maximum number of customer connections are made and retained.

Implementation and control of marketing programmes is more easily undertaken with real-time data. The effectiveness of promotional programmes can be easily measured at the point of sale from the EPOS data. If the customer is using a loyalty card and has received a promotional mail-shot then the response to the mail-shot can be accurately assessed and its effectiveness measured. Customer response to **new product launches** is also very easily evaluated using EPOS data. Similarly, web based companies can assess customer response as it occurs.

In summary, marketing software allows companies to benefit from reduced **time and effort** (and ultimately the cost) involved in targeting marketing strategies through the use of continuously updated information.

7 (b)

Many companies have become marketing household names on the basis of their marketing databases, namely, **Experian** of the UK, with its Mosaic software, and **CACI** of the United States with its Acorn software. MOSAIC and ACORN databases are designed to assist in the market segmentation process and are derived from comprehensive **geographic** (location) and **demographic** data (e.g. electoral rolls, type of property etc.) Both of these software shells have been adapted to suit the data available for many of the countries of the world and provide international marketers with **geo-demographic databases**.

Segmentation processes, and **segmentation software,** are designed to identify the particular **target groups of customers** required by the company. Manual segmentation processes are exceedingly time consuming and prone to error. Segmentation using software is very fast and is less prone to error, providing the original data and any amendments have been accurately entered. In general, the more accurate the segmentation the less waste is incurred in the marketing programme, and more profit can be generated.

MINTEL and Euromonitor, both UK companies, provide good databases for marketing research purposes, which although containing **secondary information** are nonetheless an excellent staring point for establishing the prospects for products and services.

Any browse of the **Internet** for **marketing software** will produce a seemingly endless list of companies offering software solutions for marketing planning, strategic analysis, sales monitoring etc. All companies offer similar benefits to users of their software. Benefits can be derived from the **speed** with which plans can be prepared once the thinking has been done, and the **accuracy** with which the strategies and plans can be **targeted** at particular customer segments. Some software is now available to assist in the thinking process, but most software leaves the final decision making to the user.

Some of the software developed to aid strategic thinking has become a holder for the company's **expert strategic management knowledge** through:-

(i) Identifying **drivers of long term profitability.** This will include identifying those **customers** who generate the most and consistent profit for particular products or ranges of products and identifying **returns from particular investments** in fixed assets, human assets, and marketing programmes by type of programme. Key to this identification is the **precision of the segmentation** provided by the marketing databases.

(ii) Measuring **competitive advantage**. This is effected through a **benchmarking** process comparing the company and its activities with its competitors

(iii) Undertaking **competitor analysis** to identify competing product portfolios and marketing programmes to establish the segments targeted and hence improve the company's competitive position

(iv) Performing **risk analyses** to determine the **risk and reward profile** of the various target groups so that the groups with the lowest relative risks and highest relative returns are selected as targets

The EXMAR suite of strategic marketing planning software from The Marketing Planning Process Company, and the Portfolio Plus suite from Strategic Dynamics Ltd, both UK based, will undertake the activities described above.

The SAP suite of software generically described as Enterprise Resource Planning software is currently estimated to be market leader in **business control software**.

The benefits to companies using marketing databases for planning and control purpose are derived from improved **accuracy** of data and information, rapid access to the right information, and the opportunity to work from the most up-to-date information. All of these benefits reduce waste and lead to improved profits.

Topic index

Topic index

12 Cs, 138
7 Ps, 143

Accessibility, 137
ACORN, 64, 66, 96, 109, 138
Acquisition, 73
Adaptation, 114, 115, 16
Adapted mixes, 56
Administration, 72
Advanced industrialised countries, 103
Advertising research, 113
Age distribution, 47
Agents, 73, 117
AICs, 103, 104
Air-time costs, 114
Alliances, 73
Amazon.com, 65
Analogies, 68
Appraisal schemes, 93
ASEAN, 37
Authority, 93

Balance of payments, 49
Barriers to entry, 46, 68, 69
Basic demand, 68
BERI, 67
Blame culture, 95
Brand, 104, 140
Brand adaptations, 116
Brand management, 107
Budget, 159
Business environment, 155, 156
Buyer behaviour, 57, 58, 111, 137
Buying habits, 42, 99

CACI, 64, 66
Call centres, 90
Centralisation, 107
Centralised structure, 135
CIF, 128, 129
Climate, 116
Cluster analysis, 68
Coca Cola, 115
Command and control, 93
Command economies, 48
Commercial infrastructure, 68
Common market, 126
Communication, 68, 69
Company compatibility, 137
Comparative advantage, 37
Comparative analysis, 42, 45, 64
Comparative standards, 132
Competence, 116
Competition, 68, 69
Competitive environment, 115

Competitive forces, 68
Consumer confidence, 42
Consumer profiles, 68
Contact and response, 139
Contract manufacture, 74, 85
Control, 72, 108, 117, 131, 147
Control issues, 139
Control systems, 135, 159
Convergence, 42
Convergence of consumer needs, 83
Co-operation strategies, 74
Countertrade, 126
Country attractiveness, 137
Credit periods, 154
Cultural differences, 48, 56, 106
Cultural sensitivity, 114
Culture, 54, 58, 84
Currency fluctuations, 75, 85, 125
Customers, 68
Customiser, 160

Data security, 91
Databases, 111
Decentralised structure, 135
Decision Making Unit (DMU), 61
Demand patterns, 68
Demographic, 116
Differentiated, 156
Differentiation, 78, 80
Differentiator, 160
Direct exporting, 71, 73
Direct investment, 71, 88
Direct inward investment, 73, 148
Direct selling, 137
Distribution, 68, 140
Distribution and logistics, 119, 120
Distributors, 73
Doole, Lowe and Phillips, 67
Duplication, 44
Dynamic databases, 111

Early entrants, 112
Economic development, 115
Economic union, 126
Economies of scale, 44, 56, 114
Economist Intelligence Unit (EIU), 63
Electronic commerce, 65, 90, 134
Emerging market, 68
Environmental variables, 159
EPOS, 96, 162
Ethnocentric, 44, 84, 88
EU, 37
EuroMOSAIC, 138
Evaluation, 131
Exchange rate, 54

Topic index

Existing markets, 67
Expatriate, 84
Experian, 64, 66
Export houses/trading companies, 73
Export statistics, 68
External factors, 155

Financial implications, 82
Financial risk, 74, 85
Financial services, 106
FOB, 128, 129
Focus groups, 138, 152
Ford, 44
Foreign distributor, 116
Foreign exchange receipts, 155
Forward buying, 126
Fragmentation, 160
Franchises, 136, 137, 140
Franchising, 73, 74, 85, 121, 137
Free trade area, 126

Gatekeeper, 61
GATT, 37
Generic marketing strategy, 157
Generic product, 102
Geocentricity, 88
Gilligan and Hird, 67
Global brands, 80, 82, 115, 116
Global communications media, 90
Global consumer, 41, 82, 119, 120
Global marketing approach, 60
Global marketing strategy, 45
Global position, 109, 134
Global village, 121
Globalisation, 44, 82
Glocalisation, 144
GNP or GDP, 46
Government regulations, 121
Gross National Product, 43
Growth potential, 69

Harrell and Keifer matrix, 137, 161
Hertzberg, 92
Heterogeneity, 105
High context, 58
Household expenditure surveys, 137
Human assets, 95

Import duties, 125
Import regulations, 140
Incipient markets, 67
Incoterms, 128, 129
Indirect exporting, 71, 73
Influencer, 61
Information System, 95, 102

Information technology, 42, 121
Innovation, 102
Inseparability, 106
Intangibility, 105
Integrated supply chain management systems, 119
Intelligence bases, 111
Inter-conglomerate, 88
Interconnected, 42
Interdependent, 42
Interglomerate, 97
Internal factors, 155
International communications strategy, 114
International marketing strategy, 90, 114
International trade statistics, 64
Internationalisation, 84, 120
Internet, 66, 90
Investment assistance, 155
Investment capital, 85

Joint venture, 71, 74, 85

Kenichi Omae, 133
Knowledge assets, 95
Knowledge based systems, 134
Knowledge management, 160

Latent markets, 67
LDCs, 103, 104
Letter of credit, 125
Levi's, 111
Licensing, 74, 85
Life cycles, 68
Lifestyle, 112
Local advantages, 140
Local approach, 140
Local sales staff, 94
Logistics, 124
Loyalty cards, 111
Loyalty schemes, 96

Macropyramid, 88, 97
Majaro, 97
Management systems, 132
Manufacture under licence, 70, 73
Manufacturing licence, 88
Market adaptation, 80
Market attractiveness/company compatibility matrix, 161
Market concentration, 149
Market development, 148, 156, 157, 159
Market economy, 48
Market entry, 73, 85, 148
Market entry investment, 70
Market entry methods, 156

Topic index

Market entry strategy, 150
Market extension strategy, 149
Market growth, 146
Market intelligence, 64
Market penetration, 125, 157
Market research, 64, 65, 66
Market selection, 148, 155
Market share, 146
Market size, 66, 69, 137
Market skimming, 125
Market spreading, 157
Marketing, 102
Marketing audit, 143
Marketing databases, 96
Marketing goals, 145
Marketing information system, 61
Marketing objectives, 112, 157
Marketing research, 89, 144
Marketing strategy, 146
Marlborough, 115
Mass, 116
Mastercard, 65
McDonalds, 111, 115, 120, 121
Media availability, 107
Merger, 73
Minimum order quantities, 140
MIS, 159
MkMIS, 136
MNE, 87
Monczka, 122
Monitoring, 117
Mosaic, 64, 109
Motivation, 45, 92, 134
Multidomestic strategy, 149
Multi-factor analysis, 64
Multinational, 86, 87, 108, 122, 123

NAFTA, 37
National statistics, 137
New product development process, 103
Newly industrialised countries, 103
Niche, 116
NICs, 103, 104
Nike, 112, 115
Non tariff barriers, 38
NPD, 79, 97, 98

Objectives, 139, 141
OECD, 62
Open tender, 60
Operations, 83
Organisation structure, 83, 97
Overseas production, 71
Overseas subsidiaries, 84

Packaging, 104
Pan-European brands, 141
Pan-European retailers, 157
Pan-European segments, 138
Partnerships, 73
Penetration strategy, 140
People, 143, 146, 162
Perception, 120
Performance, 128, 129
Performance criteria, 112, 129, 139, 141
Performance indicators, 135
Performance standards, 132
Perishability, 105
Physical evidence, 141, 143, 146, 162
Piggyback, 65
Pizza Hut, 120
Place, 57, 81, 147, 143
Planning and control, 106
Political and legal, 107
Political hostility, 106
Political risks, 75, 85
Polycentric, 88
Porter's five forces, 43
Positioning, 158
Premium price, 158
Price, 57, 69, 81, 143, 147
Price setting, 125
Price/quality perceptions, 116
Price/value relationships, 116
Pricing, 140
Pricing decisions, 125
Pricing policy, 124
Primary data, 68, 138
Primary information, 62
Primary research, 63, 68, 69, 137, 138
Procedures, 146
Processes, 143, 162
Product, 57, 78, 81, 139, 143, 146, 147
Product life cycles, 37
Product portfolio analysis, 50
Product standardisation, 37, 81, 97
Product strategy, 44, 139, 158
Profit, 70
Profitability, 66, 137
Promotion, 57, 81, 143
Promotion mix, 158
Promotional issues, 140
Promotional support, 118
Proxy measure, 64, 136
Push and pull strategies, 107

R&D, 79
Recognition and reward, 96
Regiocentricity, 88
Regional and cultural differences, 141
Regional expansion strategy, 149

Topic index

Regression analysis, 64, 65, 68
Repatriation of profits, 75, 85, 86
Reports, 117
Research methodology, 138
Resources, 83, 84
Responsibility, 93
Retailers, 120
Return on Capital Employed, 125
Return on Investment, 125
Ricardo, 37
Risk and control, 85
Risk and revenue sharing agreements, 76

Satellite broadcasting, 114
Scanning process, 136
Scoring model, 117
Screening procedure, 117
Secondary data, 62
Secondary information, 143
Secondary research, 63, 68, 69, 88, 136, 138
Segment, 120
Segmentation, 63, 65
Segmentation analysis, 137
Selection procedure, 116
Selection process, 140
Selective tender, 60
Service elements, 57
Service P's, 162
Services, 105
SLEPT, 51, 53, 159
SLEPT + C, 43
Social structure, 47
Speed of entry, 72
Sponsorship, 115
Standard imagery, 115
Standard price, 124
Standard product, 44
Standardisation, 80, 107
Standardisation/adaptation, 107, 114
Standardised approach, 78, 113, 156
Standardised images, 111
Standardised marketing, 80
Standardised mixes, 56
Standards, 112, 132
Strategic alliance, 74, 102, 148
Strategically equivalent segments, 63, 108, 114, 134
Supply chain, 76, 122, 123
Synchronisation, 152, 154

Tactical segments, 114
Target markets, 88
Targeting markets, 95
Tariff barriers, 38, 88
Tariffs, 38, 125, 126
Tesco, 96

Think global, act local, 44, 109, 133
Thorntons, 120
Time, 69
Time series analysis, 68
Timescale, 139
Toys'R'Us, 121
Trade-offs, 45
Trading blocks, 42
Training and development, 93
Transfer pricing, 75
Transition economies, 49
Transnational companies, 86
Transnational marketing, 86

Umbrella, 88, 97
Unique Selling Proposition, 140, 141

Variances, 132
Virgin, 112
Visa, 65
Vision, 132

Walmart, 96
Web-site, 65, 90, 134
Working capital, 85
World Bank, 48
World brands, 121
World class, 49
World youth culture, 80, 109, 111, 112
World youth market, 42

CIM Order

To BPP Publishing Ltd, Aldine Place, London W12 8AA
Tel: 020 8740 2211. Fax: 020 8740 1184

Mr/Mrs/Ms (Full name) _____
Daytime delivery address _____
_____ Postcode _____
Daytime Tel _____ Date of exam (month/year) _____

		5/00 Texts	9/00 Kits	Tapes
CERTIFICATE				
1	Marketing Environment	£17.95 ☐	£8.95 ☐	£12.95 ☐
2	Customer Communications in Marketing	£17.95 ☐	£8.95 ☐	£12.95 ☐
3	Marketing in Practice	£17.95 ☐	£8.95 ☐	£12.95 ☐
4	Marketing Fundamentals	£17.95 ☐	£8.95 ☐	£12.95 ☐
ADVANCED CERTIFICATE				
5	The Marketing Customer Interface	£17.95 ☐	£8.95 ☐	£12.95 ☐
6	Management Information for Marketing Decisions	£17.95 ☐	£8.95 ☐	£12.95 ☐
7	Effective Management for Marketing	£17.95 ☐	£8.95 ☐	£12.95 ☐
8	Marketing Operations	£17.95 ☐	£8.95 ☐	£12.95 ☐
DIPLOMA				
9	Integrated Marketing Communications	£17.95 ☐	£8.95 ☐	£12.95 ☐
10	International Marketing Strategy	£17.95 ☐	£8.95 ☐	£12.95 ☐
11	Strategic Marketing Management: Planning and Control	£17.95 ☐	£8.95 ☐	£12.95 ☐
12	Strategic Marketing Management: Analysis and Decision (9/00)	£24.95 ☐		

SUBTOTAL £ _____

POSTAGE & PACKING

Study Texts

	First	Each extra
UK	£3.00	£2.00 £ ____
Europe*	£5.00	£4.00 £ ____
Rest of world	£20.00	£10.00 £ ____

Kits/Passcards/Success Tapes

	First	Each extra
UK	£2.00	£1.00 £ ____
Europe*	£2.50	£1.00 £ ____
Rest of world	£15.00	£8.00 £ ____

Grand Total (Cheques to *BPP Publishing*) I enclose a cheque for (incl. Postage) £ _____

Or charge to Access/Visa/Switch

Card Number _____

Expiry date _____ Start Date _____

Issue Number (Switch Only) _____

Signature _____

We aim to deliver to all UK addresses inside 5 working days. A signature will be required. Orders to all EU addresses should be delivered within 6 working days.
All other orders to overseas addresses should be delivered within 8 working days.
* Europe includes the Republic of Ireland and the Channel Islands.

CIM - Diploma: International Marketing Strategy (9/00)

REVIEW FORM & FREE PRIZE DRAW

All original review forms from the entire BPP range, completed with genuine comments, will be entered into one of two draws on 31 January 2001 and 31 July 2001. The names on the first four forms picked out on each occasion will be sent a cheque for £50.

Name: _____ Address: _____

How have you used this Kit?
(Tick one box only)

☐ Home study (book only)
☐ On a course: college _____
☐ With 'correspondence' package
☐ Other _____

Why did you decide to purchase this Kit?
(Tick one box only)

☐ Have used complementary Study Text
☐ Have used BPP Kits in the past
☐ Recommendation by friend/colleague
☐ Recommendation by a lecturer at college
☐ Saw advertising
☐ Other _____

During the past six months do you recall seeing/receiving any of the following?
(Tick as many boxes as are relevant)

☐ Our advertisement in *Marketing Success*
☐ Our advertisement in *Marketing Business*
☐ Our brochure with a letter through the post
☐ Our brochure with *Marketing Business*

Which (if any) aspects of our advertising do you find useful?
(Tick as many boxes as are relevant)

☐ Prices and publication dates of new editions
☐ Information on Kit content
☐ Facility to order books off-the-page
☐ None of the above

Have you used the companion Study Text for this subject? ☐ Yes ☐ No

Your ratings, comments and suggestions would be appreciated on the following areas

	Very useful	Useful	Not useful
Introductory section (Study advice, key questions checklist, etc)	☐	☐	☐
'Do you know' checklists	☐	☐	☐
Tutorial questions	☐	☐	☐
Examination-standard questions	☐	☐	☐
Content of suggested solutions	☐	☐	☐
Quiz	☐	☐	☐
Test paper	☐	☐	☐
Structure and presentation	☐	☐	☐

	Excellent	Good	Adequate	Poor
Overall opinion of this Kit	☐	☐	☐	☐

Do you intend to continue using BPP Study Texts/Kits? ☐ Yes ☐ No

Please note any further comments and suggestions/errors on the reverse of this page.

Please return to: Kate Machattie, BPP Publishing Ltd, FREEPOST, London, W12 8BR

REVIEW FORM & FREE PRIZE DRAW (continued)

Please note any further comments and suggestions/errors below

FREE PRIZE DRAW RULES

1. Closing date for 31 January 2001 draw is 31 December 2000. Closing date for 31 July 2001 draw is 30 June 2001.
2. Restricted to entries with UK and Eire addresses only. BPP employees, their families and business associates are excluded.
3. No purchase necessary. Entry forms are available upon request from BPP Publishing. No more than one entry per title, per person. Draw restricted to persons aged 16 and over.
4. Winners will be notified by post and receive their cheques not later than 6 weeks after the relevant draw date.
5. The decision of the promoter in all matters is final and binding. No correspondence will be entered into.